Praise for *Attachments*

"*Attachments* is an intelligent and searching exploration of vulnerability in all its forms. Lucas Mann's essays attain a naturalness of form without ever losing their penetrating insight and gorgeous sensibility. Some books punish as they reveal, but Mann's generosity and clarity of vision, his humor and candor, make revelation into an occasion for connection. I was flattened and changed by this book. Simply beautiful."
—**Brandon Taylor,** author, *Filthy Animals*

"Lucas Mann's *Attachments* works itself into the fleshy folds I've spent most of my life avoiding. The writing and vision are somehow welcoming and spectacular, yet the book's greatest achievement might lay within the portals of entry created by Mann's use of the comic. *Attachments* found me at the perfect time in my life."
—**Kiese Laymon,** author, *Heavy: An American Memoir*

"The essays in Lucas Mann's *Attachments* are fierce and funny and agile, following the so-called 'smallest' moments of daily experience to the subterranean inquiries these moments have always been attached to, about the entanglements between intimacy and transformation, past and prior selves, culture and selfhood. (Which is to say: Come for the playground soap operas, stay for the acute observations about social performance!) Mann's interest in attachment itself has to do not just with love but with identity: what versions of ourselves we are most attached to, and what parts of us emerge when we betray these attachments. I love Mann's writing for its company and its candor, and especially for its ruthless battle with the twin demons of self-pity and self-satisfaction. His razor gaze slices through righteousness like a mandolin's blade slivers fruit; exposing those wry, quick-silver feelings—often embarrassing, always illuminating—tucked into the crevices of the more familiar emotions we are most comfortable making visible, even to ourselves; but always, always the animating engine of this rigor is love."
—**Leslie Jamison,** author, *The Empathy Exams: Essays*

"Lucas Mann's insights on the hilarity, devastation, and absolute weirdness of raising a child make this a book I want to discuss with everyone. It's so sharp and beautifully written."
—**Beth Nguyen,** author, *Owner of a Lonely Heart*

"Lucas Mann's essays are so funny, so endearing, so companionable, so relentless in their quest for self-knowledge and more nuanced, more generous understanding. *Attachments* reveals a mind that is always working on something, finding ways to make everything interesting, be it fandom or lost promise, social media and 'the dad space,' comfort TV or sleep training, the 'cliché factory' of parenthood in general. It may be 'impossible to feel remarkable in this world,' and yet life, in its particulars, is 'thrilling'—'thrilling!'"
—**Elisa Gabbert,** author, *Normal Distance*

"Naked and tender, *Attachments* is an eyes-wide-open exploration of everything that matters. In this twelve-essay collection that spans parenthood, culture, art, and community, Lucas Mann has embraced far-ranging and clear-eyed observation that's as astute as is it honest. A special, singular book that invites us all to participate fully in the suffering, beautiful world."
—**Rachel Yoder,** author, *Nightbitch*

Attachments

Attachments

Essays on Fatherhood

and Other Performances

Lucas Mann

UNIVERSITY OF IOWA PRESS • IOWA CITY

University of Iowa Press, Iowa City 52242
Copyright © 2024 by Lucas Mann
uipress.uiowa.edu

Printed in the United States of America

Text design and typesetting by April Leidig
Cover design by Kimberly Glyder

Printed on acid-free paper

Library of Congress Cataloging-in-Publication Data
Names: Mann, Lucas, author.
Title: Attachments: Essays on Fatherhood and Other Performances /
    Lucas Mann.
Description: Iowa City: University of Iowa Press, [2024]
Identifiers: LCCN 2023036770 (print) | LCCN 2023036771 (ebook) |
    ISBN 9781609389536 (paperback) | ISBN 9781609389543 (ebook)
Subjects: LCSH: Fatherhood.
Classification: LCC HQ756 .M3429 2024 (print) | LCC HQ756 (ebook) |
    DDC 306.874—dc23/eng/20230830
LC record available at https://lccn.loc.gov/2023036770
LC ebook record available at https://lccn.loc.gov/2023036771

For Matilda

Contents

Attachments

An Essay about Tiny, Spectacular Futures Written a Week or So after a Very Damning IPCC Climate Report

In this fantasy, it's Wimbledon and she's trying to climb over the green wall into the bleachers. Her dress is grass-stained, her eyes are wet, her shoulders—always big and round and beautiful—move like gears as she reaches up into the crowd. A voice, McEnroe's I think, is saying, *We all know who she's looking for.*

In this fantasy, I can't get through a wedding toast; her new wife is squeezing her hand as she cries because I'm crying. I think we're at the same place where my wife and I got married, but the lighting is better, softer, and there are more people, so the tent doesn't feel so big.

In this fantasy, she's thirty and still living at home, and we've all miraculously learned to both love and excel at gardening. Sometimes we have old friends over, and they're talking about how *their* kids are working at Goldman or in PR or for some clean-water charity that sounds great but is the pet project of rich lunatic narcissists, and we feign interest. We do worry, my wife and I, but it's a little background hum, and it always ends with the idea that nothing matters because the world is ending,

5

hahaha, we might as well be together so there's nothing to regret. We're wine drunk every night, rarely hungover. The dog moves around our feet, forty years old now, slow and gassy but content. I still kiss her forehead before bed.

In this fantasy, she's happy in the mornings when I get her; she never screams, *Noooooo!* and slaps at my hands. I never look down at my hands, the offenders, then put them in my pockets so she might edge back closer to me.

In this fantasy, she's a cellist, still patient enough to play along with my mediocre guitar work. I strum the rhythm of something super basic but nice—in my mind it's not "Eleanor Rigby," but that sort of vibe—and she plays the melody low and smooth.

In this fantasy, I tell her I'm dying.

In this one, I never cut back the neighbor's honeysuckle, and it creeps toward us. I see weeks as minutes; growth and decay are perceptible as they happen. The honeysuckle moves like my fingers on her back, singing "Itsy-Bitsy Spider." It smells so sweet, fully alive, but I can't stop sneezing, as usual, and I have to go inside. I close the door behind me so the bees don't get in. There are few left, but they still sting.

In this one, it rains for weeks and weeks. No one knows why. Eventually, we think it will be like this forever. We're not looking at our phones—not in a conscious or coordinated way; it just . . . doesn't occur to us, I guess—and we don't know what's going on anywhere else. She's maybe ten or eleven, staring out at the garden. The indoor air is stale.

In this one, she falls asleep while I'm holding her, the first time ever; I'm too scared to look down at her, but I feel her breathing change.

In this fantasy, she looks nothing like me and exactly like her mother.

In this one, she's fluent in Italian, and her voice is the same as her mother's because her mother sounds younger in Italian. There's a storm coming, they're watching from the deck, talking, and I don't understand them. *Let's go in*, I beg.

Her various speech impediments never leave, in this one— everything sounds like a *W*. There's no moment when we read some scolding book or pseudoscience *Atlantic* article that makes us go, *She's too old*, or *How do we fix this?* or *Why did we let it get this bad?* We decide that sounds only have meaning because we say so, evolution of language, she's literally evolving language in front of us, it's a privilege to watch, whatever whatever, and we mean it.

In this fantasy, I lose her in the crowd at the largest march I've ever seen—not in a scary way, just like I'm no longer needed; the top of her head is one of many, then it's gone.

In this one, the ground trembles, and she looks to me with fear and confusion; I meet her with the same.

In this fantasy, it never snows for the rest of her childhood. There are days when it almost does, when the air starts to taste that way I remember from my own childhood, but then it warms just enough or the clouds break. When we talk about it, for her, it's like when my dad used to say movies once cost a dime, and I was like, *Okay who cares?* but it did lodge in my memory, and there was pleasure in imagining a world before me, totally foreign except that he was in it. Finally, she's eighteen and she sees snow out the window, just a gentle sputtering, but still she's amazed. My wife takes a picture of her face reacting, and it's a picture only about joy.

In this one, I never get a vasectomy. We try again, and it's just as hard as it was the first time. No tears, just long, thick periods of quiet, save for the hum of the TV. But she's there, too, this time. She's herself—a torrent of questions; her cheeks redden when she's mad at us. We're numb after a while, which makes her madder. It never happens, years and years of nothing, until we stop trying. There's no conversation about an end, only a resignation that feels natural, at least, and as she gets older, she calls herself the miracle baby, which feels cute but also mean, like we had nothing to do with it.

In this fantasy, she's a mechanic.

In this one, I am a person who can conceive of her adulthood, or anyone's, without a job—*career*—as a definitional noun.

In this one, she never knows hunger or pure, crystalline fear.

In this one, she does.

In this one, a boy whose parents own a car dealership, whose hair is sandy, face blunt, who displays no interior life worth empathizing with and who is ensconced in enough privilege that I can say his limitations are his own fault, hurts her. I become a different type of person, and I go off to hurt him. I find him on a beach for some reason, at night. The water adds a threat, swells crash. I'm big and he's big, too. His friends are there and I'm alone. Still, he's afraid, but I don't hurt him. I almost do, but then I hold back. Driving home, I listen to a slow, dreamy cover of a Springsteen song and feel young, then old; sad, then happier.

In this one, she's trying to learn a dance for a talent show, and her concentration face is the same as it's always been. Her door is open, so I'm watching her, but she doesn't look up to see me.

In this one, she reads the whole Harry Potter series with the kind of obsession that I once did, her mother, too. She reads through dinner; we have to coax her into turning off her bedroom light. J. K. Rowling has renounced every public comment she's ever made, and anyway, Twitter doesn't exist anymore, so the whole experience is untortured.

In this one, she can do the monkey bars. She's very, very proud.

In this one, my wife dies on her way home from work, highway accident, and three hours later, it's bath time. She sees a squirrel out the window over the bath running along the gutter of a neighbor's house. *Squirrel*, she says, but she pronounces it the way she does all *Sq* sounds, which is more like an *F*. I imitate the sound as she makes it, like we always do with so much of her language, because it sounds so much better when she says it, so like *her*, but my wife isn't there to reciprocate or laugh. My voice bounces off the tile, then silence, and I have never felt more fully convinced of my own purpose, and after that thought, the grief comes, the sudden, terrifying desire for my own death, and she says, without judgment or worry, just interest, *Daddy's crying*.

In this one, I'm a person willing to explore and articulate the outer edges of what I want. What feels good. I am bound tightly, whipped hard, and it's not an awkward occasion or the beginning of something that devolves into giggles and fizzles out. My wife is wearing a strap-on, and I'm kneeling on the bed feeling wonderfully small—a trapped, feral thing. I feel my throat seize a little, my hands are gripping at the sheets. She comes in to ask for a glass of water, sees us—the ceiling light is on, undimmed—shrieks, and then laughs.

In this one, an embarrassing one, I'm on *Fresh Air*, and after Terry introduces me, I say, *Thanks, Terry—first time, long time.* And it lands! After the segment airs, she texts, *lol for realll.*

In this one, our home is loud and full of all the strangers who sleep in the park around the corner, prodded on summer days by EMTs for confirmation of life. Our doors are open, the fridge is full of water, she's on the back porch wiping dirt off freshly plucked root vegetables, tying them in bunches with purple string because purple is still her favorite color. She is at ease in this, far past her parents' mixture of fear and self-satisfaction; she merely does.

In this one, the full-body agitation that she feels so fast, this vibration of panic and anger, just disappears. She doesn't remember what it feels like; soon we don't remember what it looks like.

Her face racked, the sound of her fingernails on eczematous skin when she makes internal turmoil physical—it no longer exists in my mind, anywhere.

In this one, we're in a house I've never seen, watching on TV as the barrier wall around Manhattan bursts, and it looks like a scene from that old Stallone movie with the tunnel. She says, *At least Grammy and Grampy aren't alive anymore*, which is what I had been thinking, and I'm amazed that she's old enough to say something like that.

She's a poet in this one. She is not literal. When she describes the world in front of her, the words twist into something unrecognizable, better. It's everything I ever wanted from language— freedom, which turns into joy—that I've never managed. I'm jealous of her, and that feels nice. I ask her how and she doesn't have an answer, as it should be.

In this fantasy, she's a teenager screaming at me, *Your guilt is a useless emotion*, and I'm half standing from my chair screaming back, *Do you have a more productive idea, genius?* And she . . . does.

In this fantasy, I remember all the things I've read that have meant something to me—perfect recall. It's to the point where everyone is rolling their eyes at the dinner table, but there's reassurance in it, a database of wisdom not my own, beyond my own, scrolling by, until something clicks. It's a form of nourishment, not a burden.

In this one, they finally find a mate for the gray wolf at the zoo. We're there the day it's introduced, and the way the two animals move around one another, the nerves and the hope, the humanness, by which I guess I mean *vulnerability*, of their gestures— even the children intuit to stop pushing, shut up, and watch.

In this one, we own a vineyard on the North Fork of Long Island, organic and all that, heat rising off our compost piles like something out of a comic book. My wife holds each little grape between her finger like it has a heartbeat, and we all wander the rows on long afternoons until we lose each other. We do this until the grapes are burned out, the vines brown; we really enjoyed it while it lasted.

She's in a phase where she wants to give everything she has away, every bit of food we give her, unless she's so hungry she can't help herself. We call her a good person, an *angel*—if more people were like her, well. . . . When she's in bed, we get a little drunk and tell each other it's okay to be so proud, as long as we don't broadcast it like those fucking people with their debate-team spawn, and then we have really good sex.

In this one, there's a shooting in the park next to the ice cream truck; she hears it, and the big kids are already screaming, so she looks at them and starts screaming, too. I grab her, lock my wrists behind her back, run away from the screams. Her chin bobbles on my shoulder.

In this one, at the park, in one of those moments when one parent (a mom) hisses at another (a dad) to look up from his phone—*It's all happening out here, Kevin*—right as a guttural protest is forming in his throat, the ground opens up. We hear and feel the gears of the earth moving beneath us. Water explodes, the pressure an ecstatic moan. Nobody says anything. Parched grass returns to life. I look up. The water falling feels like a memory I can't quite place, from when I was too young to remember anything beyond feeling.

In this one, the redbud trees we planted are a hundred feet high; underneath, there are patches where no grass grows in the shape of our three bodies. Where we found shade.

Under the tree, we're burying the dog, who in this fantasy she has loved, has touched gently, has found comfort in. There's a burlap sack wrinkled around the lump of the body. She insists on being the one to place the sack into the dirt.

On a bay beach, she stands up out of the ocean, and I watch her footprints in the sand up the beach to my wife sleeping on a towel. She presses all her wet weight down, and my wife protests, seriously at first, but then joking. Their legs are stacked like uneven kindling.

On an ocean beach in Italy where her mother's family spent the summers, crabs are overheating, making a sound like a whistle, and she's crying and crying. The sky used to be clear enough to see to Croatia on some days.

We're walking to higher and higher elevation. She's still young enough to be on my shoulders. The dog is trying to keep up but tiring. My wife says she can taste the difference in the air up here, it tastes like nothing but air, and she's right. We stop to eat dried apricots on a smooth patch of granite, and I've looked up how old this granite is—395 *million* years. We're quiet, trying to think of an analogy to transform that number into something small enough to gain meaning.

In this one, the house is dark; she's asking what's wrong.

A squirrel lies down on a branch on an August day, chest heaving, almost cute.

I can taste smoke—*Hold your breath*, I say.

A whale breaches the water somewhere we've never been; she's pointing.

Legs are stampeding; I'm holding her up above my shoulders again.

The sky is tornado green.

My wife is making her funniest faces on an older, looser face. She's older, too, but she's laughing until she has to hold her belly, like the very first times, when she surprised herself with the sound.

She's with her friends and I'm not there, but I can see it—in this fantasy, she's on her own, but we're never in the dark, never abandoned. These friends are jumping off a cliff into a brackish lake. She goes last. No part of her body resists the jump. She doesn't bother to brace herself as her feet break the water.

An Approximate Hourly Record of
Thoughts and Feelings during a
Time of Intense Sleep Deprivation

1. My daughter has a sound machine for when she sleeps. It offers many bells and whistles—tinkling lullaby options, pulsing color change through a pediatrician-approved scroll of soft reds and blues—but we don't use those. We just use the sound in a pitch-black room, a drone so loud and constant that it begins to seem to have nuance. Somewhere in the code of it, there's a loop delayed long enough that each time, a part of me wonders if it won't return or if there was never a pattern at all. This isn't active wondering, just one little knot nestled into the untangleable larger knot of fear and exhaustion and tenderness and a weird new type of yearning. Within all that, the one loop sticks out— the only faithful approximation of running water that the machine produces, the gentle lap of a wave followed by a lingering trickle. The sounds paired here don't go together. They reference two totally different types of water and evoke totally different sense memories—bay beach at sunset, stream stumbled upon in bare winter woods—but before I can sort out the memories, the machine has moved on.

2. It's too obvious, and probably not interesting, to riff about the platonic nature of this anecdote, about reproduction replacing the original, about the electronic echo of nature becoming a four-month-old's only frame of reference for nature, about modern laboratory parenting and probably something about climate change—and and and. The obviousness is further stoked by how literally we try to keep my daughter's room as cave-like as possible. In the cave, filtered through the night vision monitor, she appears as something other than a person, my wife says, and that makes it easier to wait the five to eight minutes we've agreed to when she cries. It hurts less if she isn't in front of us, real, but is instead onscreen in the same fuzzy blue approximation of humanness as a reality TV sex scene.

3. Sometimes it's hard to parse the difference between imitation and memory, in that both always serve to replace. As though something happens, and then right away, the implications for how it might live on and not be lost come crushing in, repeating, competing, until the original is blurry, but everything else is blocked out. A somewhat related thought: I've been arguing with students about Harry Potter lately (the books—everyone agrees upon the awfulness of their creator). I'm not against the Harry Potter books; I really love Harry Potter and always have. But I also love and have always loved bagels, yet I still can enjoy a smoothie for breakfast or egg on toast—this is the forced metaphor I use with them. The argument we keep having is about whether we want a story or a character or a morality to mimic the ones in Harry Potter that provide such reliable pleasure, and whether, if a story or character or morality fails to successfully mimic Harry Potter, it has failed in toto. This isn't a deadpan thing where I'm trying not to be obvious that I think it's stupid to not want to read outside Harry Potter. Increasingly, I don't know.

Or I'm less sure that I know. Really it's a conversation about comfort and how much of it we think we deserve and whether we *always* deserve it and whether a book can provide comfort simply by being recognizable and therefore making us feel a little more secure, a little less alone. When my daughter wakes up and I go in to turn on the light and turn off the sound machine, there's a pause, and then into the brightness and clean, new silence, her face opens into a toothless smile. There is nothing good enough and also nothing new to say about what this feels like. Every day, the same face, one of the two or three she's learned, and how did she learn? From my face, smiling down so much that my cheeks and gums hurt, a cocaine memory, pleading to see an imitation back at me, so that imitation might resemble reciprocation. Very fast, the mornings when she doesn't smile begin to feel like a betrayal.

4. I've given a lot of poorly paid author talks where I go on about the easy comfort of narrative and life not having a narrative and writing that resists narrative being a more challenging and honest and (yuck) *mimetic* mode of expressing the experience of being human. But really, I know that order is harder than disorder—a reader, or at least the kind of reader I am, will stretch to find patterns in the scattershot while looking to poke holes in a narrative already painstakingly assembled. I read a Maggie Nelson interview in which she jabbed back at being asked about writing multiple memoirs by saying that she wasn't interested in art that looked back on a moment, then tied it up with a bow. Rather, she believes in life-writing defined only by *ongoingness*, trying to keep up with that. I love this sentiment, but I never

found my life hard to keep up with; that's always been my secret. Easier to write like you're on the edge of something, easier
to cultivate breathlessness and mess when life, the writing life,
feels ordered, full of boxes and borders where risk and anxiety
and pain cannot push through. To write a book is to fashion an
ending to the period of life spent writing it, neat by necessity,
followed by a fallow spell, and then the attempt at another. Maintain order and calm through conveying the opposite; it can fool
you into thinking you've relinquished control.

5. I think adulthood comes when there's only room to challenge
your own tastes with so many things. Very few people are con-
vincing when they claim otherwise, as though they have the
unique bandwidth to embrace omnivorous yet discerning cultural consumption. Maggie Nelson is one. Susan Sontag? Hilton
Als? I'm sure there are more, but the point is mostly everyone
else is a liar. It's important to me that I like "good" books and
movies, but the moment I graduated college, it felt like a license
to listen to a lot of music that I already knew the words to or that
sounded like songs I already knew the words to, which means
music that reminds me of me. I was holding my daughter at a
bar last week, and the two men I was talking with began going
on about the Beatles and how their whole lives, even when they
were just sullen children, they knew enough to know that the
Beatles were bad, or at least uninteresting, despite the prosely-
tizing of the people around them, who were also, they'd sensed
right away, uninteresting. This conversation made me want to
scream at them, but my daughter was sleeping, so I said nothing.
Of course, right underneath the intense urge to defend the Beatles was the need to defend myself. The Beatles meant something

to me, so to write them off was to write off the place where I chose to find meaning. My brother taught me about the Beatles, and my brother is dead—there's a Beatles lyric on his tombstone, and still, twenty years on, when I hear "Golden Slumbers," I have this sensation that everyone in the room is looking at me to see how I might react. All the elements are rote now, the echoing plunk of a single chord struck slowly on a piano, the knowledge that after A-minor must come C and F and G, at some point. When I pick up a guitar, my fingers hold an A-minor on instinct, and I strum and convince myself that it sounds significant, not just familiar— the perfect chord, revelatory each time. Sometimes I think I never liked music that much, even though, or maybe because, it makes me feel so easily, so often, so much.

6. There was a dustup in the literary corner of the internet a month ago over someone saying you should never fuck an adult who loves Bukowski. Many people agreed and said *lol*, but others cried elitism and said that those turning their noses up at Bukowski were merely those afforded the luxury of reading in an ivory tower somewhere about the problematic legacy of Bukowski. Then still others were like, don't you *dare* use claims of elitism as a way to support the continued revered status of a rampant misogynist and one of the many poster boys for self-involved male mediocrity being held up as genius. It was the perfect social media triptych—poorly thought-out statement, anger, anger at the anger. A day or two, max. At the end: lingering, pointless unease. Repeating it here, writing its movements, seems only stupid, yet clearly it's still nagging at me, so I might as well embrace that I'm invested. I was never a Bukowski guy, but I reflexively get sad at the notion of a Bukowski guy being made to feel as though what Bukowski made him feel, still makes him feel, is illegitimate. This shouldn't be important to me, maybe it isn't important to me, but that's the reflex. Also, this: every time I see a man alone at a bar, I feel sad in a good way. I used to like going to bars by myself, sitting as that alone man, and assuming that others would look at me that same way. Now, when I romanticize a before time, my childless life, I think of myself in bars alone far more than I ever was and the way I thought people saw me: shoulders curled in, elbows on sticky wood, hand swirling brown liquor slowly, like there was too much to say to say anything. I had a good friend who gave me *Post Office* as a birthday present, but I never read it because I'd already heard enough people talk about the kind of man who loves Bukowski. I didn't tell the friend that. We were both writers, but I was getting an MFA, and he worked at the liquor store I went to a lot. I got a book contract shortly after, and he was the first friend I told. We were drinking whiskey in the kind of bar that had a self-conscious jukebox. He said cheers, and then he said, *You're a real writer, and I'm a guy who works at the liquor store, and that's just who we are.* I felt ashamed and also a little jealous of the depth I saw in him then, a depth that seemed masculine in that it was expressed in only a sentence and existed mostly in beautiful, silent regret, so much to say and do that wouldn't be said and done, a tragedy that would always be more interesting than me doing and saying things that could, at best, be effortful, at worst entirely disappointing. I've been missing him, missing myself in association with him. These days, I've never felt more effortful or more disappointing, still romanticizing something I never really wanted after getting the life I wanted most. Part of me thinks I should read *Post Office*, but I won't.

7. Once, in grad school, I took a PhD class in cultural studies, an idea I should have realized was too ambitious the moment I was told MFAs were allowed to take PhD classes pass/fail. We watched videos of drag performances, first famous queens, then some kings. In our discussion, without really thinking, I said something about how much more outwardly impressive I found the drag queen performances to be, both in costuming and affect, the plethora of small observations they managed to ape into caricature. In comparison, I thought, the kings were just a collection of eyeliner goatees with some well-positioned zucchini bulge. There was instant scowling around me. The narrowness and lack of imagination in my comment was jumped on, the idea that if I thought there was no compelling imitation happening, I was *really* saying that I thought masculinity was innate, that there was no performance to study or reflect or mock. Which was me saying that I didn't think *I* was a walking performance, a set of tics that were never even my own, when so obviously I was. That particular flush of shame, a sense memory that lingers and lingers: invest your whole identity in being the type of guy aware of all the problems inherent and obvious in your identity and then, in a flash of clarity to you, if no one else, you reveal that you're not. Once, in college, a friend saw me walking toward him from across the quad and changed the gait of his own walk as we got closer. He held his chest out, hips open, shoulders stretched so broad they almost curved backward. Basically, a strut—either muscle man or bully uncle, depending on the generosity with which you chose to look at it. I asked him why he was walking like that, and as soon as I said it, before he answered, I knew, and I was even more embarrassed because I hadn't recognized until right then how easy I was to caricature.

8. Always, we read my daughter *Goodnight Moon* before bed. When it's my wife's turn, I hear them through the door—my daughter's impatient breathing, my wife's voice lowering and softening into a rasp, lingering on the best line, by which I mean the sort of throwaway literary line: "Goodnight nobody." I know people who swear their baby only gets excited when he hears Kendrick, which I think is such a transparent projection of the people *they* want to be onto a small, blank semi-human that hasn't yet had the chance to become corny like them, but also I'm a little jealous and a little anxious at how fast I've become the kind of parent who sings the least controversial Bob Marley songs to his baby, like we're trapped in the lobby of a Sandals. I tell myself that the melody soothes her, meaning it soothes me. My mother says that when I was a baby, the music I liked the best was Black gospel, which makes me think that I'm no different from her, just another generation of liberal white parent both in love with and ambivalent about their own procreation, piping in the sounds of foreign suffering turned into something reassuring—*Sleep, baby, and tomorrow our burden, such as it is, might be lifted*. Who was she pretending to be then, and who am I pretending to be now? The same blurry idea of a kind of person who might impart something soul-deep about faith, though we've never had it, though we've never been tested enough to know if we have it.

9. Every day, the gulf between the person that I want to believe I am and the person I am widens. This is another version of my definition of adulthood. The baby is not soothed when we hold her, or not that much anyway. We tell each other this is a blessing because there's no crutch, no risk of her only sleeping in our arms since it wouldn't occur to her to do that. But every morning, while my wife takes her turn getting ready for the day, I hold the baby to my chest and wait to feel something soften in her. For a few seconds, she's still and warm; her heart beats adjacent to, similar to, mine, and I waste those seconds fumbling my phone screen open with one hand, trying to catch her in the act of what would appear to be comfort in the arms of her father. I'm always too late; her body stiffens, then writhes against me. She makes a sound that's less of a cry, more of a gasp against a strangle that doesn't exist, my least favorite noise of hers, one that I sometimes convince myself I hear in the fuzzy loop of the sound machine, even when she's silent. In these moments, I have the sense that she's being unfair to me, and though I can register minutes later that it's a preposterous feeling to have, I have it again, instantly, the next time she makes that noise. It is beyond my control, which means that in those moments, holding someone that small, that helpless, I am literally out of control. It's a feeling long shelved, forever teenaged, standing close to a subway track as the train arrives, the rippling of the air, the sensation that there's no way to feel completely safe inside myself, only this time, two decades later, I'm not alone and not supposed to be fragile.

10. I've always admired people who believe differently or have different tastes than the way they were raised. My atheism, my liberalism, they don't feel like a decision. I don't believe that I'm right—well, I do, but that just means that I believe I was raised right, then I copied. When a friend describes how it feels to miss the community of the megachurch she was raised in but regrets that she ever felt any closeness to the doctrine, I am amazed, far less so by the generosity of her beliefs than the fact that she evolved into them. What I'm saying is if I was raised by racists, I'm pretty sure I'd be a racist. It's hard for me to think that my models could be wrong, even now; why, then, would they have ever been my models? My father raised me on Woody Allen movies, and when I was old enough to pretend to make up my own mind, I raised myself on Louis C.K., a slight evolution, I thought, if not a departure. Each one a model for how, if you say you hate yourself enough, it might supplant the ways you show contempt for anyone else. Or not even contempt, just disregard. You cannot make them feel worse than you make yourself feel, and embedded in that certainty is a self-defined fairness. And if that's true, what can't you say? What can't you do? For most of my life, I thought this was what sensitivity meant.

11. My wife is back at work, and I'm not, which means that multiple people have used the horrific phrase *daddy daycare* when describing my days. I like our pediatrician because she doesn't suffer from or encourage any additional anxiety, but the last time I brought my daughter in, she fought pretty hard during the undressing portion and was flailing and grabbing at that useless paper that stretches across the examination table, so when the doctor came in, it looked like we'd been opening presents in there, and her response was, *Oh, you just have the perfect helpless dad look about you right now.* She said it in a nice way—does that matter? I must have looked annoyed or hurt, so she said, *It's just a type, that's all.* I indulged in a fantasy of saying something about *her* type, which would have reflected far more poorly on me than her, but I also wanted to say, *Yes, I am helpless, so helpless, can you help me please?* The doctor said everything was normal, even the baby's skin taking on that blueish tint sometimes. She put her stethoscope on my daughter's chest. My daughter's body shivered from the cold metal, a very human little reaction, and she made a sound that made me think of her mother stepping into a cold lake somewhere, sometime, and I spent the rest of the appointment trying not to cry, unclear whether the tears I was fighting were from joy or regret. On the ride home, I played the Bradley Cooper solo song from *A Star Is Born*. A few days before my wife went into labor, the last thing I did by myself was take a bunch of old edibles and go to a noon showing of *A Star Is Born* at the mall. I was the only person in the theater. I was very moved. I'd gone in determined to be; that was the whole idea. He was just sad, sad, sad all the way through. Doomed and gifted and sad. I play the song on guitar for my daughter a lot. When I sing, I try to sound like him, the way he was trying to sound like Kris Kristofferson, the way Kris Kristofferson was trying to sound like a cowboy who could let you in on the secrets of the universe just by mumbling in tune. When we are alone and I sing, she is still, maybe happy, and I wish the doctor could see that, wish anyone was around to see.

12. There's a guy who frequents three of the same coffee shops that I used to frequent, who looks like a pained figure at the center of a tangle of bodies in a Renaissance painting. When I see him, I text my wife, *Pained Renaissance guy is here! He looks so pained!* A Google of the term "Pained face + Renaissance painting" reveals an Art History 101 primer explaining to freshmen why Renaissance figures appear so expressionless, so I may be getting my era wrong. There's a specific painting I have in mind or a composite of a few that I saw in a particular room in a museum once. The experience of being in that room remains indelible because I remember thinking that the images seemed to reflect the first captured grimace. The figures in oil looked more anguished than a human face could ever look in the wild, since there are always other concerns and impulses to interrupt any one feeling. I like to think of spending decades trying to zero in on a single expression, make it the fullest, truest version of itself. This coffee shop guy looks more unified in a particular emotion than I think of an actual person being, so he becomes more profound through consistency; that's what I mean. He looks like he's been posing for hours, and someone has given him the prompt, *Every day we stray further from God's light.* I'll never talk to him because it would only be a disappointment.

13. Maybe it's a cop-out, but when I think of ever trying to make art of any kind again, it feels simultaneously overwhelming and boring to do anything but focus on a single feeling, one note out of however many human notes there are, and just hit that note over and over. Maximalism, by any definition, upsets me in a way that I'm almost positive is more than simple jealousy. I was reading Han Kang's *The Vegetarian*, and loving it, and then the perspective changed, and I got so personally offended that I gave up on the book. I stopped reading Valeria Luiselli's *Lost Children Archive*, which I was also loving, because someone warned me, though they meant it as a compliment, of an impending shift into an almost entirely distinct story. Virtuosity is impressive, but often I think impressiveness is the opposite of beauty. I went to a museum in Iceland running an exhibit of their preeminent modern artist, Ragnar Kjartansson. The work was cool but sort of all over the place, and I remember nothing except a video installation where he filmed the National playing their song "Sorrow" on a loop for six hours. The singer's voice grew hoarse; sometimes the tempo changed a little, nearly impossible to notice if you weren't trying to. The crowd cheered each time the band started again, but the cheers became increasingly lackluster as they, too, grew tired. The song itself is a drone, three minutes of repetition stretch out into six hours; to watch it didn't feel repetitive, it felt like a lens focusing until the image becomes so crystalline that it blurs, then deepens. When there's nothing else to expect, the thing in front of you expands to fill the space you need it to fill.

14. Can you imitate a feeling? Can you imitate something that can't be seen? There was a conversation five or six weeks into her life in which we both said that we didn't love her. What we were saying, I think now, is that to love her felt like an imitation, and we needed to admit that. To call a newborn beautiful or perfect feels both rote and hopeful, but not accurate. Very soon, it seemed impossible to have ever not loved her, but when did the change happen? I don't remember changing my mind—nobody ever remembers changing their mind—so I find it hard to trust that I didn't just do the impression of how I should have felt until it stuck. *I love you I love you I love you*—not as an expression of truth but an attempt at manifesting. I like to think I can discern when my daughter is in real pain from when she's repeating and honing a performance of how pain should look and sound, but

I can't, and that's the worst thing. It seems necessary to try to create a hierarchy of how bad she might be feeling, terrifying that she might always, in her body or her mind or both, be feeling everything her face suggests. Immunizations—this was real, obvious pain, from the moment the needle punctured her thigh. Her face skin moved like pinched dough; there was silence and then an explosion of sound. Maybe this is giving her too much credit, or not enough compassion, but it seemed like the first time she found the feeling she'd been performing whenever she was bored or confused, or edging up to the beginning of hunger. We've been telling everybody about the way the pain looked on her, unlike, we try to emphasize, any pain ever felt or expressed. Or really, more like pain than any depiction you've ever seen— pure pain, isolated, with nothing else to feel. It's tempting to find relief in what is so excruciating for her because there's no question, there's nothing muddled or frustratingly conscious about what she's feeling and what she wants: pain and someone to hold her until the pain stops. And it's easy to be the person to do that, at least until the pain subsides and there is quiet, and a face that once again is trying to figure out what to express.

15. It's hard to think about badness being an imitation of bad influences, because that means that goodness, too, is just an imitation of someone else's version of goodness. I was reading the apology of a poet today, who thirty years ago was the front man of a skinhead punk group. Another pang of sympathy for this stranger whose work, both the early evil and the later respected versions, I had never interacted with. I read an article in which he said that, at the time he was a skinhead, he was a young man without models, for whom self-expression was only ever introduced through this vessel of rage and cruelty. He has learned. He has found a community with new models for what it means to make art, and he's followed those instead. The subtext is that he cannot be blamed for what he didn't know, that the contrite, decent-seeming person he found his way to being should erase the person that he was when he was lost, and he's sorry. To write or think that sentence, it seems unimpeachable—I've always been a sucker for the vulnerability of even a half-decent apology— but then it's impossible not to wonder how a person could not know better than to be the worst kind of person. Or how an apology can be anything but an imitation of other apologies.

16. Before the baby was born, my father asked me what I was afraid of, and I said anger, and he said that's what he figured because of him and the speed and the force with which he got angry. I don't mean to suggest he was *that* angry—I was never hit by anyone, or if I was, it was such a weird occasion that it's become a joke in memory. I never faced anything within even the newly expanded definition of *abuse*. But I remember his anger prominently, as silly as it feels to say, given the scope of angers in the world that his didn't live up to. He is smaller and older now, a more reflective version of the good man he's always been, and when he's angry, it fizzles into mournfulness. We were visiting my grandmother—very near death, porcelain. She was so fragile, and he was getting there, and it seemed so impossible there in the nursing home for anyone to be anything other than quiet and brittle, and I felt myself looming, still capable, we were agreeing, of causing harm. The first time I heard my own anger at my daughter, she was maybe a week old, howling as we tried to bathe her. I said *Shh* in a way that moved from an attempt at calming her into an attempt at drowning her out. She screamed louder. You should have to pick between saying something happened on instinct or that something happened because of the ways you've seen and internalized how to be in the world. Both make a similar claim to helplessness, which is a kind of inevitability, and that was the claim I made, even though I didn't believe it. I left to sit on the stairs under the window. It was a black night out, nothing to see in the window but the reflection of the light inside, my body big and hunched, monstrous. When my wife brought the baby back over, she was wrapped in a towel, like something rescued from the side of the road, a million internet videos of a hand squeezing milk from a washcloth into the pink mouth of a stray kitten—how hard should it be to love that the right way?

17. This can't be true, but from what I can remember I've only read one version of fatherhood that felt worth emulating: Reverend John Ames in *Gilead*. An old man, written by a woman, a man of quiet, patient faith, though I've never been quiet or patient, and I've never had faith. There's a passage early on where he describes honeysuckle, the act of smelling it, then biting and tasting it with his son, and that sense memory spans his whole life, the sweetness and stillness of it, and the enormity of everything he'd ever wanted and had and lost and still regretted. The child in *Gilead* is vague, mostly just an audience for his father's monologue, the only image to remain blurry in a novel whose whole bit is to render every detail so fully that it begins to feel like a miracle. Ames's love is vivid because he's writing his own elegy. Love seeps in through regret—not the love of being with his child, but the love of anticipating what he'll miss. *Gilead* is the best kind of first-person novel, in that it wouldn't be good if retold in third. What Ames thinks and feels is so much more compelling than what he does, which is nothing, really. Too old to have a good catch with the boy, he thinks but does not say, and I reread and am moved by what he wishes for, so much more resonant than anything he could have done. If the novel was in third person, he would be stiff and silent; there would be no evidence (and this is the most painful thing to think about) that he cared at all.

18. When the baby was about a month old, we watched *Eighth Grade*, which I thought was remarkable—paced like a horror film, the good, old kind, before every horror was rushed in an effort to get to the next one. The scene I loved the most, though it was probably the worst one in the movie, or at least the most out of place, was the sudden, overwhelming catharsis of the single dad next to a fire in his backyard with his daughter who was so sad and frightening, so foreign to him, but in that moment he told her how much he loved her, the strength he saw in her, and she accepted that, leaned into him, and you realize watching that it's the first time in the movie that two bodies touch in a way that isn't furtive or cruel. It's a release valve in a narrative that maybe isn't supposed to have one. It makes the whole thing feel like it was never about the eighth grade girl's loneliness, but rather the loneliness of the father seeing her alone; it's as destructive a moment as it is generous. To be a thirteen-year-old girl remains full of unsolvable pain, but the movie lets us think of the triumph of what it feels like, even in a single moment, when a father cares the right way.

19. It's not a coincidence that the most indelible renderings of a father come in a narrative in which the mother is gone. This goes way back to *Lear*, at least in my memories of a literary education. There's Atticus Finch, there's the man in *The Road*, there's the guy in *The Curious Incident of the Dog in the Nighttime*. As a boy, I read *Danny the Champion of the World*, the only stab Roald Dahl ever took at a sympathetic adult, a father alone with his son. Every other caretaker Dahl invented was either evil or an idiot or both, but not this one father, who was instead the barrier between his son and all the evil idiots. Sometimes the fathers aren't solo, they're one better: gone, a memory, a disembodied guide, like in Foer's *Everything Is Illuminated*. Either way, the father shines through in absence or because of absence. As though, in a narrative full of characters alive and where they are supposed to be, he would fade.

20. For some reason, I tried to teach the Mary Gaitskill story "The Girl on the Plane." A middle-aged businessman returning to his family sits on a flight next to a young woman who, if only for her youth, makes him remember a girl he knew as a teenager. He drinks and speaks to the young woman, and slowly you start to realize that he's confessing to a gang rape that he's unable to identify to himself, still, as what it was. The feeling of reading the story is mounting unease, until it's excruciating. I guess I taught it to say something about craft, that imaginary vacuum. *Look* *how she paces the revelation to twist the knife! Didn't you feel it twisting?* The easiest way to write off the ensuing conversation is to say it was about sensitivity, but really it was about pain. If literature is supposed to make you feel, then it's just as foolish as it is cruel to minimize the feelings it provokes. A lot of reactions to the story were, *I hate it,* but I think that can often be a stand-in for, *It makes me feel awful—*a roomful of students of whom I'd required something that made them feel awful. This class happened right around the time I stopped reading *Butcher's Crossing,* a novel about buffalo slaughter, once the buffalo slaughter started. On my own time, it's becoming harder and harder to remember the argument for reading or watching through the awfulness, once you know the awfulness will happen. *An examination of something is not necessarily an endorsement of it,* yes. *Empathy and curiosity shouldn't be reserved for the good,* yes. *Art isn't supposed to be affirmative—*that's something I know to be true, but more and more, it seems like the highest compliment you can pay to a piece of art is that it affirms you, that it provides a blueprint for how to be better, or at least feel better. And I like to feel better; I want to feel better. Still, it's hard for me not to read that as weakness, especially as a teacher—that line of thought I was taught with and lapped right up, about how steeling yourself through something is more intellectually valuable than turning away. Then there's this: the fact that I just compared the trauma of being made to read about rape with the trauma of voluntarily reading about buffalo slaughter during the gold rush—what can I possibly know of the difference between discomfort and pain? So much of the silly, nebulous claims of a *culture war* hinge on a refusal to ever say the phrase, *I cannot understand.* I know the familiar rush of shame at the idea of admitting that you have no frame of reference for what could be painful enough to trigger someone else—why? Some admission of lost expertise in suffering? There's that Margaret Atwood quote about how women are afraid that men will kill them, and men are afraid that women will laugh at them, which is a great quote but also makes me feel unfairly attacked, so there you go. Anyways, in the few quiet moments of paternity leave, as the baby lay soft and still, breathed evenly, I found myself replaying this interaction, which wasn't a *bad* one exactly but ended up at this predictable place of me talking about art like it was vegetables, or the naps she never wants to take—*Go ahead, hate it, but it's good for you.* How much of the way I was taught, and the way I teach, breaks down to this idea of some earned authority, then the student going through discomfort to try to approach it? How often does that seep out into the rest of my life? How many times would it have been better for me to say, *I don't understand, and I'm sorry*? When does challenge, even growth—emotional, intellectual, physical—veer into pain?

21. She made the sound *yum* very clearly once, though not intentionally. She made it after I squirted treacle-sweet liquid Zantac into her cheek to try to quell her constant spit-up. *Yum!* We say it to each other back and forth, then down at her. *Yum! She said it! Yum!* Now we call her Zantac her yum. *Do you want some yum? It's time for your yum! Say it, with your lips like this—the way I'm saying it—yum! What a sweet tooth! What an excitable girl! Look at you, just like a person!* How many times a day now do I say *yum*? Hold the *M* until the vibration makes my lips tickle. She's maybe six inches away from me, propped up on my legs, her heels kneading my stomach. I've never been watched like this before. The complexity of moving lips from open to closed. The little twitches across her face as she tries to mimic mine. In this position, I play music and she dances, which means that I make her dance. We binged that show *Umbrella Academy*, which I reflexively said was stupid but watched with great investment. It's all about adults who still feel like children who resent the adults that made them that way, which I am realizing most everything is about. Superpowers, yes, world saving/destroying and all that, but also, always, childhood. There's a cathartic group dance scene to Tiffany's "I Think We're Alone Now." I play that song on a loop, the way I've always listened to music, but do even more so now that the baby seems to demand recursiveness in anything she likes, or at least recognizes. I'm looking for that glimmer of recognition, feeding it. I think she wiggles the same way every time she hears the plunky eighties electric drum pad at the beginning. I make us dance together, my fingers around her chubby wrists, pantomime running just as fast as we can. She's happy while the song plays, so it plays again. *We're dancing*, I tell her. Her eyes carry so much flickering life that it makes my breath catch. Again, dance, again. Once, when I let go, there was a reddish ring where her skin absorbed the force of my holding her—it was that easy; I was horrified, ashamed, and then her skin bounced back blank.

22. When I remember my earliest childhood, I remember fear. I remember the red vacuum cleaner in my mother's apartment, the sound it made so close to me; in the memory, there's the red and there's the sound and my mother isn't there, so there's the feeling of abandonment, though it's very unlikely that she would've turned on the vacuum and then left the room. I don't remember my father at all until I'm older. When Maurice Sendak died, I listened to and read a lot of his interviews. He'd spoken to Terry Gross about fear and how his work resonated because of the memory of, and commitment to acknowledging that, the experience of childhood was only terror. Sendak never had kids; I think that was an implied foundational aspect of his legend, especially as it was retold around his death—his relationship to childhood remained pure to the experience of being a child. *I refuse to lie to children*, he said. That's the role of the parent: lie to them or to ourselves, either way for comfort. As my daughter gets older, with each successive month of further resembling a human being aware of the world, I have imbued her with a personality based around fearlessness. The child that wants to put her whole hand in a dog's mouth when it sniffs around the stroller. The child at the bar, who we can hand to a cooing stranger while we go order and who meets their gaze. I say often that I don't know how she's mine—I was afraid of everything, and she's afraid of nothing, as though I can speak it into truth. The only time I've seen fear on her face is when I've made her feel afraid—that's the truth. And I wonder how that feeling will linger, how many times it's come back that I haven't even noticed. And I think of that Plath poem "Daddy" and how the heart of it, the turn, is the simplest line among all the Auschwitz metaphors: *I have always been scared of* you. Despite our commitment to giving the baby at least a bottle a day, a month before my wife went back to the office, she began to refuse it. She would scream as though I was choking her, scream until she actually began to choke on the milk she was rejecting, proving herself right. Sometimes, I'd hold her for an hour until finally, mostly by accident, she finished the bottle. My wife began to take walks during these moments, so there would be no visible presence of the person who could make things better, and also because the sounds of the baby's cries caused her such visceral pain that it became like I was torturing two people instead of one. Alone, I'd say to my daughter, *I'm sorry, this has to happen, this is happening.* Even if she could understand any of that, what would it tell her? I recognized that this caused her pain for some reason, and the recognition wasn't going to stop me. It's the same image, over and over: her eyes shut tight, then slowly opening to look up at me again, the bottle looming. And what of my face? Every inch of skin strained, eyes turned up to the ceiling like I could disassociate. *This hurts me more than it hurts you.* I've really thought that so many times, but there's no way to know if it's true. Once, I set her down in the Rock'n'Play, put a pillow over my face and screamed because my wife told me that a mommy blog suggested this as a guilt-free way to vent. I screamed until my throat hurt, but I felt no catharsis, and when I pulled the pillow away, she was staring at me. I watched her face turn slowly from blankness to terror. *No no no no*, I said, and I reached to hold her, and she cried. A few days later she stopped hating the bottle; she lay soft in my arms and blinked up at me as I fed her. I tried to make my face look like the opposite of a scream.

23. The last concert I went to before the baby was Julien Baker, at one of those perfectly sized old theaters with a marquee outside. She played in candlelight with nobody else on stage, small and hunched in the glow. I'd first started to listen to her during the many months that my wife and I were trying and failing, and every new day was beginning to feel the same except a little worse. I love Baker for a lot of reasons, but mostly I think it's structure. There is absolute precision to the way her songs do not resolve. When she finds the note or the refrain that captures the feeling of the moment, she hits it again and again. Sometimes, when a song is swelling in a way that suggests a return to the chorus, a quiet and satisfying comedown, she ends it—not exactly a crescendo, just the feeling of being almost at the top of the rollercoaster, still afraid. Maybe my favorite song of hers is "Sour Breath," which starts off ambient and searching, beginning to tell a story, but by the end hits a refrain like a dirge: *The harder I swim, the faster I sink.* Over and over, and each time it changes, clarifies, like a fist closing on a feeling, finally holding it. I think the possibility of not having our baby, how slow and sad time had begun to feel, made us believe that having her would be like a fever breaking. As though the flash of hope of her existing would mean only hope moving forward. Julien Baker was the soundtrack to the earliest mornings with my daughter, after sleepless nights, her head on my chest, the weight of her so insignificant that I feared if she started to slip off, my body wouldn't feel it enough to react to the change. I like to think that when I sing along to something, she enjoys the vibrations off my skin. I guess this is like being those parents I hate who swear their kid is a Kendrick fan; most of comparative parenting is being grossed out by the thing someone else is doing because you so clearly recognize the impulse. And also the need to believe that sometimes the thing that soothes you can be the thing that soothes them. The way Baker's voice can command at the same time as it trembles. The way she distills fear into a looping guitar riff. I swear the baby loves music.

I swear her eyes are so alive when a voice turns to melody. Music hasn't been this constant since I was fifteen, and every song is a revelation. Four minutes is very fast and very slow, and then I hit repeat. When it's time to put her down for a nap, she fights it, but we're letting her cry it out, so I don't comfort her. I turn the music up and watch her on the monitor—glowing eyes, body writhing against the swaddle, mouth open, and it looks like she's singing. The other day, my mother asked me if I feel any different, and the real answer is *In every possible way and also not at all*, but I ignored the question.

24. She likes to be outside. In the house, she's uneasy, caged, but almost always the air and the wind soothe her. We walk and walk and walk now. When I'm trying to get her to sleep, I walk her in the stroller, but I hate this because it takes her forever, and the sidewalks are so uneven in our neighborhood that usually I'm walking in the street. The best times, she's awake when she's supposed to be and strapped to my chest in the carrier, facing out, her still-soft skull under my chin. We walk the same blocks, past the old Victorians and the deli, all the smudgy windows where I try to make her know her reflection, into the park with the row of trees that someone once told me were London plane, so now I say, *London plane, remember? Like from yesterday.* Everything is like yesterday, sometimes beautiful. The sweat seeps from the front of my T-shirt onto the back of hers. We stick together. Sometimes she gets restless and begins to wriggle, and I try to sing to her, but softly so that people walking by don't hear—what a silly thing to be embarrassed about, but I am. I sing softly, a plea for her to settle, not make us have to turn back home. I tell her everything is a song. The fire engine: a song. The car alarm: a song. The squirrels fighting, the birds, the wind. She loves the wind more than anything. When it hits her, I feel her body taken over with sensation, like she's forgotten how good the same thing felt yesterday and the day before. When this happens, I think I've never been so purely happy, and when it comes just seconds after she's fussy and I'm panicking, it makes me doubt the feeling, and then it's gone and I long for it again. The other day, she was stuck to me and I'd forgotten her hat, so I had my palm out over her face to block the sun. A heavy breeze kicked up. I whispered, *Wind song*, and tried to imitate it, and then I heard her voice, a screech, but I like to think there was a melody in it, imitating the breeze, imitating me.

An Essay about Watching Brad Pitt Eat
That Is Really about My Own Shit

The first movie I remember watching Brad Pitt in was *Meet Joe Black*. This was also the first movie I ever saw on a date—seventh grade, with a horse girl who took great pains to let everyone know she was an other-side-of-the-tracks sort of horse girl, one who had to ride someone else's pet, and they never let her forget it. I remember she showed me her father's empty liquor bottles under the sink in their apartment, which felt important because it implied a certain darkness to her life, and she talked about how, to be an elite show jumper, they made you ration your food, so there was this whole thing with her regimentation versus her father's neglect. When we hugged, I could feel her ribs. I didn't offer any glimpse into the darkness in my own life, though I could have, but that felt out of the emotional range of my self-presentation. None of this has to do with Brad Pitt, but also, it does.

It was a group date, Friday after school. I had been on an unofficial fast for most of the day, which I then broke at a bodega where me and the other boys with dates were buying flowers. I picked out my flowers, went in to pay first, grabbed a Hershey's Cookies 'n' Creme bar and crammed it into my mouth before anyone saw. I could feel white chocolate all over my teeth, so I was rubbing my tongue along the borders of tooth and gum while keeping my mouth closed.

In the theater, everything was about mouths—what you could or should do with them and how you could or should do those things—and of course bodies, either touching or not. It was one of those supercharged moments when normally slouched and silent tweens puff up and laugh louder than necessary, secure in the pack. I hadn't bought popcorn because of the candy bar. My date sucked a Diet Coke and didn't offer me any. I watched the other boys shovel snacks into their mouths while the girls plucked single kernels; both parties looked somehow correct. I felt a familiar mixture of jealousy and hunger. Onscreen, a young, clean-shaven, mop-haired Pitt gleamed. He played Death.

I don't remember much of the movie, other than him getting hit by a bus (which turned him into Death?) and the scenes of him eating. These were a running bit, an attempt at levity in an otherwise humorless slog. Brad Pitt, Death, eating a lamb sandwich while Anthony Hopkins monologues about cilantro. Brad Pitt, Death, accepting a spoon of peanut butter, sticking the head into his mouth, closing his lips, and working his tongue over it, eyes flickering with pleasure as his jaw flexes. Eating as an activity both naive and erotic, like a first kiss. The bit is that Death has never had the pleasure of tasting anything, but it only works if Death looks like Brad Pitt, the impossible ideal of what a man's body could be before any sustenance is added or taken away. Even as Death, he's Aphrodite being born, rising out of the water fully formed, simultaneously perfect and nonexistent, a vessel only.

Onscreen, like a child, he asked, *Can I have more?*

We never had peanut butter in the house because my mother said it was one of those fake healthy foods. At friends' houses, I'd eat the Oreos first, but at some point, I'd see the jar of peanut butter, not even shelved with snacks but a *staple*. I'd open the silverware drawer as quietly as possible, take a tablespoon, force myself to swallow it all in a rush, and then wash and dry the evidence. In the theater, I put my hand on my date's hand and hoped it wasn't too heavy.

Rewatching the movie, I think it might be the blankest performance Pitt's ever given, which is saying something for an actor whose most positive reviews usually include the word *understated*. The eating scenes are the only ones he perks up for, like he's finally got a chance to do something. Him and Anthony Hopkins interviewed each other decades later and barely brought the movie up, even though it was one of only two times they worked together. Pitt said, *I was actually going through a difficult time during that film. I felt pretty shackled. I didn't feel very free.* Hopkins said, *Oh really? I had no idea.*

There are many options available if you want to watch a supercut of Brad Pitt eating. They range from three-minute collections of the obvious clips to the more satisfying twenty-minute epics that trace his consumption across three decades. His two greatest eating performances, in my educated opinion, come in *Moneyball* and the entire Ocean's franchise, primarily because nothing about the character or plot seems to call for food, but Pitt makes the choice to turn food into a central component of both. Casing a luxury casino in a silver leisure suit? Eat an ice cream cone in violent lunges and gulps. Pacing the bowels of a baseball stadium during the late innings of a crucial game? Shove half a hero sandwich into your mouth, let mayonnaise and lettuce leak onto your trapezoidal chin, chew for an impossibly long time before delivering your line. These scenes blur into a sort of magical realism for me—this particular, painstakingly captured hunger incongruous with every other data point given by the movie.

What I'm talking about is watching a body that is made to be looked at, that is professionally looked at, behave as though it's simply doing something natural, unconcerned with what we might see. It seems I've just described the concept of acting. What I mean, though, is when the incongruity feels gratuitous, or at least pointed, and the lack of acknowledgment of that pointedness becomes part of the pleasure or tension—the one nude person on a non-nude beach rolling over for an even tan, an act of defiance made nonchalant.

No man in my lifetime has ever done nonchalant beauty better than Pitt, certainly none of his immediate peers. Someone like Matthew McConaughey seems to want very badly to be that kind of chill hunk, but he's so insistent that it becomes shtick, which is not nonchalant at all. Keanu Reeves doesn't want attention, but he doesn't want it to the level that it just makes everyone kind of sad that he has to deal with it, and sometimes I want to be like, *Hello, he's rich and beloved, good for him that he takes the subway, but let's move on!* These are all Gen X examples for a reason. I grew up watching these men, pushed toward their films by my older brothers who wanted to be them, and I was unquestioning of my brothers and their desires, no matter the darkness that swirled around them. They were perfect, unattainable, and so too were these heartthrobs, vessels for both desire and envy. I think of them now as the last of a type. Now, beauty in general, and for the first time male beauty, is sold not as some brooding, enigmatic, otherworldly quality, but as constantly documented work. Cheerful, inclusive, attainable progress.

Sometimes I look at Kumail Nanjiani's cheat-day Instagram posts, which exist only to reinforce the gym bro monasticism of every other day, since even the act of holding up a fork sparks sinuous ripples across a body pushed to its very limit, and I feel only contempt. I got into a hole recently of people looking at Nanjiani's old face next to his new one (from one of those photos where he smirks over his once-a-week cake) and speculating about steroid use. I felt enormous satisfaction, the same as when people turned on Chris Pratt—long before he became overall hateable, I hated him for the transformation, the supposed-to-be-humanizing profiles, the gosh-look-what-a-regular-guy-can-do-if-he-cuts-out-beer workout pics.

Even with a genuinely magnetic star like Michael B. Jordan, part of the appeal lies in seeing how he was made—the story of the skinny, sweet-faced kid from *The Wire* contrasted with what he has become, though not exactly that because there's passivity in the idea of *becoming* and that's not what's being sold. In *Creed*, we watch him make the body we're watching, an instructional montage for hotness, with a soundtrack attached begging fans to emulate him. I have, stumbling through jumping jacks, trying to ignore myself bouncing, then settling, more ashamed than exhausted. When Michael B. Jordan eats in a movie, it is infrequent and purposeful: pure fuel.

There's a way of looking at stars as something aspirational and a way that's the opposite. It's akin, I think, to looking at a wealthy person and seeing a benevolent future peer or looking at a wealthy person and seeing a monster forged from luck and evil. For a long time, I was obsessed with reality TV, in large part because the distance between the original person and the person made to be watched was collapsed. Instead, I got to watch the effortfulness—some alienating, some seductive, all of it, in at least a small way, familiar to my experience of being in the world. The reality show obsession that has lasted longest for me is *Love Island*, and I think that's because of the amount of time dedicated to men with perfectly engineered bodies thinking and talking about those bodies. The gym is a central setting in the house they all share. It's where the men talk, or really groan, to one another, about their lives and their feelings, which are often related to the bodies they're working on. If a man is absent from a scene set elsewhere, we know where he is and why. Sometimes, they bob into the background of a conversation, in their tiny, sweat-drenched shirts, shaking protein mix into water, scrambling up enough eggs to overflow the pan. When they dress for dinner, they stand in front of the mirror and pull at their shirts, try to move their body so the fabric settles haphazardly but in the right way, vacillating between frustration and satisfaction. When I'm watching this, I am free of envy because they look so worked up about it all, so small and human, even as they don't want to be.

In 2008, the film critic David Thomson mourned the death of stardom, pointing at Heath Ledger and saying that the *cult* calling him a superstar would last maybe through the opening weekend of *The Dark Knight*. His essay is that wonderful combination of crankiness and nostalgia, whittling down to anger at us, the viewers, who *gave up [our] affection for stars . . . and replaced it with mounting cynicism*. He situates true movie stars, from the old studio era, as the timely American replacement for gods and royals, an image of *a chance at happiness*. The more we see of them, the constant accesses of modernity and all that, the closer they come to resembling us, or at least some cursed middle between us and gods. Then his ultimate thesis: *We don't like our stars—but we don't like ourselves so much [either].*

He wrote this over a decade ago, and the years since have continued to move in the direction he pointed, though I think a counterpressure has emerged. Stars are more muscly, more oddly and inhumanly beautiful, more famous, while also becoming more streamlined, more constantly accessible across platforms, more needy of every little glance—ultimately interchangeable. It's the simultaneous celebration of commonness and perfection. A movie star doesn't feel that different from a *Love Island* star to me at this point. Both clearly know I'm watching all the time and depend on that; both make me feel weak and fat and mortal, but also like they would be, even would *want* to be, my friend.

I want to be a different person a lot of the time, but really that means I want to be in a different body. It's hard for me to watch someone and see the emotion they're performing in some vacuum of intellect where their body doesn't exist in the performance. It's hard to separate depression from vanity. When I was at the heaviest I've ever been, I got into a fight with my father that culminated in him holding a belt and yelling that if I *really* didn't feel like I'd become obese, put it on and see if any of the loops fit. The worst part of the memory is that I did it. I put it on and sucked and clenched everything, and it did fit, and it took a few moments for me to realize how much sadder this was than if I'd walked away. I thought about it every day for months. When good things happened, it was the caveat lurking immediately behind them; when bad things happened, it felt like the reason. I lost a lot of weight through starvation, and one of those CouchTo10K apps. When I saw my father again, he said, *Now you can't write about being a fat person anymore because people will*

get mad about appropriation, which was meant as a compliment
but felt like silencing, and also served to prove my suspicions that
everything I'd ever felt or expressed was really about what was
wrong with my body.

My wife and I have a pact to not make our daughter feel the way
we felt as children, which was an acute awareness of the size
of our bodies in relation to those of our peers and a sense that
what we saw in ourselves was not what we wanted, that what we
wanted was something to be earned, attainable yet always out of
reach because we never reached hard enough. Loving her body,
telling her to do the same, turns out to be easy, but I don't trust
the ease, because when I see her lovable body moving around in
the world, mine is always next to her.

Sometimes, she's naked before her bath, sprinting the hallway
in the apartment, and I catch her, wrap my hands around her
belly, drum her skin with my fingers and say, *Look at this beautiful body.* The spot right under her top rib makes her ticklish.
She bucks and writhes and giggles. Sometimes she'll repeat, *body
body body*, through the giggles. In these moments, I very often
will have a rush of emotion so intense that it's literally destabiliz-
ing. I'll sit down and squeeze her until she says, *I wanna go back*,
which is a throwaway line from a random scene in *Moana* that
she uses to reference all forms of displeasure.

My daughter is in love with the way her body looks and feels.
She's old enough now to understand when we tell her that we love
it, and that has increased her love because of the validation she
can receive simply by lifting up her shirt. When she's upset, she
runs away into our bedroom, finds the full-length mirror that

is a source of great anxiety for me, and stands there watching herself until her image settles her down. When I go get her, I crouch so that we're both in the same image, but then instinctively look away. She thinks I'm ignoring her and says, *Daddy Daddy Daddy*, until I smile.

The relationship between a toddler and reflective surfaces is all possibility. She's still surprised, I think, by just how many different objects can become vessels to bring her back to her own image, her own body moving through the world, always moving. Everything blurs, and then suddenly, wonderfully, there she is again, mimicking herself. Sometimes I see her move past a reflective surface and only realize what she sees when it's almost out of view. She's like a cartoon, freezing for a moment before springing back to look. If she has food in her hand, she'll shove it all into her mouth to watch her cheeks expand, and then she'll lean in close to watch her jaw work. We have an advent calendar going, and when she eats her daily Hershey's Kiss, a line of muddy spit trickles out. In her reflection, she follows the spit down her neck and torso, finally pooling in her belly button.

I like to talk about her stats every time we come back from the pediatrician. *Ninety-ninth percentile—in a room of one hundred toddlers, there might only be one taking up more space than her!* I worry, though, that this is starting to become as performative as so many other aspects of parenting, like every pixelated friend on the other side of FaceTime, every stooped and hurried playground acquaintance, is paying keen attention to whether I'm expressing the correct sentiment. It's in line with when she got obsessed with a baby doll at daycare, and I took her to buy one, and, faced with a row of dolls identical in every feature except for skin color, she picked a Black baby because that's how her daycare doll looked, to reflect the racial composition of the school, and for a while I couldn't stop posting photos of her holding her Black baby doll. It's that weird gray area where an aspect of your child is not staged but . . . *highlighted*. She loved this doll and carried this doll everywhere, and I was—I'm not sure if *proud* is the right word, but sort of—proud of the implication that I encouraged this, which really just means that I wasn't such an absolute asshole that I demanded she get a white doll because she's a white kid. To mention it outright is gross enough to ruin any good implications, so it was left for me to perform without comment, hoping that someone else might. It's *that* feeling, all too specific, all too recognizable, that I get when I express yet again my joy at a big daughter, who holds her belly to feel the shape of it and likes to watch her skin jiggle in the mirror—so *beautiful*, I say again, so *hungry*. I pull a banana from my back pocket; she eats in gulps. I hand her pieces that are too big, and she pushes a new one into her mouth before finishing the last one. She's overflowing, but she's smiling at the sight of her body and her eating, our closeness through it all.

Hooray, I say, *hooray my big eater, my best eater*—leaping over that lowest bar of not making a toddler feel anything toward herself but love.

In an interview alongside Margot Robbie during the press tour for *Once Upon a Time in Hollywood*, Pitt was asked if he'd seen any of the supercuts of his eating. Robbie appeared more interested than at any other moment in the conversation. *I . . . have noticed*, she said, smiling but pointed. Pitt, of course, claimed to be entirely unaware of the fact that there was any noticeable pattern; he was just behaving the way any human might. He had his little incredulous half grin.

I'm a grazer by nature, he said, which, okay, sure man—I imagine him grazing quite literally on grass.

Robbie, bless her, pushed him. She brought up *Ocean's Eleven* and asked if there always just happened to be food around during his shots.

Here, Pitt jumped into actor-discussing-craft mode. He said, *Oh, well, there was actually a method to that. I thought, he's always on the run, always on the go, he never has time to sit down and have a real meal, so he'd just have to grab something.*

I love how implausible this explanation is. The idea that, in a movie designed to be pure fun and fantasy, all shimmer, playing a barely 2D character who seems to have no motivation or distinctive features beyond beauty and poise, Pitt would drill down on this central question of, *My God, how is he supposed to get his calories in mid-heist?* And none of the other characters, all keeping the same schedule, under the same stress, respond by eating, so the result is the *very* noticeable (just ask Margot Robbie) juxtaposition of his costars doing what people in movies usually do—not eating—while Pitt polishes off a hot dog and an ice cream cone, chomps down on a nearly unlicked lollipop, shovels jelly beans from a crystal tumbler at a hotel bar as though that's the sort of thing that would come gratis at an upscale casino. In a cynical read, it's a particular kind of bad acting that conflates being noticed at all costs with creating character, like the kid in my college production of *King Lear* who did a Mike Myers Scottish accent for three hours while nobody else did any accent at all. But Pitt isn't a grandstander; again, part of his seduction is that it doesn't seem like the desire to steal a movie would occur to him. If anything, he believes he's out there performing a perfect approximation of a regular man doing regular things, a regular body covered in flesh in the midst of that regular act of shoving sustenance into his face hole.

In the interview, I don't think he realizes that his tone becomes anthropological. He's fifty-five, still sitting the way popular high school boys sit, which is easy to confuse with self-satisfaction but is really lack of concern so pure that the question of whether or not to feel satisfied wouldn't ever come up. He doesn't shift his weight. He doesn't tug at the white shirt tapered around his arms and waist that offers no cover for whatever might spill out and over. He wears a cap that on any other aging star would be the ultimate white flag to pattern baldness, but with him it just means he likes hats. All of this is so expected, has been repeated seamlessly so many times, that interviewers never really comment on his looks or clothes or lifestyle choices. He is as he has always been—what is there for him to say about it? It's not just that his body has remained static over thirty-five years of fame (other than a quick detour into even greater buffness for *Troy*), it's that he inhabits that body in the same way, both as a character and as himself talking about his characters. Brad Pitt on press tour in 2019 sits just like Brad Pitt shirtless in *Thelma & Louise* in 1988, a purely physical, entirely uninternalized gesture that makes him seem almost neon compared to those around him, memorable for his pure act of *being*. The critic Manohla Dargis described it best: *A sublime lack of self-consciousness and self-doubt about taking up space. . . . This isn't swagger; this is flow.*

But none of it is interesting to me. None of it is worth remembering beyond simply knowing I saw it, like a better-than-usual painting in the lobby of the building where you work. I only care when his flow reaches for food, makes a show of it, invariably breaks down into self-caricature. There is nothing less human to me, nothing more strange and showy, than eating freely, constantly, without noticing yourself, and without any physical or emotional consequence. It's not even that I don't believe the character, it's that I don't believe Brad Pitt. I believe him lounging and talking and having whatever little tics he chooses for a given role and smiling and fucking, but I don't believe him eating. Always, still, to not believe him, to find that crack in him, is a relief. I remember only the unacknowledged incongruity, like a TikTok of a bulldog skateboarding or a cop being kind.

There was a brief period when my father bought and used a camcorder. Most of the material was long ago taped over or lost. I've only seen two videos—my grandmother's eightieth birthday, unearthed because it was at that restaurant on top of the World Trade Center, so it later took on a dark novelty, and my own second birthday, which I scrounged up to watch after my brother overdosed, since he was the one holding the camera and you can hear his voice. The video is mostly of people I don't remember, just milling, saying random things when my brother prods them to. When I appear, he moves the camera in through a little crowd that has assembled for the ritual of watching children eat cake. Quickly, the show becomes only me, round, blond, and unmoving, as my peers lose interest and wander off to play. I'm left alone at the table with the cake, cupping my hands to scoop in a way that suggests a more advanced dexterity than I've often been told I had. I eat and eat. I don't say anything to anyone, I don't look up to acknowledge the camera or my parents laughing out of the frame.

My brother films himself for a moment—aviator sunglasses, clean-lined jaw, swoop-necked weightlifter's tank, all the totems of his attempts at a modeling career. He grins, then turns back to me, the big baby, too concentrated to be happy exactly, entranced by taste and texture, food in mouth, how much I could consume and still find more. Laughter continuing from all around; me oblivious to the laughter—how soon would I become conscious enough to no longer be oblivious? When I fill in the blanks of early memory, the image that remains most indelible of my brother is this one, when he turns the camera on himself, brooding, fleeting, and the image most indelible of me is the toddler eating amid the laughter. This is unfair, of course: reducing his unknowable pain to a before picture of beauty, elevating mine because people generally like to laugh watching a chubby kid eat. But to remember admiration for him, how good it felt, I need to remember his once-sculpted body, find the power there in this thing he had that I never will, as though seeing him that way is an act of generosity.

I don't know why this particular video was saved when so many others were lost. Probably, almost certainly, there was no nefarious intention, and yet. . . . However it came to be, this is the only video recording of my body and my brother's together. I knew all its beats before I ever watched it; that's how central it was in family mythology. It was told alongside the jokes about how my father gained a lot of weight when I was little—these were the stories that most linked *us* together in the time before I remember much. Always, I wanted to eat, and sometimes, when my mom was busy, he fed me, and when he fed me, he succumbed to temptations and ate, too. Baby food—sweet and mushy—it went down without making him think. *You know I'm a grazer*, he has always said, and now I hear myself saying it, too. So many childhood memories, everyone's hand in everyone else's plate—*If I didn't order it, the calories don't count! Stop me, I'm so full, it's disgusting! How could I still be eating?* There should be different plateaus in memory, one up high to keep real grief, real love, away from the superficial maw, yet there is my brother, still inseparable from a general idea of appetite and why it's wrong, always the conflation of petty shame and danger.

I pilfered the nursing snacks I bought for my wife when we got home from the hospital. All the trail mix, too many of the peanut-butter-stuffed pretzels, even though those were the ones she liked best. Breastfeeding was hard; the baby rejected it and she never slept, so the first month of nights went in shifts—my wife would wake to pump, leave the bottle, wake me to feed her with the bottle, then I'd set her down, and she'd be up again for more before my wife was done with the next pump. There was a feeling of shared purpose and burden to this time that was the only nice part about it; we were made as close to interchangeable as possible, rotating in and out of the same Ikea chair, writhing warmth pressed back and forth to each of our chests in a steady rhythm. It made me feel like I was doing more than I was. The physicality of my wife's year had been so stunning in its endurance and elasticity, all the extremes absorbed. There is nothing to say about it that won't now sound trite; somehow I'd never considered the athleticism of birth. I'd been trying to cut weight in the months prior. I'm not sure why, exactly—because the literalness of my wife's need for sustenance allowed me to frame mine as superfluous? Because something life-changing was going to happen, and this is the way I'd grown accustomed to marking change? Because I was trying to budget for the parental weight gain I'd been warned about, that I once caused? When she was born, I cut the cord and took off my shirt for skin-to-skin, the way they tell you to. She was so small on my chest. The doula took a picture, and I felt myself try to tighten, felt my weight shifting, such a clear wish amid the chaos that the newborn was a bit larger so that she might cover more of me. I was crying from fear and love and pride for my wife; still, phone turned on me, there was my body to consider. Back in the nursing chair, feeding the baby the bottle, one hand in the pretzel bowl in the dark, wondering if the baby was settling into sleep, wondering how few pretzels I could leave while avoiding the panic of my wife bringing it up.

Will I ever tell my daughter about this? I've imagined the conversation the way I imagine so many versions of her being older because it's nice to dwell in only possibility. In my mind, on an optimistic day, it's a throwaway line that holds so little weight that we won't remember it—we're on a hike, we're on the way home from a movie, we're just passing time together. I'm planning it fifteen years out, hoping it doesn't mean anything.

Pitt is taken seriously now, which I'm mostly happy about. He is the last of the beautiful Gen X leading men to receive this treatment, probably because he's the most beautiful. At some point, people stopped thinking it was silly that Ethan Hawke called himself a novelist, and there was the *very* hyperbolic and ill-conceived McConaissance moment; now we have Pitt, who is a better actor than these peers but is also so much nicer to look at that it's taken him a decade or more to catch up.

Manohla Dargis's essay makes this explicit: *Beauty can be as much of a trap as a benediction, even for men.* Then she doubles down: *There's nothing new about how we punish beauty*—again, she makes a point to say that while this notion is more readily exemplified by female stars, Pitt proves that a man, too, can be pretty enough to make people want to see him eat shit. She's right, though it's a touch ironic that this essay ran alongside Pitt's lauded performance in a Tarantino film as a near sixty-year-old, still peaking in a career that has provided him choice roles with no fallow period and *only* a single Oscar—how many of the actresses he's been associated with over that time would consider this a punishment?

But then there's Dargis's point, perhaps: I am much more willing to be sympathetic to the obvious biases foisted upon famously beautiful women than I am to accept that anyone has the power to make Pitt feel something other than chill. It remains important to me to believe that Pitt never has to think about the power of beauty if he doesn't want to, even though his whole life has been defined and bankrolled (and, sure, I guess maybe pigeon-holed) by people marveling at the beauty. I've been searching for an interview where he talks about it, and there's hardly anything, which is like LeBron James never talking about basketball, though of course in Pitt's mind, his basketball is acting, but who cares about his acting? All I want to do is talk about his body and how noticeable it is to me, how noticeable every body is—that's the problem—and how insulting to think that nobody makes him account for himself. This is the greatest privilege afforded in my fantasy of thinness: that it eventually might allow you to disappear—to other people, sure, but most of all to yourself.

I always wanted a daughter—some misguided hope that the particulars of the shame baggage we try not to saddle her with wouldn't exactly be mine. Also, more insidious: I don't trust myself to be kind to a son. I can recognize and reject the cruelty done to a young girl's body by reinforcing what it isn't, what someone else thinks it should be. There's an obvious track record for that cruelty, a consequence baked into every bit of society. Fat men have power, and sometimes it seems like nobody has ever made them feel shame; fat men do bad. I have known fat men whose fatness was a show of strength, or even a performative joy—*Look at all that I can consume; it's a joke to me, so you can laugh, too.* I've felt hatred for these men and a great deal of jealousy but never kindness. If I had a two-year-old son in front of me sizing up his birthday cake the way I once did. . . . The thought trails off, or I don't want to follow it.

I never get the tone right when talking or writing about men's bodies, least of all my own. Despite (because of?) that, I won't let myself stop. In graduate school, I turned in an essay that organized a day through calorie counting, and in my mind, it was a fun, sometimes funny experiment, dipping my toe into *lyric essay* land. My peers liked the piece, but in the way that people like the most morose memoir material, when admiration and pity become indistinguishable. A classmate called it one of the most courageous but self-loathing things she'd ever read, and I was like, *Whoa, wow, haha, just a chubby goof over here, did you get to the bit about forgetting to wipe my hands after the Tostitos and then rubbing my eyes?* Right after, I wrote another weird piece that (surprise!) underneath the experimentation ended up being all about my body, and this time I thought I was leaning into the darkness of it all. But when I read it in front of a crowd at a bar, I got such big laughs that I pretended humor had been the goal.

When you're in the community of people who believe it's valid, even valuable, to write about one's self, there's a lot of talk about trauma, and always I nod along but don't see myself in the con-versation. It's hard to call any of these invisible scars of fat boy-hood or yo-yo diets a trauma; I still don't really believe they are. I think it's my choice whether or not this pain over my body is real, is earned, is worthy of having ever existed, yet it always has. To consider life without it doesn't feel like a choice at all. When I'm asked to empathize with people's addiction or depression or illness, this is the only frame of reference that comes to my mind for feeling out of control, unable to find catharsis, but I never say that.

When my daughter was maybe nine months old, a spherical cherub who'd just barely begun crawling, a well-meaning person said, *Don't worry, when they start walking, they become bean-poles; it's amazing the way things change.* I felt the kind of stunned anger that only clarifies into a response too late. But I also worried about whether I'd been complicit. Had I spoken of her size like I was complaining? Had I suggested that I might need some as-suaging? I tried to imagine my own expression as we watched my daughter; what in my face could have sold her out? I've heard my parents say, *The way she eats!* and if I don't respond fast, they rush into the silence with, *Healthy things! All those healthy things! You're lucky!*

In high school, I watched the girls with conspicuous eating disorders, noted their changes and their fastidiousness, which I confused with dedication. I felt misplaced envy that they had the capacity to feel bad enough to *do* something about it. The boys doing push-up contests at lunch until one of them collapsed; the girls consuming nothing but coffee and SlimFast shakes pilfered from a mother's stash—I saw two halves of a general idea of what personhood looked like for the non-lazy. I knew better than that. There was pain that I at least somewhat recognized that made the girls different than the boys, or maybe even that was wrong, but I couldn't begin to consider that the boys doing push-ups felt anything bad, anything at all. I just watched. Let myself think, *At least she's getting something out of it.* I tried bulimia a few times; no, it was more than that—knees on the tile floor, fan wailing to cover the noise. I couldn't ever pull the trigger enough to fully purge. Even now, rereading that sentence, the judgment appears to be more on the failure to complete than the impulse to try.

One thing I've always appreciated about Pitt is that he's never played ugly, and he's never played fat. Even during those years when all an A-lister had to do was put on a prosthetic or gain forty pounds to get an Oscar nod, he never did it. George Clooney was a reliably good actor for a very long time before he flaunted a burgeoning belly in a shirtless torture scene—*commitment* to craft over image, got him his recognition, though rewatching *Syriana*, he looks pretty much like himself. There's Theron in *Monster*, Kidman's Virginia Woolf nose in *The Hours*. Whatever various overrated extremes Christian Bale has taken on over the years.

Pitt has never chosen to not be Brad Pitt in the image onscreen. Even as he's taken strange, anti-careerist roles, earned that character-actor-trapped-in-a-leading-man cliché, each performance comes attached to the promise of Brad Pitt's body. He may have done a wacky Irish traveler accent in *Snatch*, but he was still a boxer, and there was a slow-motion break in the movie's frantic comedy to watch him pull off his shirt. It's almost as if he's set himself a lifelong artistic challenge—*I can believably be anybody, even when I look like this.* Or there's that lingering possibility that he hasn't considered his body enough to wonder whether it's a gift or a hindrance. Or maybe it's a moral decision, honoring what has always been the moneymaker, refusing to take on that greatest and easiest bit of artifice, the physical kind, even in a profession all about playing pretend.

I watched *Ad Astra* recently, which felt like the closest Pitt has ever come to nodding at the fact of his body, by removing it as much as possible. The movie groaned with the effort of profundity; it's the first Pitt vehicle I've ever seen where you cannot escape how badly he wants critics to use the word *brilliant*. This bummed me out, but it worked for some. Dargis fawned over his *wounded, crumpled humanity*, hailed the film as *an exploration of masculinity and all its discontents.* I try to imagine the words *wounded* or *crumpled* or *discontents* or even *humanity* being applied to a Pitt role where we see more of him, where it's not just his aging baritone mumbling through a voice-over, his partially visible face floating in endless, weightless black. Did he think he couldn't tackle all the failure and pain of what it means to carry the broken legacy of manhood if we saw him?

He had a long conversation with Christiane Amanpour on CNN about the film, and it's the only time I've seen him even briefly uncomfortable in an interview. Amanpour says he's never done anything like this, without a gesture at the upward tilt of a question in her voice, and he wriggles in his chair. He looks way from the camera, seems to consider pushing back, but settles on, *Well . . . no . . . maybe not to this extent . . . I've always been a little more . . . physical.* He forces that word out, like he's been looking for the least obvious way to say it. Later, the talk turns to the themes of loneliness that the film explores, and Amanpour gives him the chance to get autobiographical. He demurs, tries to find his footing as the artist, vessel for universal emotion: *Well, we all . . . feel great loneliness . . . sadness . . . grief.* I don't believe him.

He's in all gray for the interview, including a gray cap, everything a little baggy—a look chosen, I think, to make him blank, make him anyone, like the outfits they put on a stuntman in front of a green screen. Maybe, finally, he seems burdened by himself. Maybe the goal all along has been to have his art become as little about his body as possible. Maybe his fantasy is the same as mine—that satisfaction will only come when he feels like he's disappeared and he no longer must confront what is seen onscreen, in the mirror. But who knows? The point is never to know what it feels like for him, right? The point is what it feels like to see him there. Maybe it's changed for him, maybe he's changing all the time; the problem is it hasn't changed much for me.

Brian Phillips puts it well in his essay on Pitt: *The secret to [his] stardom has always been . . . to make watching seem like a more alive version of itself.*

There is something active to it—the steady brightness of his star over a whole life, returning to him again to reengage. But all this engagement, and what has progressed? Ask me about Brad Pitt, and I'll still make fun of him eating onscreen, like a lot of people do, but in a way that is a little too invested and a little too offended. And I'll hope that the tone reads funny. And I'll worry that it never did.

When I remember my brother now, which is a less and less frequent occurrence, too often I'm thinking about vanity, and always I'm doing the thing where vanity stands in for, or maybe subsumes, pain. Despite all evidence to the contrary, there are still the two archetypes of his memory—clean, dazzling, fit; fat, helpless, gone. I didn't understand track marks or slurred speech or giant pupils as a kid, but I understood a body that, depending on whether we were mad at him at a given time, deserved either pity or ridicule.

A junkie should at least be skinny—I remember that joke, or whatever it was meant to be.

In his last, lonely years, he'd go through a sleeve of Oreos like nothing was happening. He'd drink a two-liter Pepsi like it was water. Conversations revolved around these details, as though they gave something away. As though the truth, the shame, lay there.

In the year before my wife got pregnant, I got back into therapy to talk about difficulties conceiving, plus my brother, plus the usual making-art-into-the-void, world-dying stuff. The way I remember it, there were all these conversations about fatness and how to think about it or not think about it, and it felt like my therapist kept harping on this, looking for openings to cram her body-posi, self-love message down my throat. In retrospect, I'm pretty sure I was always bringing it up, and she was like, *Wow, this is toxic and annoying, we should probably work through it.* She was talking about disordered eating, and I was like, *No, are you listening? I'm just saying I need endorphins.* That sort of thing—back and forth. I left for a residency, only ate breakfast and dinner, ran every day until my knees started to throb, felt briefly amazing at the lake because I was around strangers who had no context for my body other than this slimmer version, and when I came home, I never returned the therapist's calls.

Now everything is physical. More is needed from my body than has ever been, for the pacification and safety of somebody more important than me, somebody whose every move we feel compelled to document. So, there I am—ass crack peeking out as I crouch to hold her back from an irritated goose by a river. Looming over and around her on my lap to read a book, that crease in my shirt between chest and stomach, my least favorite of all the creases. Hoisting her above my head when she demands *Shoulders*, my belly button exposed the same way I love it when hers is. I had hoped that needing to simply act so often, so fast, would take away the chance to think about my body, but there it is, there I am. When I tickle her now, she tickles back, and we are two people, big and little, with bodies familiar, bodies that bring each other joy, and I wish I could feel only joy, a blinding light.

We want her to eat without thinking about it; my wife and I have been discussing this since before she was born. Eating as just a thing one does, both a pleasure and a necessity, nothing else. We buy cookies and string cheese and goldfish for her. She knows the words *cookie* and *cracker* and *pizza* and *waffle* and *chocolate* and *cake*. She knows and loves the word *bagel* so much that it serves as an umbrella term for all circular baked goods. The other night, she was finally down, and my wife and I were doing that hunched thirty-minute dance of retrieving her toys from around the apartment, and I held up a bowl still half full of the cookies we'd given her. She'd lost interest at a certain point.

I finished the cookies with my back turned to my wife, then pretended to dump them into the garbage. She said, *I'm proud of us for this.*

We don't say that a lot parenting-wise; I don't know, either we're not proud in a given moment, or we don't want to jinx it when things feel good. I didn't respond, so she said, *The cookies aren't a thing for her. They don't mean anything. She eats until she's done.*

I wanted to ask my wife jokingly if she was tearing up, but then I was tearing up. Happy tears, proud tears, layered on, or really mixed into, those of regret. That ultimate sensation of parenthood—the simultaneity of something beginning and something ending, constant potential only solidifying what has been lost. Think so hard about how fragile this little person is, and you forget your own fragility until it floods you, like a migraine, creeping, creeping, ignorable until it's not.

This isn't a climactic moment, just one of many that ebb and flow, that feel the same way. The question is how to end a narrative that hasn't changed and that I still can't envision changing, no matter how much I want it to, and no matter what in my life has changed around it. When my daughter sleeps, we scroll through pictures of her awake. There she is; there I am. I don't want to change anything about the pictures except my body in them, and sometimes, when I think that, I can almost convince myself that it's reasonable. I've tried so many times to change my body, but it's never changed the way I feel about it, just distracted from the effort it might take to love myself the way I want her to. And I want her to so badly, but what does that desire mean if I lack the imagination to even approach the feeling for myself.

I'll end on a desire for a smaller change, an end that can hopefully be a beginning. In the morning, when I pull my daughter from her crib and hold her, and her little fingers search across me, then finally squeeze, I don't want to flinch.

On Boredom and Vigilance and Addiction and Other Everyday Occurrences

Once, when I was scrolling, I came across the headline "Your Kids Think You're Addicted to Your Phone" from the *New York Times*. I copied and pasted it to the place in my Notes app where I put all of the essay ideas that I mostly never write. Next to it, I put **, which is my number one symbol for *This might have legs*, and wrote, "DO THIS ONE," just in case I missed the symbol. Six months later, I finally read the article, which pretty much said what the headline said, while referencing a specific study from an organization I'd never heard of, and now here we are.

The problem with these sorts of essays is that often something born of out a pop-social-science-driven *Aha!* moment can never get any deeper than the original *Aha!* The thing has already been "proven," so the job of writing becomes an act of extra confirmation, which turns anything that might have felt like a revelation into the opposite. There are too many anecdotes to pick just one. Or really, the problem is that the enormity and sameness of these anecdotes don't add up to create what feels like a mountain of evidence but rather a redundancy of an idea that was probably too obvious to begin with, or it wouldn't be that easy to exemplify. What frightens me the most are the things that are so plain to see that they don't quite seem worth acknowledging.

A potential starting place, or at least the most recent memory: we were trying to potty train. It didn't work, so this is not an essay about potty training, as there is nothing more to say beyond, *Wow, horrible,* and also, potty training books can be predictably sexist and almost effortfully racist, even when they come recommended by Subaru types. One of the things that this potty training book demanded was a chunk of consecutive days in which you don't take your eyes off your kid, since they are forbidden to wear clothing of any kind. We set aside Presidents' Day weekend, and for good measure I canceled my office hours the following Tuesday. The book says this is supposed to be hard, don't pretend it isn't hard, but try to find the joy in the closeness and unfiltered attention that modern society usually robs from us.

In the days prior, my stress kept ratcheting up, but what I couldn't manage to say out loud to my wife was that it had almost nothing to do with the piss and shit that would end up on the floor or the emotional toll of the I-am-causing-you-pain-but-for-a-reason fights that hadn't occurred since sleep training, or even the great possibility of failure. Those looming intensities felt muted in comparison with the thought of a four-day weekend in which I would be with my family and not with my phone at the same time. At dinner, when we'd talk about what our plan was for different scenarios, I'd also be attempting to anticipate how time would move through those phoneless hours, and it wasn't that I was certain those hours would be bad; it was that I could not conceive of that passage of time and how my brain might process it. I couldn't imagine myself like that, the same way that I couldn't imagine my daughter ever pulling down her jeggings and taking a clean piss in the appropriate location. It seemed inevitable that these two failures of personhood would come to a head in a moment when I snuck off to greedily tweet just as she began to diarrhea all over the couch. Excruciating—her shame and mine, all at once.

Long before parenthood, I began leaving my phone charging in the kitchen at bedtime so that the last and first thing I saw each night and morning was not a screen, and that's been the most continually successful act of self-care I've ever undertaken. But the night before potty training began, I found myself not wanting to put the phone in its safe place. I was standing with all the lights out but one, plus the screen light, and I don't remember what I was looking at, but I was looking at it long enough that when I finally glanced up, minutes had gone by, though I would have guessed only seconds, that sensation of falling asleep when you haven't meant to, not long enough to find anything restorative, and then the gasp when you wake up, as though you've slid underwater. My wife was standing in the hallway in the dark. She said, *Should we. . . .* Her tone was gentle, which made it worse. We both speak to each other about our phones gently now; I'm not sure exactly when that started. It used to be fun—*Gotcha, you fucking spaced out robot!*—and then it was full-on annoyance, but at some point, we decided to go easy, which was the best way to say without saying it that we think the other one has a problem.

As the study in the *Times* (and a casual Google search revealing a million similar articles) suggests, the language of addiction feels appropriate here, but it brings diminishing returns. Well and good to say, *Yeah, duh, we're all addicted to our phones, man,* but it gets clumsier and more toothless the longer the parallel extends. If I'm honest, I think I had a shred of hope that the potty-training experience and the days of pure, vigilant parental care would create a detox environment—some sweating, the shakes, a vomit or two before naptime, followed by the fever breaking and then a newly bright world. Did I even fantasize in the shower of one day telling people that my daughter and I shared a moment of mutual evolution fostered by my devotion to her? Who can remember, but the reality of that first morning, and the days after, too, was that the lack of my phone in my hand and my inability to glance at it every ten seconds didn't cause extremes of any kind. The world was not harder or brighter; I didn't feel more present in it. I was sludgy. My eyes had their familiar medium-sting, even though there was no screen to blame it on.

The whole point of this exercise was that the moment my daughter showed any signs of soiling herself, I'd be so accustomed to her little tics and tells that I'd be able to grab her and carry her to the potty on time, but often she'd be standing there with piss running down her leg, and I'd be looking directly at this, as though from a great distance or from behind a pointlessly frosted glass door, and only when I heard the trickle on hardwood would I be aware enough to move. I was staring at her so hard I was staring past her.

My daughter was aware of what potty training meant and vehemently disagreed with the whole process, but what seemed to upset her most of all was the surveillance. Often I'd realize that she was looking over her shoulder back at me, tracing the way my eyes dutifully traced her, and the attention emboldened her to want to do something to earn it, which invariably made me annoyed at her, though as in almost all cases of me being annoyed at her, the root of the emotion was me: the novelty she clearly felt at my exclusive attention. I crawled over to her and sniffed her face like a dog, which made her laugh for fifteen seconds or so. She always smells like some version of toast, and I told her that, which made her want toast, so I made toast, flipped her over and drummed on her butt while she got impatient waiting for the toast. Then she ate the toast, and we shared a banana. Six minutes. On the kitchen island, I could see a notification light up my phone screen, a dopamine rush too predictable to attempt to describe.

This isn't working, my wife said periodically over those days. I'd get mad because that correct observation didn't exactly change things, and also, we were in this deep already. What were we going to do, go through it again in the future? Yes, of course that was the answer, and when we quit, I snatched up my phone, and already, somewhere in the back of an ambient yet still crowded brain, I began to worry about the next stretch of days. My daughter pointed at my screen and yelled, *Baby Shark, Baby Shark,* which is this sort of unspoken agreement we've come to that if we get to have our phones, she can at least get her songs out of them. I played "Baby Shark," set it to repeat, felt everybody in our home exhale back into normalcy. I thought about how good she'd gotten at singing not just the words but the melody, so I filmed her singing for a while; she looked back at me, my phone between us, trained on her, playing the song as she sang it back to the phone.

There's a way to talk about being a parent to a young child that emphasizes *boredom*, said like that, an italicized weight on the shoulders. This implies a gritty, unromanticized beauty, introducing a narrator of the experience that, if not cuddly, can at least provide candor, which is less cringey. *Boredom* occupies outsized space particularly in the language of dads, I think, because boredom is a riskless emotion—not even an emotion, but rather a way of articulating the opposite of whatever seriousness the presence of emotion implies. *Boredom* stands in for *depression*, for *helplessness*, for *resentment*, for whatever the feelings are that mothers have and acknowledge and investigate. My dad has often told me that on the occasions he took his kids to the park solo, he'd look at another dad grinning through children's games and feel certain that this man was trying to so hard to act like he wasn't bored, a story meant to frame my father as imperfect yet at least honest and imply that this honesty was better than being an engaged liar. We have the kind of relationship where it's important for us to think no one is bullshitting, and I don't mean to make light of that value system because I've cherished it for a long time.

My father, my father-in-law, really any grandfather-aged man just now beginning to accept that there are some potential reasons for guilt—they often say that you cannot overstate how different expectations have become. *Good* different, but wow: another world. Yet *bored dad* is a trope that has stayed consistent into my generation, despite everyone wanting to be seen as the opposite of how our fathers were. The ideals flip, but the muted affect and the language for it remains—the old-school man is bored by and removed from children in a way he thinks his wife could never be; the modern liberal man doesn't want to seem like he's presuming to understand the depth of what a mother feels, so he deflects to something less. Either way: boredom, a compass that no matter how you turn it reliably points north to *dad*.

There's this moment in the second *My Struggle* book, when Knausgaard has been riffing on trying to get his daughter home from a birthday party, all of her weirdness and shyness and the way she looks for him but then runs back to the action, doesn't eat but wants his food, her legs wrapping around his waist as he carries her, and her shoes, where did her shoes go, he can't bring her home barefoot. Pages and pages—his eyes are on her, she is magnificent and weird and common, and then suddenly he says, *Irrespective of the great tenderness I felt for her, my boredom and apathy were greater.* It's like a rug being pulled out from under the reader, especially upon revisiting the passage. There's this attention, so thorough that it can only be full of love, and that feels all too remarkable on the page, totally naked, but then we're snapped back into this misanthropy that's supposed to be risky, yet is far less so than the care. I guess the thing to love in Knausgaard is the honesty, but sometimes honesty is the easiest thing. Or maybe I mean that it doesn't even read as honesty, just meeting the expectation of what honesty should sound like.

There's an arrogance to boredom. It implies that there are things more worthy of your attention, a focus and a purpose that you've had and will again in a different situation. Very often when I'm with my daughter, I feel the opposite of boredom: an ever-present tension, a churning even when nothing is happening. Fear, timid hope, white-knuckle anticipation of . . . something. What I'm looking for, what I'm stoking with my half attention, is not the desire for something new or different, just the chance to make this experience in front of me a little softer. *Are you ever bored?* my father asked me once, watching me try to coax my sick daughter into drinking Pedialyte. I felt a murmur of annoyance, but it was overcome fast by silly, loud pride, at the chance to say, *No, not at all, I can't even imagine what you're talking about.* This is its own kind of semi-honesty.

For a long time, my daughter didn't sleep, and I broke my no-phone-by-the-bed rule. In theory, this was because my wife and I each needed to have separate quiet alarms that could go off close to our ears, so as not to wake one another and also not wake the baby, even though the baby was invariably already awake and louder than the alarms. When it was my turn to give her the bottle, it was just us in the dark. I heard her little chokes and guzzles, her mewls tapering off into brief satiation, then hopefully sleep. The length of these minutes was unfathomable to me, unlike anything I'd ever experienced. I remember saying that they felt like a recurring pre-death moment, in that, faced with the silence and darkness but the ongoing need to have my brain awake, I'd start scrolling through what seemed like my entire life, replacing the algorithmic scroll with an autobiographical one. *I'm sorry you feel like you're dying,* my wife replied when I said that, and I got a bit huffy because that felt like a willful misinterpretation; plus, we were huffy about everything in those days.

My wife didn't talk about her own stretches of the night, a silence that felt important but impenetrable. I grew to dread these montages of extra consciousness that I had no control over, which always seemed to slow and delve in on memories that I had no desire to revisit. Everyone in our household feared the nights. The baby's mood would darken along with the sky, and then my wife would start crying. I would look at my phone so hard that I could feel my brow furrowing, my whole face pinching. Sometimes, we'd commiserate over the fact that nobody had been honest with us; either nobody remembers or everyone is a liar.

For a week or so, I tried to hold myself to not bringing my phone with me when it was my turn to tend to the baby in the night. This was my first stand, I guess, and first fast loss—but against what, exactly? I didn't believe that the experience would be better if I had no screen to look at; rather, I thought that if I suffered through it without a buffer, I'd have more legitimate ownership over how difficult I found it to be. If I was to be more ill-equipped for this most important job than I'd ever let myself consider possible, at least I'd do it the *right* way. If you're going to call it misery, earn the misery. The baby's ability to be roused from sleep by any slight change in environment was at superhero levels, so I was able to create this binary choice: do the parental duty of allowing my baby any morsels of rest without which she would die—worst-case scenario, but still—or look at pictures of people from high school who had all remained friends, at a holiday party in an apartment with exposed brick, and risk it all.

When I broke, I sat with one arm wrapped around the baby, propping the bottle against her lips, the other hand holding my phone directly above my head, angled in a way that the light didn't reach her. I craned my neck backward, held as still as I could, and the phone beamed down, almost blinding in the blackness around it, and this felt like sitting in the dentist's chair with that spotlight on you, hearing the drill. I read most of an article about how modern parents were screwed by late capitalism and posted it with some comment that was meant to come off snarky but was really looking for sympathy, and a friend with an older kid said something dismissive about *Just you wait*, and I remember vowing then, at four a.m., to never speak to her again.

We had an app to track all the functions that might prove that the baby was alive and normal—we entered in every shit, piss, meal, stretch of sleep, any change in height and weight, any time my wife pumped and how long we could store the milk. It broke her down into measurable particles of human life, converted her to data, then presented that data back to us in flat, harmlessly cheerful emojis, a muted palate of pinks and blues. I scrolled to this app when the other apps felt raw. Holding my daughter, the most comforting distraction was this evidence of her life and my care for her. Those weird, maple-syrupy diapers changed, recorded, saved to the cloud; her soft breath as she slept and the warmth of her in that brief stillness, all saved, each minute accounted for, even the minutes I was living through as the blinking red circle reminded me that I'd begun to record this feeding.

The actual baby wriggled. I closed my eyes and wished as hard as I could that she'd settle. She did, just briefly, and I imagined sending the friend who had commented dismissively on my tweet a screenshot of the baby app, a little taste of my nights in case she'd forgotten what these times were like, and then I could tell her to go fuck herself.

Five years ago, there was a series that went viral by the photographer Eric Pickersgill, where he took images of people together in intimate ways that people often are, then edited all phones out of the images. The couple facing away from one another in bed, staring at the palms of their own hands; the newlyweds leaning against the hood of their *Just Married* car as though unaware of one another; the family of four around the dinner table, heads bent in what we're invited to see as the modern bastardization of prayer. I think the photos are good—some of them are beautiful and clear in my mind years later—but it's hard to know. They fit into one of the two extremes available in the increasing polarity of content—does it show a world entirely unrecognizable to my own, or does it show me literally myself? Escape or mirror; nothing too complex in between. Look at these photos, get that feeling of yourself unmasked, grotesque but at least grotesque in the way every single other person is, and then what? Part of the ubiquity of the technology is that it begins to make you think it's interesting, the way old drunks talk about drinking, and even if the point is critique or regret, that's never what it sounds like. The art that's easiest to remember is seen, then reseen on the device that it's commenting upon, tailored to it, meant to evoke shame in the viewer but also dependent on the fact that the shameful behavior will continue. *Look how empty they look (I look). Look how detached.* Copy the link, send it—*Seen this? Yes.* Multiple times over the years, these photos have been shared across my screen on some platform or another, recycled into the loop, and to reencounter them doesn't deepen them, just reminds me how much time has passed while this central thing hasn't changed.

It's the famous McLuhan line—the medium is indeed the message—but now the message is how much the medium hates itself. It's the only vessel available for its own critique, which makes the critique seem more profound than it is, pre-weighted with the knowledge that it won't change anything. We're all standing at the bottom of a very deep hole, drawing pictures of the hole, and the pictures of the hole get better and better, what with all the practice, so it's still moving to point at the picture and say, *Wow that is a very accurate representation of the hole we're in.*

To think about what we want for our kids is to place tracing paper over the childhood we remember having, deciding what lines to match, where to turn away. It's never clean, of course—the ink bleeds; all the decisions our parents made that we feel hurt us or stunted us begin to blur in memory, until all we have is this certainty that we don't want to repeat that pathology without any concept of what an alternative looks or feels like.

An example: we don't want our daughter to feel that her whiteness is the unspoken center of the universe, because we, in our mid-thirties, still do, as evidenced by this hand-wringing about what to do with our whiteness and hers. We send her to a daycare where she's the only white kid in hopes that she'll be less cloistered than we turned out to be. This is the beginning of what I assume will be a deeply fraught, constantly shifting process, already well documented by others in its ambitions and flaws. At the heart, though, is the reckoning with our own childhoods and the way they centered our comfort, our parents' comfort, and our potential achievement, above all, and trying to hold to the belief that such an ingrained ethos is bad and to not progress past it is a failure. Ultimately, we're asking our daughter to experience and internalize as normal something we still have no frame of reference for.

The way we think about kids and technology is the opposite but operates within the same stifling parameters. It's the rare arena in which we can romanticize the customs of our childhoods, mourn what she'll never have on her behalf. We can, often do, say, *Remember how nondependent we were on screens? Remember just* playing *in your room? Remember* imagination? *Remember how* weird *and* bored *we were?* And we can feel, for once, like we have wisdom to pass on about a better model for living. But amid that self-satisfaction, we're still desperately foisting expectations on our daughter to live better than us—not better than we were at her age but better than we are *now*. Sometimes, she sort of floats in the hallway between where her toys are and the TV is, and tries to lean toward the TV without moving her legs, watching us to gauge our reaction. We say, *Not yet*. We say, *It's morning, baby, come on, we're all hanging out, isn't hanging out better?* We say this, of course, with personalized screens that we've been nursing in little sips along with our coffee since the moment we woke up.

When she starts screeching and goes to the mirror to watch the machinations of how upset she can be, we say, *What's P for, baby?* And (bless her) through tears, she screams, *Patience!* When I go to her in these moments, hold her little shoulders and breathe with her, tell her it's okay to wait, to not get what feels like the only possible soothing thing right away, often I'm rushing to slide my phone back into my pocket like a kid caught in school, and in my haste, I might miss my pocket. The sound of plastic on hardwood is a gavel bang. She looks down, then up at me; sometimes, she points at it without comment. She's old enough to understand that we're trying to keep her from succumbing to an impulse we feed in ourselves. If a toddler understands anything, it's injustice.

We've noticed recently that when she reaches for a wire and says, *Is this a wire?* in a cheerful yet threatening manner, it's usually when we're both on our phones at the same time. We snap our heads up and she smiles. What does she see change on our faces? Where does she think we've been? How long has she been holding the wire? How fast did she learn that the most efficient way to win a battle for our attention is to cry danger?

If you're trying to read about the relationship between technology and child-rearing, you will face a mountain of thought about the pros and cons of technology's usefulness. The history of technological intervention in parenting has always been fraught with guilt, but that guilt centered a cost-benefit analysis of labor—how much attention could/should be paid to a child at all times; should a parent (always read *mother* here) feel lazy for outsourcing more work to the newest available machines. New technology promises safety, or at least less uncertainty, so the moral question becomes: If you can keep this precious child just a little bit safer, why wouldn't you?

The scholar Hannah Zeavin writes about techno-parenthood and, among many examples, teases out the complete norm-shifting power of the invention and evolution of the baby monitor. The parts of your kid's life that were theirs alone became not that; you could first hear, then see them even when they didn't know it, in the times when anything at all could be happening, in the dark when the risk felt greatest but existed least. Each evolution has been a sea change, instantly swallowed by the next wave, and now, only a few decades after the first little walkie-talkie monitor, Zeavin points out that the industry has blossomed into so many options where video surveillance of your child's bedroom can stream on your phone at all times, on multiple phones even, available to any interested parties at a great distance, sometimes in partnership with local fire and police departments. *Care,*

Zeavin writes, *is a mode that justifies surveillance as a practice, framing it as a social good rather than a political choice.* How could vigilance be a bad thing?

I think this is all further complicated when the nag of potential surveillance plays out on the same device that offers us the most and easiest ways to ignore our children. So you can be obsessed with your child but also looking at an infinite amount of other things, keeping them slightly safer and endangering them slightly more at the same time. The feeling of surveillance is easiest to ignore when what is happening resembles something more along the lines of content. The device in your hand is the only hub for vigilance *and* distraction, and on top of that, it's the best medium through which to perform care, not in the way of hugging or listening, but in projecting the image of your care to the most people. So, when my daughter sleeps, the feeling is there that I can, probably *should*, be checking on her at any moment, and I'm on the group text, and I'm on Facebook, and then I'm on Instagram, and I see the stories of other parents I know, and sometimes those stories are the night vision streams of their children in their beds clutching a bed-inappropriate object as they sleep or doing something goofy other than sleeping, their little eyes glowing, all of which signifies that these parents are chill and have a sense of humor about the whole thing, even though they have a twenty-four-hour live feed of their kid going just in case, and I'm watching as part of my diffuse and numbing and necessary entertainment, but at the core of the entertainment is the reminder that my own child's image awaits, and maybe it's time to check.

Labor and leisure are inseparable, and the only certainty is the feeling of exhaustion, and suddenly it's time for bed. The first image I see of my daughter in the morning will be on a screen. Sometimes she's just sitting there talking contentedly to her stuffed animals, and on those mornings I will pick up where the night left off, plowing through waiting notifications while glancing at her image and feeling a mixture of joy and dread at the thought that, right now, I could see her for real. Sometimes I do this until she gets upset, and then I rush to fling open her door as though I'm saving her from something.

When the pandemic hit, my wife still had to go into the office, and with the added urgency of knowing that everyone but her had been temporarily laid off. Suddenly, it was my daughter and me alone again, finding a new routine for a shared existence that this time had no defined end. I set it up so that, ideally, I was doing all my Zoom teaching while she napped, though sometimes I was teaching while she mumbled and flailed in the dark or screamed herself hoarse. Sometimes, I held her while trying to lead a discussion; a student later confessed that she and others were live streaming our image onto Instagram, which should have felt like a violation, but honestly, amid the loneliness, I was flattered.

The rest of the day, we wandered around the neighborhood while my daughter learned to walk or hung out in the park because being trapped indoors made us both restless and combative, and she's always liked being pushed very hard on the swing and having to decide whether she's terrified or delighted. A little park crew solidified before the governor shut down all public gatherings, so at a given time, I could expect certain mothers to appear from different directions, each with a unique beleaguered gait, some with the kid audibly wailing from a block away, others in reliable tense silence. We greeted each other's children loudly and cheerfully from a distance, and these stood in for our greetings to one another, like dog owners. I enjoyed that for some, you could tell they were really smiling at my kid, genuinely thought my kid was cute, even from behind the mask. I have nothing shitty to say about these encounters; I grew to crave them as the only daytime hours in which I felt like I existed and people could confirm this fact.

One thing about bringing my lonely kid around other kids, though, was that, while there was less claustrophobia, there were different pressures. The collective exhalation that all us parents felt upon seeing other humans at the park was almost always followed by one kid hitting another in the face. We'd attend to the necessary parties, and all put our phones away for a while, an ebb in anything not child-focused as the howling quieted and the tears dried.

One day, my daughter's favorite pal came to the park with two teeth broken and a puffed-up lip. The day before, she'd wandered off the pointlessly dangerous bridge between slides and taken a header into the wood chips below. Everyone hovered extra close that day without realizing it. At a certain point, I was the only parent with the mom of the injured party, since our daughters had gone off alone to flirt with the idea of hugging one another, scrapping it at the last minute. Silence for a while. Then the mom said, *I was on a work call, then I had to answer an email, and I was just looking over my email, and I don't know, I guess I was looking down too long—I don't even remember what it was about—and then she was on the ground crying. There was all this blood. I thought something really, really bad had happened.*

The mother glanced sideways at me, waiting. It felt as though this preemptive admission had been planned on the walk over, maybe even the night before, after they'd returned from the hospital without bad damage. I'd always admired this mother, probably the least granola of all us gentrifiers, whose kid's adorableness came in the package of whatever gendered Target clothes were easiest and who often heard the word *no* but had a general feistiness that felt like it had to speak in some way to her parents empowering her. They seemed like a family that maybe said grace at dinner, which is the sort of thing I romanticize only because it's so far from my experience. All of this to say, I liked her, but we didn't know each other well enough for this level of vulnerability. I felt enormous sadness for her, then relief that it wasn't me giving this prepared statement, then choking certainty that someday soon, it would be, then the thought that I was risking my daughter's life, or at least baby teeth, to occasionally check email but mostly just fuck around, and at least this mom was suffering through a busy professional day while mothering, so the real culprit here was capitalism, whereas in my case, the culprit would be a little bit capitalism but mostly me.

Our daughters looked very beautiful together in morning sunlight, super busy and perfectly candid. I wanted to pull out my phone to take a picture of them, but the mother was still looking at me like it was important for her to know if I thought she'd endangered her kid, so I said, *Honestly, if mine was a better climber, she'd probably be dead by now.* I wanted to apologize right away for bringing up the possibility of death, which was what we were talking around but should never have been voiced. Then I tried to say something about how I admired her for managing to schlep her kid around while working what seemed to be an important job, though I didn't remember what her job was, and we were too far down the road for me to admit that and ask. She said, *Well, it's the hand we've all been dealt*, gesturing around at everyone, especially the mom who was always in a Zoom meeting, muted, but whenever she heard her name, she'd have to drop whatever she was doing to quickly unmute, and say, *I'm here, I'm here, just thinking about what you said, so interesting.* The worst thing to cop to in those days at the park was happiness, because happiness implied ease, and ease either suggested that you were judging everyone else or, more likely, you were doing something wrong or lazy, and everyone should make themselves feel a little better by judging you. Often, with my daughter, I feel both wrong and lazy. This mother didn't feel lazy, just selfish to the point of neglect.

When my mother talks about being with me as child, she describes it with the tone of magical realism, a sensory lusciousness, the world as she'd always known it, except not quite, this feeling that it was just me and her in a vacuum that magnified every sound, slowed time and expanded it. But also, somehow, she doesn't remember much detail; whenever I ask what we did, she can't quite say. So the way we were together is an ideal whose existence is unconfirmed, a taunt—the way I remember the fertile boredom of childhood as an idea, not an experience. The overwhelm of this reality makes it impossible to remember the previous one, so all that remains is the suspicion that things must have not felt so overwhelming then.

This mom and her daughter moved to the suburbs not long after, and I don't see them anymore, but I remember this moment very clearly because it's hard to come by honest moments between parents. Our kids were both mercifully sweet that whole morning. The mom brightened along with the confirmation that her daughter bore no emotional scars. Before going home, we hoisted them onto the big swing shaped like a disk, and they seemed content to stay there while we furiously photographed them. Our arms held the ropes, then let go but hovered, then finally pulled back to get the shots we wanted, each of us cooing different versions of, *You look so happy, you look so happy!* My daughter wobbled and clutched the other girl for balance, then there was a moment where it seemed they could both topple, so we dove forward, phones still in hands, to save them. They blinked up at us. Somewhere in my thousands of pandemic photos (I had to pay two dollars a month for extra data storage), there's a series of my daughter and her little friend—half smiling, half vacant—on the big swing, and in one of them, the blurred specter of my hand and this mother's hand breaking through the cheerful plane of the image.

For some reason, the *Baffler* let the novelist William Giraldi publish an essay about how he was so bored during paternity leave that he developed a drinking problem. He, as so many have, wrote of boredom as though he alone had worked up the courage to articulate this taboo, like a white comedian dropping the n-word. He likened the brief period of time without a job to go to, and with a baby, to the end of his productive life, full stop: *Think of the tremendous ennui or earthquakes of personhood that can occur when men are laid off or retire.*

If there's anything interesting to engage with in the essay, I think it's the binary created by a life that's either dedicated to professional labor (writing/teaching) or personal labor (parent-

hood), and the rest is wasted (in his case, literally). Giraldi reduced personal labor to something born into his wife's marrow—
*Her apparent willingness and capacity to do almost everything
for [the baby] flooded me with awe*; whereas writing was his
purpose, so he didn't feel any shame not caring for his kid but
felt all the shame when he wasn't tending to his work. This is,
of course, particularly gross, but even participatory *writer parents* chronicle the frustrations of parenthood in a pretty similar way—a life comprised of competing works of varying significance, and the only excuse for not doing one is the need to
do the other. Being with the child makes the writer long for
the laser-like creative purpose they had before the child. It's a
central tension of parenthood lit. But reading about this clarity
and focus, or the resentment of the *loss* of once-pure clarity and
focus, increasingly feels to me like reading historical fiction. If
it's contemporary writing, it reminds me of Pickersgill's photos, a
scene of life that should be recognizable, but with its most central
component erased—this porous membrane between distraction
and purpose, work and leisure, living and documenting, where
the majority of a day is actually spent. How can you write about
tending the child or tending the book as though each is a room
in your mind that you walk into, with a sealed door and sound-
proofing, and your mind is a two-room house?

It's tempting for me to think that these books are lying by
omission, but interpretation is further complicated and smushed
by the fact that the speed of techno-dependency has accelerated
so much faster than books move as a medium. I was thinking
about how weirdly timeless and slow Rivka Galchen's *Little La-
bors* is, meandering through classical references alongside moments of visceral early motherhood, brain versus body, how pri-
mal yet clean and elegant each little fragment, and then I was

like, wait that was published seven years ago and probably written two to three years before that, and it's totally reasonable that
she wouldn't have had an iPhone and still maybe felt excessive
making a weekly Facebook post on her laptop, giving herself an
hour to scroll. This is a deeply reductive way to think about an
amazing book, but then the intense access and diffuseness of this
current lived moment makes reading way harder than anyone in
my circles wants to admit, so to look for yourself in books, even
the newest books, ultimately feels like another scolding from
some long-lost time of purity in which people were better, which
is such a loss of imagination, turning literature, turning all past
experience really, into a *Remember When* listicle.

I've been reading Tove Ditlevsen's heartbreaking trilogy about
girlhood, poverty, motherhood, art, and addiction in postwar
Copenhagen. She writes about this joy that her typewriter provided, the only real joy in all her life, an unwavering truth about
who she was and what she valued and what she was *meant* to do,
which was only heightened when she had a kid—she pined for
the typewriter when mothering, then attacked writing moments
with the kind of focus that only new scarcity could provide. Seventy years later, in a near unrecognizable world, came Knausgaard, another Scandinavian, blunt and unsentimental, except
when juxtaposing parenthood with the divine productivity of the
moments alone with his computer: *The happiness that filled me
and the feeling of invincibility they gave me I have searched for
ever since, in vain.*

I'm not trying to play the better parent here, only to say that
the way I love being with my daughter and the way I sometimes
love to write feel linked, in that neither is fully present, and the
possibility of being fully present in either seems so exhausting
that I find it hard to believe I wouldn't deflect into something far

more destructive. Now, as I'm writing this, I miss my daughter at school, so I look back through old pictures of her and find a good one—sitting on the grass at the park, eyes peeking up at fat clouds—and send it to my wife, then post it to Instagram like, *Can't believe she was ever so young*, and that banal observation feels more important and real to me than anything else I could write, despite its speed and ease and exact similarity to the posts of every other parent I know who's hit a lag in their workday. When I pick my daughter up from school, I'll pause in the car before going in and regret how disengaged I was from my working moments when I had them, flagellate as a way to avoid the other responsibility, then see her out in the courtyard, cheeks red, running toward me, and regret having ever paused.

A poet and essayist I know and admire wrote a piece in the *Times* about quitting her smartphone by using the technique from a famous book on quitting smoking that my wife has used four times now. This is not a failure on the book's part, because the book says this might happen, in which case you just have to read it again, and when she does read it again, she always reminds me that I, too, am a smoker, and I say that I've only ever smoked other people's cigarettes, I can and have stopped smoking any time I want, and she says that's what the book says all addicts say, and I say, *Well it's true for me!* I digress—again, stuck in the tropes of addiction talk. Smoking seems impossible now, like something an entirely different person once did, but I'm sure that will change if I ever get a few nights away from my daughter and around booze.

This poet wrote in the voice of one who has made it to the other side, AA-voice: *I am free again to enjoy the things I have always loved,* she writes, *to worship the God I choose.* The essay begins with the phone as a wedge between her and her partner, or not a wedge exactly, but that same image I keep coming back to of a rippling, invisible barrier, something from a superhero movie that absorbs the force of the world, converts it into a mumble. She writes about not fully hearing the person she most loved to hear in the world, the sense that love was less of itself with the phone in the way—*Where'd you go?* he'd say to her when they were next to one another, touching even. Love of her person, but also love of the books she read and wrote, words she'd spent a life entangled with, a once-great intimacy.

When I read the essay, my daughter was a year old, and I remember exactly that she was home sick, so I took her to the little kid room at the children's museum. (This was pre-COVID, so that was only a medium fucked-up thing to do.) She couldn't walk, but she was heavy into that shuffling sideways while balancing phase, as the bigger kids stampeded around her. The room had this little plastic tunnel they could explore, and she was around the corner, working her way toward world's slowest surprise, and I was sitting in the dark reading this essay on my phone, listening enough to hear any evidence of her falling or being run over or crying from the cruelty of her limitations. I was rushing to finish the essay before something terrible happened or another adult came around the corner and found me; I remember being jealous of both the freedom the poet described and the byline. Just then, my daughter appeared. She has always been (sorry, I know this isn't exactly objective) a wonderful smiler, free of the odd woodenness that some kids get when they try to perform emotion; in this moment, she broke into her best smile, the sly grin of suspicion that she'd done something worthy of pride, which then expands across her face when she gets confirmation from my reaction. I remember it all because I have a picture of it; my hand moved instinctively to bring the phone from the reading position to the photo position, and there she is, backlit at the mouth of the tunnel, eyes right at the screen because she's looking for me, and the screen is between us. I don't think the distraction, the barrier, makes what I felt less real, and I don't want to suggest that to love a child (or anyone) means only to suffer through constant attentiveness, but I also don't like that the prospect of that attentiveness feels like suffering.

The poet was pregnant when she published the phone-quitting essay; after she had her baby, she was right back on Instagram. Every week or so, I catch a glimpse. There's the baby as a skeleton on Halloween or in a night-light glow in one of those four a.m. pictures taken as a missive—*Is anyone else there, in the dark?* Two weeks ago, her baby saw its first snow, and the poet had her phone on the baby's face in profile, held in her partner's arms, and I replied with the emoji of the cat with heart eyes. Her kid is beautiful and bigheaded. I don't know where she lives now, but there's a nice front porch, a rug like the one we have, a pumpkin patch within day-trip distance. A scroll of a life with tired eyes, an unmade bed, captioned in that tone meant to convey, *I'm sorry to be doing this again, but look at me, here I am.* I don't feel any glee that this poet is back on the phone, only tenderness. Of all the infinities of lives that your phone can show you, the most reliably moving remain the lives that look like yours and look nice, which means maybe yours looks that way, too.

My daughter loves to be read to, probably more than anything, which you know if we've ever met or if you follow me online, because I don't shut up about it. I can't quite put into words how important this is to me, how I'm always a little nervous that this quiet, satisfied love will go away. There's a book that should be too old for her that she sits through, and this is a source of enormous, pointless pride for me, and I think a source of joy for her. My mother brought it in a haul of what she used to read to me; I don't remember it, but I can imagine her voice steadily moving through these exacting descriptions of weather, all the native plants in a lonely bog. My daughter sits on my lap and leans all her weight back into my chest, I hold the book up in front of our faces, and sometimes with my off hand, I touch the softest skin on the nape of her neck until she gets annoyed. She whispers along to the words she knows, and I coax her to say them louder; she's beginning to take on this agonizing perfectionism, whispering any word until she feels confident, and only then opening into a bellow. A couple of pages before the end of the book, she starts preemptively going, *Again again again again,* and will only be pacified by agreement. This can stretch on for hours. That's not true—this can stretch on for what feels like hours but is, at the most, maybe forty minutes, though I still think that's a lot. It's the longest I'll go without reaching into my pocket.

In a too-on-the-nose metaphor, my child is literally sitting on top of my phone, desiring nothing more than continued closeness with me, and to reach for my phone would be to shove her out of the way, so thankfully I don't do that. During the failed potty-training days, she was naked, her feet cold, and the rest of her body very warm. She'd eventually decided to fight the training by refusing to pee at all, so I wasn't worried about a disaster on the chair, and she was less likely to get enraged and pee spitefully when confined to my arms, so we stayed like that. If I had a simple, romantic idea of what fatherhood could be before I was one, it would be this image—the physicality of this unself-conscious little body wriggling into mine, a child hypnotized by words the way I like to think I once was, and the way they reverberate from my chest when she lays her head on me. I felt the weight of the beauty and the need to somehow be worthy of it, which in my mind means to not think of anything but the beauty that's happening, and by then I was out of it. I didn't feel myself already longing for some next activity; I just felt the anxiety of knowing that I might quickly want this moment to be diluted, and then the anxiety manifested the desire.

Reading with her has become like driving to work—making the turns without realizing until suddenly you're parked—so I could hear my voice carrying on, but my mind was revisiting the days when I researched my first book and didn't have a smartphone, and it was just me in a beat-up hatchback driving through the Midwest, taking notes in a marble notebook in the bleachers of minor-league baseball stadiums, watching the sun trace noon to night across the sky. I cannot remember what it felt like to be that person, to be that alone, alternating between focus and some ideal of productive boredom. I think of that person a lot, wondering what he thought about, and I get to the point where I'm so certain he was better than me, able to observe the world, record it, create within it, with a clarity I'll never get back. But that person had a pretty severe anxiety disorder and must have found the time trapped in his own mind to be excruciating. I'm not romanticizing clarity here or patience or presence; I'm romanticizing a life unencumbered enough to be productive, which was a life that I didn't enjoy as I lived it. Back to the most central, and also maybe worst, part of phone life—the way even the moments without the phone, reflecting on what might be bad about the phone, centralize the phone. And I'm left thinking in the tonal extremities that this dynamic instills: either the slog toward self-optimization or the retreat into jokey nihilism.

And there was my daughter, still in my lap, listening away, maybe because she loved that engagement with her imagination or maybe because I hadn't given her any other options. A combination—I think part of what she loves so much about books is that they're the only space we've allowed in her life where she can be away from herself, that doesn't come with any sense that she needs to ask permission, or that she'll be told to stop. She can just sort of zone out, and we can feel like she's *doing something*, and we are, too, because she needs our attention to do the thing we want her to do. She was still going, *Again again again*, but beginning to rub her eyes. She was impossibly adorable like that, the way she often is, but I didn't want to lose it. I asked my wife, *Can you take a picture? Can you send it to me?*

At the Playground

At the playground, we say, I'm sorry. We say, Please say excuse me, and then eventually we say, Excuse us. We say, Good job! We say, You're doing it! We say, Watch out! Watch out! We say, Are you okay? You're okay.

We say, No water today. We say, Remember, honey? The city shut it off—no more water in the pump. We say, A pump with no water, isn't that silly? We say, They didn't like people washing their clothes, isn't that silly? We grow quiet, try to discern the different quiets—sadness, guilt, discomfort, maybe annoyance. We remember when the pump was on: the sweet, zigzag tracks of muddy footprints, the slips and small mouths filled with blood.

We watch the big girl pour sand in the little girl's hair, and we feel mad, but we say, Where's your mom, sweetie? Sometimes, they fall off the jungle gym like rat-poisoned sparrows, and there's the beat of silence awaiting a cry or a laugh.

At the playground, we take pictures of blur, feel bad for missing the moment as it happened. Someone screams, You're not my friend! and we say, Everyone is a friend here, this is everyone's community. Everything belongs to everybody. Everybody deserves a chance. On a good day, we say, Is there anything more perfect than this?

On a cold night, when the hippie mom with the pet rats won't tell her kid to be nice because that's intervening on their autonomy, we seethe. When kids run free while their parents sit in the van with the heat on and the music, and sometimes weed, we say, Hey, God bless, but we feel uncomfortable, and we also feel uncomfortable for feeling uncomfortable.

When sirens go by, we stop to perform awe. When one child is wailing, we say, It's fine, they're fine, we're fine.

At the playground, when the lonely older boy makes a kingdom in the dirt, we tell him it's nice, and he smiles shyly. When we ask if his kingdom has a name, he says it doesn't, but he's built a ditch that will be a moat when it rains and he's from Florida and he misses it and he's not scared of cold but he'd rather be warm. We say, What's *your* name? but he mumbles it.

In a lull, we do pull-ups on the monkey bars, and an ache spreads in a crescent around our shoulder blades. We say, Getting old, and we glance around. We remember triumphs and bruises. We talk about metal slides, how they burned, how kids today should be grateful for temperate, non-splintering plastic, but also how we pity them for what they've never experienced. We watch them pretend that the floor is lava, watch the fear on the little ones as they slip and the big ones jeer, You're dead now, dead, you're dead.

At the playground, the ice cream truck looks like it could be from any time in the last fifty years, like if you took a picture, it would feel as though you were living inside something you missed. When the children flock to the truck parked on the street, we reach out our arms like we can hold them from far away, as pickups slam speed bumps without slowing.

When a hawk drinks from a puddle and the children move closer, we hold them back. When the toddlers keep tugging like the only thing that makes sense is to touch it, we're a little proud but also disturbed at the lack of basic self-preservation instinct. We think, but don't speak about, beak on flesh, talon in eyes. When we drag them home, they cry.

At the playground, "Baby Shark" emanates from an after-work khaki pocket. The kids with Arizona ice tea guzzle all twenty-four ounces, and the kids who will never have Arizona ice tea look jealous.

On a frozen evening, when a man sleeps with all his belongings under the slide, some kids laugh and some don't notice. On a hot afternoon, when a man is doing donuts on a dirt bike next to the swings, someone says, Call the cops, and someone says, Don't ever call the cops, and there's a conversation to be had, but we don't have it.

At the playground, our children move toward one another, and we ready ourselves for violence, and sometimes there is violence, but sometimes there is tenderness. Hands in pockets, we smile, bashful and sad and silly and hopeful. We say, Maybe they could be friends.

On a morning when the sun is still low over the buildings, so early that no one else is out yet, we say, All ours now, baby, and always, in the quiet, there's a stab of relief.

Attachments, Wild and Tame

For a while there, I was taking my daughter to look for ducks twice a day every day, pre-nap and post-nap, bright cold morning ducks and hazy sunset ducks. They put something at ease in her, however briefly. *She loves them*, I would say often. We live in a small city in the smallest state, cut down the middle by a river, in proximity to the ocean at a hundred different angles, a lake ten minutes away. Our duck odds were good. Still, if we traced a bend in the river with no sign of them, she'd get frantic and I would, too. When they did appear, she'd gasp, a mixture of relief and surprise.

They were so beautiful—with her, I felt that. What can you say about the color of the streaks on a mallard? Each one, a miracle. When they sunned themselves on rocks, squinting, I thought the ducks looked like leather-tanned old women on a beach in Italy, a memory from long before my daughter was born. She walked at them as gentle as she could make herself, hand out, palm up, the way we taught her with dogs. She said, *Hello, duckies, are you smiling?* Before waddling away, they craned their necks up to look at her like she was a giant or they were children. Sometimes, with glee, she would shout, *I see their eyes!*

The Tale of Jemima Puddle-Duck is one of the darkest Beatrix Potter books. Pretty, stupid Jemima, doomed from the beginning, in her little bonnet, head always tilted up like a child, eyes blankly trusting. She is not human, nor is she wild; she is at the mercy of both the humans farming her and the fox stalking her. Her only motivation is to keep the eggs that she lays; each day she tries and fails. Like in every Potter book, the possibility of violent death looms. If the protagonist escapes, this comes only after vivid references to all those who didn't, the descriptions half joke, half warning. Even the child reading knows more than Jemima, knows well enough to see the soft feathers on which she lays her eggs as evidence of something awful out of view.

When we get to the end and Jemima has made it through alive with a tiny flock of ducklings behind her, I say to my daughter, *Hooray!* I ask if she remembers when we saw ducklings in cold early spring by an otherwise empty lake. We went back three days in a row; they were learning how to swim. I was over the moon. I kept saying to her, *I've never seen a duckling, either! We're seeing this for the first time together!* I was trying to film, my hand shaking the phone with excitement—their squeaks, her squeaks, the implied potential of the whole thing. Life! Life! She wanted to touch one so badly. She was scolding herself preemptively: *Gentle.*

A doll was made of Jemima Puddle-Duck shortly after the book was published and became a runaway hit. The originals are a hundred years old now; one is housed in the Victoria and Albert Museum of Childhood collection: soft, downturned beak, coal-black little pupils. I think it looks shy.

Potter referred to the plush animals made from her characters as *sideshows*. She complained of the quality, anticipated the various knockoffs that did indeed flood the global market. She reported encountering some *very ugly* rabbits at Harrods. Every animal she drew and story she invented was born from the mice and rabbits she trapped and kept as pets as a girl, or the working farm she lived on as an adult, wandering, watching. I like to think it's the intimacy that makes the characters timeless—not a general idea of a duck but a fantasy of this *one* duck, stupid and helpless but real and particular, worthy of chuckling compassion.[1]

I've never seen a white duck in real life; it would shock and thrill me, I think, to come upon one. But in a children's book or a cartoon or a movie, they are always white (this goes from *Jemima* all the way to that duck randomly kept as a pet in *Friends*), just as a rubber ducky is always an unnatural, unexplained yellow.

In his seminal work on fairy tales, the psychologist Bruno Bettelheim bemoans the increased popularity of lifelike illustrations in children's stories. He says any added imagery robs from them true meaning-making, true imagination. He quotes Tolkien: *Every hearer of words will have his own picture, and it will be made of all the rivers and hills and dales he has ever seen, but*

1. Linda Lear. *Beatrix Potter: A Life in Nature.* New York: Penguin Books, 2008.

especially out of The Hill, The River, The Valley which were for him the first embodiment of the word.[2]

I find some comfort in the idea that people were always romanticizing a purer version of childhood—at least since the Romantic period, when the idea of childhood as a distinct time in life and consciousness was first introduced (for those wealthy enough to not rely on their children's labor). An Edenic past with less filtration between reality and imagination, between the fullness of nature and a child's conception of their place in it. But it's a little annoying, too, like even the anxieties of modern parenting—everything a *product*, a reproduction, yada yada—are themselves unremarkable.

In her first minutes alive, my daughter was wrapped in a hospital blanket covered in illustrations of ducks, each with a patch of water rippling out behind. The first book she cared about follows a little chick the day it hatches. We thought she had the same face as the illustrated chick in the book; of course that was intentional. We called her our little chick. We called her our *gufo* (Italian for owl), our little goofy gufo, because we thought she looked like that, too. She had a book about owl babies, waiting for their mother to return, eyes round in perpetual awe and fear. She still sleeps with so many stuffed animals that in the night

2. Bruno Bettelheim. *The Uses of Enchantment*. London: Thames and Hudson, 1976.

vision monitor, a few invariably appear to be staring back at the screen as though alive, cornered, and caged. If she isn't yet asleep, I watch her hand probe around until it feels a soft ear or trunk or wing or antler, then snatches it to her. The intensity of that comfort, visible even through the screen—her whole body slackens into an embrace. Sometimes, when I open her door in the morning, she shoots her hand out, holding her raggedy polar bear—*Bear is awake! Good morning, Bear!* Bear is the conduit for our conversation until she's ready.

The first illustrated book for children, *Orbus Sensalium Pictus*, resembles a lot of what you might get for little kids today—part is simply the alphabet, with each letter corresponding to an animal image, putting language to the natural world and putting image to words. This was in the mid-1600s, and all the animals that a child might encounter were there: see the cat, the snake, the baby chick, the goose, the toad, the deer, the hare. But also, just like now, animals that already only existed in European imaginations, or sometimes freak-show captivity: lions, crocodiles. Jump two hundred years, and there's Alice, through the looking glass with the grinning cat, the anxious hare, her arm gently hugging the neck of a little fawn who tolerates it. The history of these texts, these images, is the balance between knowledge and imagination.

A detail I love about *Orbus Sensalium Pictus*, from the British Museum, which houses some original pages: *Despite the book being incredibly popular, few copies have survived. Because the book was so well-used, the pages got torn or wore out as children returned to the pictures over and over again.*

My middle name is Whitcher. Apparently my mother had a pilgrim-era ancestor named Sarah Whitcher, who is semi-famous for getting lost in the woods as a toddler, kept alive for days by a black bear. My mother has never been a sentimental woman, certainly not for any part of her family, but she wanted me to have this name, and she wanted to tell me this story. There's a kid's book about it; she read it to me as a boy and now I read it to my daughter. The bear in the book licks wild berry juice off Sarah's fingers, blood off her knees; its snout is wet and its fur warm and soft. I remember my mother reading it to me and feeling my body pressed into hers, like in the image of the girl and the bear. I remember thinking, when rescuers finally find Sarah, that the bear looks lonely, watching at the edges of the illustration, eyes big and round. *I see him*, my daughter says. *He's hiding.*

When we read the book now, I realize that most of it concerns the family certain their little girl is dead (*She'll have been ripped to pieces!*), a community tracking through dark, untamed woods with their muskets, ready to kill. The bear's motivation goes unexplained; it exists in useful kindness, then recedes back into a secret.

When I asked my mother why she named me that, she said it had been nice to think of something miraculous but also real. That's what a baby feels like; that's what you want the world to feel like for them. She was planning to be alone with me, and everything about my name was hers. I don't think of her as an anxious person, more someone worryingly unaware of danger as she moves through the world, but she must have been terrified, the way I often am now. I don't ask her if she remembers that feeling, and she doesn't offer it.

Last year, a highway marker was put up in New Hampshire around where Sarah was lost, then found. The driving force behind it was a Christian school. There's a version of the story that's made its way into Christian schooling curricula, framed as the tale of a father's belief keeping the searchers searching until his daughter was saved. The bear, then, is incidental—just another vessel for a story about what man can overcome through faith. I find this information infuriating. When I read the story to my daughter, we talk about the kindness of the bear, the instinct to love and protect, something innate, and I tell my daughter that she is kind, just like the bear, as though there's some connective, universal ideal of kindness to embody, but of course, that's its own myth.

We flew to California when she was three, drove the coast, stopped in Monterey with friends for the aquarium. There's an exhibit called *Open Ocean*—we already knew this from the Pixar movie *Finding Dory*. The open ocean swirls above and around you; it makes you feel like you're underwater but also looking up at the stars, and also, mostly, like you're inside the movie *Finding Dory*. All the kids say, *Woooooow!* in that particular way that is a top-five most-satisfying kid sound, used to justify any hassle or expense.

There's a tank at the aquarium filled only with the fish featured in *Finding Dory*; crowds throng here like red carpet paparazzi. Children scream, *There she is!* My daughter was very happy that Dory (the one she determined with certainty to be Dory) was not alone. Dory is a blue tang with memory loss; she exists in a constant state of grief and panic, eyes protruding, huge, glinting pupils conveying hope and inevitable disappointment on a loop. Also, she's funny? Or she's supposed to be; I have a hard time watching *Finding Dory* without crying. Sometimes I have to walk away and leave my daughter to watch alone, worried that she'll become as inconsolable as me.

On the beach in Monterey, my daughter and her friend went right down to the crashing Pacific, then ran away as the water chased their heels. As they came toward us, we noticed a bloated sea lion carcass sitting on top of the sand. Its whiskers shuddered in heavy wind. I couldn't look at it; the little girls went right up to it. My daughter seemed to not see it as something that was dead or had been alive—it was an object; I was relieved. The other girl, a year older, wanted to get as close as she could to its milky eyes, wanted to smell. Her mother said, *Just wait, there's a point when they can't get enough of death. You have to talk about it so much with them that you get desensitized.*

My daughter's a little older now, and everyone at school is talking about death. They pass a still pigeon on one of their walks—*Is it dead?* Some kid will interrupt a book at story time to ask if, on the next page, the animal protagonist finally dies. They're around so many things that are alive, and any one could just . . . not be.

This makes the world newly potent—the stray cats smushed by traffic; the rat-poisoned robin upturned, cute as a picture, feathers still and intricate.

In his Caldecott Medal acceptance speech, Maurice Sendak quoted a friend who said, after reading *Where the Wild Things Are*: *So we remember once again, as in so many times in the past, that the children are new and we are not.* In an interview years later, he said something which feels like an addendum: *I refuse to cater to the bullshit of innocence.*[3]

That summer, a lot of sea lions were washing up dead in California—the Channel Islands Marine and Wildlife Institute, near LA, said they got fifty to one hundred reports a day. Crowds on a packed Ventura Pier watched a sea lion seizure in the water below; some posted videos.

I've been doing a thing where I read beautiful accounts of environmental collapse and extinction, then get enormously sad, then get pissed and think, *Duh, everyone knows this, what's the point of saying it?* In Elizabeth Rush's *Rising*, it took me to the end of the first chapter to realize it was set at a coastal Audubon preserve where we often take my daughter. Rush describes decaying trees in the marshland, hanging ghostly out over the bay.

3. Emma Brocks. "Interview: Maurice Sendak." *The Guardian*, October 2, 2011.

I'd thought they looked like Dr. Seuss trees—silly and almost unreal. Back and forth, we said to each other, *Aren't those trees silly?*

On the bare tops of these trees are the osprey nests. I was with
my daughter and my parents during summer break. We looked
up at the ospreys: the fuzzy bed head of the chicks just visible
above the tangle, mouths open to the sky, then the elegant swoop
of a mother above us, carrying a fish to the nest. I will always
remember this: the divine predictability as she returned to them,
the intimacy, the thrill.

My mother read out a plaque about how the ospreys migrate five
thousand miles to that spot where we stood with them. Each
year, they start at Lake Valencia, in Venezuela, and they find
their way to us—what a *gift*. Think about everything they see,
and everything they know, in a way of knowing that is so inborn
we couldn't possibly understand it. I tried to say some version
of all this to my daughter, though so often when you're coaxing
appropriate awe out of a kid, you realize you're just reminding
yourself, over and over, that you can, should, feel it, too.

It was late August, when ospreys prepare to head south, so we
talked about them like they were packing up the house. A long
time ago, I'd driven by Lake Valencia without knowing its connection to this place where we were then. I said, *Isn't that* amazing? I must have seen them there, five thousand miles away. Time
and distance were collapsed around the osprey; the world felt big

and small. We told my daughter to wave goodbye. She did, but she also made a sad little noise from inside herself. We told her, *They'll come back, they always come back.*

Before his name was synonymous with preservation, John James Audubon was famous for his illustrated book *Birds of America*, still a remarkable historical compendium of man looking closely at animal. Most of his renderings were done using dead birds as models—propped up in poses of flight or fear with wood and wire. A recreation of what he may have observed or wished he'd observed, mass-produced for the observation of others. They're still beautiful: the long slope of a neck, a talon's grip, the fullness of a beating wing and that particular combination of delicacy and strength.[4]

Even then, two hundred years ago, when every image was a primary document, rendered by a man whose stated purpose was scientific, there's question as to how much humanity seeped in. In *The Art of Natural History*, S. Peter Dance wrote of Audubon's birds, *Most human of all are the eyes.* He describes the mixture of fear and steely resolve in two mockingbirds fighting off a rattlesnake, the bulging menace of an owl's eyes contrasted with a clasp-pawed squirrel.[5]

4. S. Peter Dance. *The Art of Natural History*. New York: Overlook Books, 1978.
5. S. Peter Dance. *The Art of Natural History*.

To render an animal is always going to be, in some way, an act of imagination; every act of imagination is always going to be, in some way, a chance to reflect the self.

There's an ongoing argument about the value or danger of anthropomorphism. When I talk to Marc Bekoff, a renowned evolutionary biologist at the University of Colorado, he tells me that in the past decade, people in the field don't turn their nose up at it the way they used to. Why not call an ostrich shy? A mountain lion mischievous? It's a question, really, of whether it's more arrogant to think you can relate to an animal or to think the animal can't possibly be anything like you.

Bekoff says his friend Jane Goodall was so revolutionary because she was the first to name an animal she studied, like she had with stuffed toys as a child. It was the act of a novice who didn't know any better, but the not knowing is what made her brilliant. The science grew out of love. I didn't tell him that I already knew all this from a picture book about Goodall that my daughter reads, where she sits with Flo and Fifi, the whole crew, like children at circle time, their smiles matching.

The last line of the book is: *If chimpanzees can live in harmony with their environment, then we can, too!* In the illustration, Goodall, now grayed, sits in a circle in the same spot in the Gombe with her chimp family, all of them looking out from the page with gentle, imploring eyes. I say, *That could be you*, to my daughter, though I don't specify which character.

In the forties, a Disney animator named Preston Blair wrote about how to make a cartoon lovable, and in particular how to make an animal cute. He made a diagram of "The Cute Character," a page with a human baby, a pig, a rabbit, a raccoon, and a chipmunk. Each has pupils upturned, hands or paws or hooves clasped or touching their own face. With arrows, he annotated the rules. Arms: short, never skinny. Neck: nonexistent. Head: huge; forehead: proportionally even huger. Legs: fat, tapering down. Belly: bulging. Eyes: round, low on the head, wide apart. The result: harmless.[6]

The lead animator for *Bambi* said that in his initial sketches, he drew a human child's head onto a deer's body, and that was the model for the character. So, when Bambi's ears prick up, eyes widen, when his father says, *Man has entered the forest*, right before the crack of the gun, we see the contours of a human face grieving the violence from human hands.[7]

My daughter has started to do the thing where she says, *I'm cute.* Then, if we don't respond, she asks, *Am I cute?* And so we have to say (well, are very eager to say) yes. *Cute* is the highest compliment; she uses it to mean *lovable*. *Silly* has become important, too, the distinction between *silly* and *serious*. If she's unhappy, she calls herself serious. When she's unhappy with me, she calls me serious. In her idealized moments, we are a silly family, and

6. Rebecca Stanton. *The Disneyfication of Animals.* New York: Springer, 2020.
7. Rebecca Stanton. *The Disneyfication of Animals.*

the dog is silly, too—we can all be silly together, which I think means we're all a little bit wild.

She isn't a clingy kid, but now she likes the drama of missing us. If one of us is going out to run an errand, she makes her eyes big like a cartoon animal and asks if she can come, then asks if we'll come back. I kneel down and hold her and relish the chance to say, *I'll always, always, always come back.*

The parenting moments that feel best are the ones when I can provide reassurance. Sometimes, I know, reassurance, even comfort, is the opposite of truth. Every time she imagines something nice, something beautiful, I want her to believe it forever.

She wants every animal to have a family. She is frantic in her organization, overcome with the responsibility of being the one to ensure that no one is alone. I'll hear her rooting around in a bin in the other room, hurried breathing, then a scream: *I found the mama turtle! She's going to teach the baby turtle to swim!* Then, impersonating the mama turtle, *Baby! I was looking for you! I found you!*

We were at a zoo, and there was a sea turtle in a tank that was too small, gliding its white underside against the glass. It looked . . . sardonic? Though that's the vibe I've ascribed to all turtles since the chill-bro sea turtles in *Finding Nemo*; plus, once I was snorkeling and came upon one, and it really did seem bemused. My daughter laughed and laughed at the turtle's white belly and the lackadaisical wave of fins that didn't have much use for propulsion. We'd been talking about how long they can live, a number large enough for us to round up to forever. She asked why the turtle was alone and how long it had been alone and how long it would be alone, and I felt my body tense the way it does whenever I think a whole day might go off the rails. But she dropped it; we moved on. It seemed like a choice—she was suspicious of the situation, then pushed past it for the benefit of the group, which is the way I experience the zoo. It felt like a marker of growing up; I was weirdly proud but also grieving something, or maybe I invented that whole thought process for her.

In the same week, I sent my wife a clip of a giraffe father at a zoo meeting his calf, and she sent me a clip of a chimpanzee mother at a zoo holding her baby for the first time after an emergency C-section. We both cried at both. The giraffe father flitted his eyelashes, then glanced at whoever was holding the camera, like looking for permission, then lowered his head to touch his calf's cheek. The chimpanzee mother grazed the baby with her fingertips before swaddling. Our daughter is a full kid now; it's hard to remember what holding a newborn even feels like. We said we'd never miss it, but sometimes we do. I think we sent the giraffe and chimp videos to one another as a reminder, a chance to see our own memories in them, with no visible ambivalence, just an unimpeachable instinct we could call love.

Most of the comments on these clips are of a similar vein—*Look, they're just like us!* But then there are those focusing on the human hands onscreen, or voices off screen, what it must feel like to be the one who helped these babies survive, who could give this gift to the animal and bask in what we can imagine to be their gratitude.

It's well known that the term *teddy bear* comes from Teddy Roosevelt. I hadn't realized, though, that it references a specific act of mercy. On a presidential hunt, he *refused to shoot a small, bedraggled black bear*,[8] a decision dramatized in a popular newspaper cartoon. The bear was called "Teddy's Bear"—he could have killed it, but he didn't, so it became his, a testament to both his power and his benevolence.

He had someone else kill the bear, a mercy killing. It wouldn't have survived, but it wasn't worth a sportsman's hunt.

Roosevelt was a conservationist and is still held up as a responsible hunter, one who railed against gratuitous death. But there are images of him readily available, next to a dead rhinoceros whose chin rests on the ground as though just tired, a yak, a lion, a cheetah whose face he has pointed at the camera, his fingers seeming to tickle the fur of its chin just beneath the bared teeth.

8. Sheldon Cashdan. *The Witch Must Die: How Fairy Tales Shape Our Lives*. New York: Basic Books, 2014.

I'm the type of liberal person who points to Donald Trump Jr.'s big-game hunting as the embodiment of, and maybe even greatest extreme within, his cruelty. This is an embarrassing impulse sometimes. It feels like when I was the kind of liberal person who got so very sad and angry at the image of a plastic straw lodged in a sea turtle's throat, and vowed off plastic straws, and then other people were like, *Awww wittle turtles make you wanna use a glass straw? What about boycotting Chase or caring when humans are gunned down in the street?*

Often, I think serious adulthood is predicated on the belief that care is a finite resource, not one that builds momentum. That to care too much or in the wrong direction is childish, therefore worse than not caring at all.

When you walk into the New Bedford Whaling Museum, there's a model of a sperm whale's heart in the lobby. It's the height of a tall child, bulbous enough that if you tried to wrap your arms around it, you wouldn't even get halfway. It's hard not to imagine what it would look like beating, the force of it and the sound. When children stand in front of it, often they touch their own hearts. It's not hard to make a child fall in love with a whale, the museum's education director Jeannine Luoro tells me. To be so grateful they exist. Then she takes me to the second floor, to a room where the tour changes tone. A sperm whale skeleton sits next to a preserved whaleboat; the walls are covered with harpoons. There's a painting dramatizing the hunt. It all clicks. Louro says, *When they start crying, we try to give them context: this was how people survived, they didn't know any better, we wouldn't do this now.*

There's an observation deck at the museum where they take children to look out over the harbor, then the bay, and imagine what was there, what's still there in the depths, life beyond what we can see. Imagine a whale emerging out of that, this eruption of consciousness. What would you feel? Terror? Thrill? Connection? Once, at a crowded beach, a whale breached in the distance. Everyone was briefly unified, pointing and hollering. I held my daughter up and asked, *Do you see? Do you see?* She lied and said she did. She was mostly interested, I think, in the transformation of the adults around her—suddenly rapt, grateful, making eye contact with strangers. Then it was over. At the museum gift shop, you can buy a plush whale family—mom, dad, and baby, mouths grinning, tails flicked up in a wave. I do.

I don't think my daughter distinguishes between rarity and abundance. She doesn't have a frame of reference for what is worthy of wonder, what is saddled with the weight of former commonness, what she should feel lucky to see, what she can see every day until she stops looking, what she might never see again.

There are children who want to know facts, who want to define what *is*, and perhaps even more importantly what cannot be. I was one of those kids. I was a *Zoobooks* subscriber, a cheetahs-are-obviously-the-fastest-animal-but-do-you-know-what-the-second-and-third-fastest-are type of kid. My daughter is not. Sometimes, she'll want to linger at school when I pick her up, so as not to miss the last story time. I obediently crisscross-applesauce to watch a teacher try to make it through a book about a jungle or elephants or the deep sea, stopped every few seconds by a torrent of information from eager four- and five-year-olds.

Sometimes I catch myself wishing she would say, even prodding her to say, what she *knows*, like that's the ultimate sign of appropriate maturation. But she won't; she just likes the stories.

As she gets older, I feel this increasing responsibility to arm her with knowledge—both in the traditional, annoying look-at-my-gifted-child way and in a newer way that feels like a performance of my own political progressiveness: *We won't let her look away from all the awfulness.* But I do want her to look away from the awfulness, or rather, I at least don't want to be the person to show her. She nods her head with satisfaction when she calls something or someone *nice*, like she's identifying again that universal animating quality that anything can have—animal, person, object. Sometimes I think this is the most beautiful thing, but sometimes now, the generosity of her wonder reads to me as babyish, and I hate that thought.

Even thirty years ago, the back pages of each *Zoobooks* issue were devoted to miserable facts. Every animal covered was endangered. I have such a clear memory of the rhinoceros issue: the diagrams of their armor-plated flesh, the sharp tips of their horns contrasted with these baleful horse eyes, the downturned face shape, the nuzzle of a mother to a baby. Then, at the end, the descriptions of poaching, a mutilated face with the horn cut off, a four-digit number for how many were left *in the whole world*. I felt sad and angry and helpless, though somehow more serious and adult for the knowledge. I wanted to see a real one so badly before they were gone. To treat it with tenderness.

I began researching this essay because everything about the way my daughter experiences animals, seeks them out, has them curated for her, matches my childhood experience, but the world feels different now. It feels beyond whatever that long moment was of *Look into the baleful eye of the rhino and know that its land is vanishing and be inspired to save it.* That whole concept seems too unlikely, and also too small in scale, to even write down—their extinction is near inevitable; to indulge in weepy infomercial environmentalism is just nostalgia for a simpler kind of sadness. But watching a kid flicker with curiosity, with care, for something alive and unknowable still stokes memory and hope, all at once. Still falls so pleasurably into a timeless, beautiful, doomed routine: see the animal, imagine that animal, look into its eyes, find love in your idea of it.

She wants to see everything. She wants to believe that everything is looking back at her.

She got obsessed with the book *Stellaluna*, about a lost bat raised by birds. Then she cajoled a friend into giving her a plastic bat off a Halloween decoration, which she cherished. She'd only ever encountered them still, in pictures, with faces resembling a little dog, clutching fingers resembling our own. Then we visited friends in the country over the Fourth of July and stood outside to watch fireworks beginning in the distance. In the foreground, bats crisscrossed the sky between old oak trees, distressed (maybe?) by the sound. Their movements were jagged and strange. She wanted them to slow down. She wanted to know what they saw; we were looking for the gentlest way to say she never would. She isn't afraid of the dark, but sometimes, when I turn out the light, she asks, *Why can't I see? Stellaluna can see!*

Sometimes she screams, *I can't see its eyes!* This will refer to the dog facing away, or a squirrel that she's followed with her gaze up a tree. For a while, she'd reencounter the realization that she could not, in fact, see her own eyes, and this caused brief, operatic bouts of distress. Like she couldn't prove to herself her own being. She'd find a mirror, look at herself as though she were the animal in the zoo, or onscreen, say, *There they are*, and smile again.

When she encounters an animal in captivity, in the wild, in the imagined relationship she's built with a stuffed toy, she says, *Hello, are you looking at me?* It feels like the world slows down, simplifies, becomes newly manageable then—all intimacy, no context. At a book swap, we snagged a copy of *Owl Moon*, another of the old outdoorsy New England genre that I was steeped in by my mother. A kid and their father trudge into unsullied winter woods; everything is quiet but for their owl calls, and then finally one appears. The climax of the book is just the owl's eyes meeting theirs, shared breathing, the enormous elasticity of time and love and silence. The father is big, the child is small; it's just them and this still-wild world, and I leave her room imagining myself as that father and her as that child.

It's hard to talk about animals in a way that isn't nostalgia for a place and time we've never been. A lie for the sake of comfort. John Berger wrote about zoos as a setting created to repeat the lie over and over. They provide the chance to feel that there is some connection, some love, something preserved, to dilute the reality that humanity has only ever been, in his words, *remorseless*. Berger describes interactions at a zoo like this: *At most, the animal's gaze flickers and passes on. They look sideways. They look blindly beyond. They scan mechanically.*[9]

Look, I love John Berger, I have a pretentious Berger-inspired tattoo, but he doesn't know if the animals are looking blindly beyond any more than someone else knows that they're connecting. He's choosing righteous anger over saccharine denial, but that's its own seduction: the chance to grieve and tell yourself it's on their behalf.

Anthropomorphism is connected to human loneliness, or really the human fear of loneliness. In a Harvard study, pet owners were asked to watch a movie meant to make them feel sad and

9. John Berger. *About Looking*. New York: Vintage Books, 1980.

alone (*Cast Away*), or a movie meant to make them feel distrust-
ful (*Silence of the Lambs*), or a neutral movie (for some reason,
Major League). When the movie was over, pets were brought in,
and they were asked to describe them. At far greater rates than
the others, those who watched *Cast Away* began to describe animals like their friends: thoughtful, sympathetic, kind.[10]

One night, after my daughter was in bed, my wife and I watched
The Banshees of Inisherin, which is a beautiful movie about sad
people whose sadness is only heightened by the constant presence and love of animals. I adore this genre in any medium—
Sigrid Nunez's *The Friend*, Michelle Williams's performance
alongside a yellow lab mix in *Wendy and Lucy*. In *Banshees*,
Colin Farrell has a sweet black donkey named Jenny with the
best eyes you've ever seen. Ten minutes in, I said to my wife, *That
poor little donkey is going to die*. An hour and a half later, she
did. There's a scene of Colin Farrell sitting with the body, its head
and neck draped on his lap, a pose my daughter will only tolerate
when she's so sick that she needs the comfort.

I loved the movie, but it does the thing that plenty have done
before it—equated an adult who loves animals overwhelmingly,
free of any cynical self-awareness, with a certain *simplicity*.
They feel deeply for something that appears so simple, and it *is*
a simple kind of love, one built on unsubtle, unspoken devotion

10. Hal Herzog. *Some We Love, Some We Hate, Some We Eat*. New York:
    Harper Perennial, 2011.

and need, and that's easy to turn into a metaphor. Think of big, helpless Lenny in *Of Mice and Men*, and the rabbits he loved, then accidentally killed. The animals exist—in their blameless-ness, then death—to allow humans to feel. In *Banshees*, people go back and forth calling Farrell's character either *simple* or *nice*. They're used as different ways to frame the same type of person, a man who wants the world to be as it felt when he was a child.

The anthrozoologist Hal Herzog describes being at the world's leading conference of animal behaviorists when a speaker asked the question, *How many of you went into this field because you wanted to know what it was like to be a member of the species you study?* Herzog was in the back, sneering at the childishness of the question, but then, he writes: *I was completely wrong. More than half the researchers raised their hand.*[11]

Sometimes, we're too hard on my daughter, and when we're ask-ing her questions about school—*Did you pee when they asked you to? Were you loud during rest time? Are you even listening to me?*—we double down, instead of taking her decision to become nonverbal as a way of saying, *Not now, please.* Lately, in these moments, usually at the dinner table, she slides out of her chair onto the floor. She says, *We have two dogs now.* She disappears under the table, on all fours, following the dog as she looks for scraps. It's like she's identified non-humanness as a space that is

11. Hal Herzog. *Some We Love, Some We Hate, Some We Eat.*

less annoying, where what you cannot say, or don't want to say, no longer matters. It *must* feel better than what we're asking of her.

She has begun to remind me (remind herself) that animals can't talk. She used to ask what an animal was saying (real or stuffed), as though it was information that grown-ups had that she one day would. Sometimes she sounds disappointed, sometimes almost like she's scolding herself; lately—and this breaks my heart—she's at the point where she says, *Animals don't talk, that's so silly.* But then she wants to know what they think yet cannot say. If they can't say that they see her, do they still see her? Is the interaction happening that she believes is happening?

When a bird chirps, it's talking in its way, we tell her; when the dog howls at the mailman, she's saying, *Hello, I'm in here!* Some favorite animals don't have a recognizable sound—a giraffe, for instance. I looked it up, and they do occasionally make a guttural moan, usually at night, if one can't find the rest of the herd. We played a YouTube video of just the sound on a loop—*The giraffes are talking!*—but she was disinterested. It was not the sound she would have wanted them to make.

I took her to a deserted zoo on a cold day. The giraffes were inside a building, staying warm and getting fed. We sat on a bench for nearly an hour; she was rapt, satisfied to watch their jaws working, their silly black tongues. The zoo had just gotten a new giraffe in, and we watched keepers teaching it how to accept leaves from a human hand—clicking, petting the muscle of its neck. My daughter wanted to know how it was feeling. I asked, What do *you* think? She didn't answer.

I thought the giraffe looked miserable, but also, what did I know? Part of me thought my daughter had the same inkling, but again, what do I know? I felt a heavy melancholy, but also, I felt so close to her, which was ecstatic. She tiptoed as close as she'd allow herself to the giraffe and the zookeeper, waited for acknowledgment that didn't come, and then we left. At home, I knew she'd find each of her *three* stuffed giraffes (two were gifts, I swear), hold their necks, put their faces up to her own. They range from faithful realism to pink-spotted goofiness, but these distinctions don't matter. Each looks pleading, a little ashamed, with long, arcing eyelashes—my favorite feature of a real giraffe, so seemingly unnecessary other than for expression. She stations the largest by the sink to watch her brush her teeth.

Susan Sofia-McIntire, a plush-toy designer, tells me you learn early on that eye proportion is the key. Render the animal as realistically as you like, as long as the fur is soft and the eyes large and open enough to become a defining feature. In recent years, she says, this alteration in scale has pushed into the ridiculous, with toys like Beanie Boos, where the eyes are half an animal's face, perfectly round, filled in with hypnotic, multicolored glitter. My daughter has one from a rest stop during a miserable stint on I-95. She was briefly obsessed with this hard-to-parse animal—cotton candy color, giant shimmering eyes that she held up in front of her own—but now it's lining the bottom of a bin by the TV.

The secret, Sofia-McIntire says, is that a child will love the ugliest thing if you give it to them like it's beautiful.

In a moment when parents (me) are often terrified of the warp-speed evolution of their own relationship to technological pacification, there's a certain blind acceptance of, then weird satisfaction in, the idea that a child should love old, simple things better than new and complexly digitized things. It's the ethos of *The Velveteen Rabbit* continued into the twenty-first century. (Surprise, surprise: I cannot make it through that book without weeping.) So I can say, *Look, my kid doesn't need* Paw Patrol, *she finds placation in the original Cinderella's kind mice or Beatrix Potter's woodland tales*, and in the right moment believe that means something. *Look, she can find wonder in the animal totems of my childhood*, a simpler-ish time that was itself mimicking another world, my mother's, that was closer to the ideal, or maybe I mean the *real*, but was still mostly a construction of nostalgic faith.

She has the same brand of stuffed polar bear that I had. She loves it with the same intensity. I remember a point when I was old enough to grow obsessed with images of starving polar bears stranded on thin ice. Maybe I loved my bear more for it. Maybe she will when she knows. I remember my mother saying she was proud of me for feeling bad about it, like I'd passed an empathy test, and I can imagine myself saying the same thing.

When I speak to children's literature scholar Wesley Jacques about the way modern kid lit attempts to provide fraught, complex political critiques through the remove of adorable animals, he tells me about a subgenre of books in Civil War times built around one plot: white child gets covered in mud, mistaken for Black, stolen and brought to auction, where the mud is washed off just in time, and a lesson is learned. Capitalism has always commodified its own critique, Jacques says. You can allegorize shame, ambivalence, empathy; repackage, resell.

The question, then, is whether these ciphers for feeling are made to evolve into catalysts for change. And I don't know; I've always been stuck on feeling. Mostly, I'm content to watch my daughter feel.

She loves a book about a bat who knows that inside he's a butterfly and even gets caterpillars to make him a cocoon, out of which he springs as a metaphor for gender-affirming surgery. She has a book in which fish encounter an unmovable pile of garbage polluting the ocean and, in the climax, come to the conclusion that, *The problem is . . . US*, even though the *us* isn't really them. She got obsessed with the movie *Zootopia*, about a bunny cop, which was ultimately a metaphor for racial profiling that still has the cop as the hero, and the only part that I could watch comfortably was the genius bit where everyone working at the DMV is a sloth.

Jacques tells me he recently spoke with a children's librarian who decided to stop ordering any books that use the appeal of animals to teach a lesson. The idea is, at a certain point we need to say what we mean.

Sofia-McEntire says she's seen a million trends come and go, but it's usually some combination of adorable and impending tragedy that makes a new animal pop. So the sloths, the pandas, the giraffes—all those that have recently become ubiquitous—appear kind yet very strange, have gentle, sleepy eyes, move with whatever the opposite of menace is, *and* they need rescue. That's something else to market. Hug them tight, and it feels good, feels necessary. But then the stuffing material used hasn't evolved much ecologically, she says. They won't break down. My daughter's stuffed polar bear will likely exist on earth longer than the species; her three separate stuffed giraffes might all outlive the existence of giraffes in Africa.

This is another one of those facts that feels both too obvious and too sad to write down. Will there be a point when rendering the animal loses its wonder? What I really mean is: To feel wonder, must there be at least some glimmer of hope?

The inventor of the stuffed animal was a disabled German woman named Margarete Steiff, who built an empire at the turn of the twentieth century. It was her design, showcased at an international trade fair, that captured Americans' imaginations and exploded as the teddy bear—the first with movable arms, up and down, soft-clawed paws always reaching out in demand of a hug.

The word *bear* dates back to a Germanic word that means only *the brown one*. In Scandinavian languages, too, the name for the animal was a vague descriptor, as though it was too frightening to conjure with a specific word.[12] It was a universal symbol of a monster, then it was hunted and tortured for entertainment, then, once beaten down, there was that face, that belly when up on two legs, those individuated paws, like our fingers, those eyes.

In her fantastic book *Animals Strike Curious Poses*, Elena Passarello writes about Sackerson, the only bear who survived enough rounds of bearbaiting to be name-checked by Shakespeare. He's famous for his ferociousness, but only because his death was inevitable in front of a frenzied human crowd. Passarello writes, *They saw it in his stance—up on two legs, the forepaws spread, the ten claws digital. They saw it in his low slung hips and gut. The way his pupils, round and beady, lived inside a circle of expressive white. And milliseconds prior to the bite,*

12. John Green. *The Anthropocene Reviewed*. New York: Dutton, 2021.

they saw it as he bowed his head and sighed. What did they see? They saw themselves, of course.[13]

When I speak to Passarello about what she remembers from touring with the book, she talks about how often readers, even ones meaning to be complimentary, said they couldn't finish parts of it. Particularly the bear essay. The story of this bear tortured four hundred years ago, in a manner of torture that's not a secret. I had that reaction, too. But then I had that reaction watching *Game of Thrones* when the CGI *dragons* died, which maybe invalidates whatever care I might have had about the historically real suffering of a bear. What I'm curious about in this universal wince is whether it hurts more to see ourselves as the animal in pain or as the humans causing it.

Sylvia M. Medina writes and publishes children's books because she fell in love with grizzly bears hiking the Rockies—the unlikelihood of spotting one, then the magnitude of their presence. She tells me grizzlies, aware now of the odds stacked against their survival, will often kill off young bears when there are too many. She saw the aftermath once, a cub the size of a human teenager bloodied and lifeless. She became a mother around the same time.

13. Elena Passarello. *Animals Strike Curious Poses*. Louisville: Sarabande, 2017.

Medina combines real anecdotes from animal welfare NGOs with illustrations done by a Disney animator—tales about canned hunting of lions, chimps abused by medical testing, one specific grizzly in Yellowstone who journeyed through human towns searching for enough food to keep four cubs alive, unwilling to give up. *Think of the courage of this mother*, Medina says to me. In her book, the mother talks her cubs through their survival. The National Parks won't sell the book in gift shops, not even Yellowstone, where this real bear family still lives. They don't consider it an educational tool the moment an animal speaks.

One thing she never does, Medina tells me, is show an animal dying, or the moment of a kill, even if the story is about mass death. That's an image drained of any possibility for hope, and what's the point of telling a child a story that's hopeless?

We end up talking about Werner Herzog's *Grizzly Man*, a prime example in my mind of when an adult thinks about an animal the way we encourage children to, and how easy a person like that is to call pathetic. Timothy Treadwell—a man who loved grizzlies as though they loved him back. He's killed by one, of course. Herzog has a famous bit of narration, spoken near the end, over Treadwell's close-up video of the bear that would soon kill him: *What haunts me is that, in all the faces of all the bears Treadwell ever filmed, I discover no kinship, no understanding, no mercy. I see only the overwhelming indifference of nature.*

There's a Maurice Sendak quote about Beatrix Potter that reads a bit like a precursor to Herzog. Sendak was a devoted enough fan to dub himself a *Potterette*; he described reading her work as a child and finding in it *the exact quality of a nightmare: the sense of being trapped and frightened and finding the rest of the world . . . too busy keeping itself alive to help save you.*[14]

I can conjure so many images and stories of animals from my childhood, both real and imagined. Some remain as vivid as my own lived memories. It was overwhelming, what they made me feel—longing, terror, sometimes grief, so that if they found any safety or comfort at the end, I was ecstatic all over again. The first stirrings of what art can do.

Another Herzog clip went viral a few years back, in which he monologues about chickens and the *enormity of their stupidity.* Before I was a parent, I thought this was the funniest thing. Now, I think about saying those words to my daughter—*Look at the stupid chicken, look at the absolute nothing in its eyes*—and it seems impossibly cruel. There is a way of being when I'm with her that's easy to frame as compulsory *for her sake*, but more than anything, it makes me feel good.

14. Bruce Handy. *Wild Things: The Joy of Reading Children's Literature as an Adult.* New York: Simon and Schuster, 2017.

She grew to love a hippie neighbor's chickens, and over the span of that love, many new chickens were swapped in for old ones. Then the hippie neighbor got quails, and we squinted through chain-link to catch sight of the babies. Very quickly, one froze, and a few were eaten by rats. The whole thing was a bad idea; he carried a lot of guilt over trying to force something to happen that shouldn't. He whispered this to me, eyes on my daughter so she wouldn't hear, which I thought was sweet. He lured the chickens over to the fence with food. My daughter crouched so that she was almost eye level with them. One cocked its head at her, and she reciprocated. The neighbor said, *That's nice*, and it was.

We talked about getting chickens and then didn't, and I said it was because I didn't want the work, and while that's true, it wasn't the reason. They would die—that's the reason, of course. Annually, at least, maybe in bunches, and I didn't think I could take that, which is so ridiculous, I know. It's letting the lines of tenderness and fear blur, which is too often how I experience parenthood.

Once, she was helping us out in the garden, in early spring. There was a crunch under my boot, and she came over to see a snail dead, shell shattered. I froze, but it was okay. We found more snails. They were slow enough for her to ask a question, and they'd still be there by the end, which she loved. She was terrified of what she might do to one; she tried to hold her body so still that she was vibrating like she had to pee. On instinct, I said, *Do you see its eyes?* On cue, antennae moved like fingers, and she laughed.

I spoke with Calef Brown, an illustrator, about all the animals he'd drawn over the years. He showed me an instructional book he'd published for children that revolved entirely around snails. At first, he shrugged when I asked, *Why snails?* but then he launched into an anecdote of when he was younger, newly a father, in a rented home, looking out into the garden in down moments, watching snails methodically trace the leaves on the bushes. His landlord brought salt over to kill them, and he ended up pleading with the guy not to; he'd pay, he said, to replace the bushes the snails ate. He felt strongly, suddenly, that it would hurt to not see them.

When you draw a snail, he says, all you need are two ovals, perpendicular, and then a circle on top for the shell, and it is recognizably itself. Isn't that amazing? Can there be a simpler way to render distinct life? And then whatever other detail you want to add, it's yours—this bare template of reality, then only imagination.

By the river, the ducks mingle with swans or a flock of big, loud geese. Once, in the distance, a white stork completely still. I felt my breath catch. Once, much closer, on a small rock, a blue heron. I was whispering, *Can you* believe *it?* I've cared about few things to the degree that I wanted her to care about that bird. An old bird-watcher was near us with a long lens camera. He said to my daughter, *Are you the luckiest little girl in the world?* The heron disappeared its head into the water, then pulled up with a fish half-gone down its throat. The bird-watcher whispered, *She's feeding,* with reverence. He asked my daughter if she wanted to look through the lens, but she didn't—not, I think, out of fear, but because she just wasn't as interested as we wanted her to be. I was disappointed and relieved. I looked: the heron's jaw was all muscle, a feathered snake.

The other day, I asked her about it—*Do you remember?* The giant bird so close to us on that rock? The color of its feathers, like dark water, the way it balanced on one leg? She said yes, but the look on her face suggested I could have been talking about any animal, any time, any place. She knew she would like my reaction upon confirmation that it had made an impression. We were out again by another spot on the river. There were ducks, geese, seagulls, a flock of pigeons on the ground near us. We were talking about what *wildness* meant, how all of these birds fended for themselves, lived in a way that didn't involve us. We were lucky to watch them, that's all. She was still concerned about their eyes—how close she could get to them, if any would meet her gaze. They flew off and came back. Eventually, we got cold. As we left, she said that all those birds didn't know her or talk to her or look at her, except one. A gull that didn't flap away immediately, that stared back. There were hundreds of birds there, and she knew enough to say they weren't talking to her, they didn't love her, but this one; she held onto the idea that something different, something miraculous had passed between them. And why not?

You are so kind, I said. *The gull is kind,* she said. *You're* both *kind,* I said. I told her I would remember everything about this moment forever, which didn't impress her to the degree it impressed me. Her polar bear was waiting in the car. She snatched it to her and said, *I missed you I missed you I missed you.* I watched her in the rearview mirror, her perfect, unaware, animal self, until finally she asked why we hadn't started driving away.

Dads Being Dudes Making Jokes

The first time I consciously engaged with a dad meme online, an old spin instructor shared it. She was a new mom. There was a moment when my wife and I had been almost friends with her, in that we were loyal attendees of her class and kept going right up until a week before my wife gave birth, so everyone was invested in us, or it felt like that. By then, the instructor was beginning her own pregnancy and was picking my wife's brain. It was an early example of the sincere, supportive, fellow-traveler type relationships that came in and out of her life during pregnancy and early motherhood. They were instantly bonded by the enormity of this new responsibility. My wife was determined to be generous in her mentorship but also as no-bullshit as possible, to prepare the spin instructor not only for joy but also hardship. She was incredible in this role. I loved watching her from the edge of the interaction.

We had the spin instructor and her husband (a football coach, intimidatingly trapezoidal in both chin and torso) over to hand down all the things our baby had outgrown. My wife and the spin instructor talked; I helped the coach schlep everything out to their car in silence. They marveled at our daughter, then a round, smiley six months, who sat on the couch and appeared to be listening. They said her eyes were very *there*, very connected, and we said, *Thanks, that's so nice to hear.* By the end, she melted down and they left fast. We waved goodbye, my wife holding what had gone from a cherub to a snot-streaked angry tomato. I watched something pass between my wife and the spin instructor, this look of rueful knowingness. They both said, *If you need anything* . . . like they really meant it, and just because we never saw these people again doesn't take away from the fact that they did mean it in the moment.

Anyway, we were still struggling with sleep training a year in, and I was on Instagram trying to ignore the monitor, and the spin instructor shared this post that was a picture from a movie of a zombie—clothes in tatters, eyes blank, face bloody—shuffling away from an explosion. The caption was something along the lines of: *Dads after the bedtime routine.* It was from an account called The Dad, the most prominent aggregator of all things *dadness*, which had just climbed over two million Instagram followers. The spin instructor had tagged her husband with a string of crying laughing emojis.

I was a little embarrassed by how funny I found this meme to be. It was so nakedly dweeby. But . . . you know . . . it *did* get at something real. I *did* feel like that zombie whenever I tiptoed out of my daughter's room—*Dead inside! Ha!* It was the perfect balance of ridiculing the drama of how one might experience something so quotidian, but underneath that, then, the implication that such drama, if it's worth ridicule, is common, so if you see yourself in it, you're not alone. I don't want to spend too much time here analyzing why a meme works; it works because it's more fun than analysis. You don't have to say anything, just point and giggle, hold your phone up for someone else to see.

My wife was more of a pacer during post-bedtime panic, always ready to spring, while I anchored myself to the couch. I held my phone up as she passed. *Look*, I said. *Isn't this exactly right?*

She stopped for only a second. She leaned in and said, *Seen it, babe; pretty good.* I followed the account.

It's an easy target to point out the way fathers and expectant fathers are spoken to, or not, in the books, websites, classes, and Instagram accounts that exist to help a certain type of overeducated thirtysomething prepare for the early days of parenthood. I stopped reading *The Birth Partner* when, fifty pages in, other than tips for an effective perineum massage, the book had mostly made me spin out about how expensive a college education would be if inflation continued at its current rate. In the face of the birthing parent's physical trauma, emotional upheaval, the entire reconfiguring of life, body, and self-conception, the birth partner could fret over budget, a responsibility that felt both too small *and* burdensome.

Years later, when we asked around for the most practical, non-preachy book on potty training, we were recommended the same one, over and over—irreverent enough to have *crap* in the title. Upon purchase, we discovered that that it included a *very* short section on page 263 specifically addressed to fathers, with the assumption being that the first 262 pages—full of statistics, warnings, commiseration—weren't meant for their eyes. Page 263 begins, *You're probably already the chill one. . . .* A few paragraphs later, we get to the father's primary directive: keep vigilant moms from going *crazy.*

These characterizations are insulting, yes, but they also provide a bar of expectations so easy to clear that a merely present father can feel not only annoyance but righteous superiority. On a group chat of dads, there's no more reliably fun topic than anecdotes about neighbor dads or fellow pre-K dads or dads at the park who behave like the cartoons conjured in these books. Everyone can get on board with saying, *At least we're not that*, and even though an awareness of the lowness of the bar is essential to not being a total prick, it's still fun to pat each other on the back while pretending we don't mean it.

Underneath, there's the nagging question: Just how different am I from the archetypes I mock? How often, no matter the eye rolls, am I another dad customer living up (down) to the limitations sold to me? For instance, despite being someone who *professionally* overthinks and overreads about any subject important to me, I froze at the prospect of doing much research pre-baby. Sure, *The Birth Partner* felt retrograde, but also, I wouldn't know—I couldn't be bothered to finish it. All the nuts-and-bolts, is-your-home-ready, will-this-kill-the-baby, power-through-knowledge stuff? I assumed that wasn't for me. I read as many emotionally vivid portrayals of parenthood (read *motherhood*) as possible, and that was a genuinely informative, nourishing thing to do, but the nitty-gritty of planning? The weight of being the person who, in minute one, had to know what was required for survival? I recused myself without even stopping to acknowledge it. I didn't ask anyone's advice; nobody offered me any. I'm amazed that I was allowed (allowed myself) to be so static in these before shots. I cannot believe that was me, though the incredulity makes no sense, feels like its own performance now.

In retrospect, I experienced so much of early fatherhood as the journey toward not feeling like a joke. The word *joke*, like the act of telling one, is a quick and easy header for all the complexity swirling underneath. Really, everything was *too* serious, entirely overwhelming, yet it was hard to shake the sense that whatever I felt or expressed, did or didn't do, resembled a punch line. When I first held the baby, it was wrong, like I couldn't make the crook of my elbow do the job it needed to. I preferred the method of draping her across my chest and shoulder, limp and damp as a steam room towel. There's months of near duplicate pictures—large man in dirty sweats, tiny baby, spit-up on large man's shoulder, large man rocking tiny baby back and forth, sweating, failing to console her, glancing helplessly at the camera. Each tortured move was slapstick. Everything is funnier when the butt of the joke isn't laughing.

It was the most enormous gulf I'd ever experienced between the way people responded to me and what it felt like to be me. I was so tired, so short-fused, so disappointed in myself for the flaws mounting each day. I felt isolated, even when surrounded by love, simultaneously closed off and needy. I began posting more than I ever had. The baby in my arms clutching a Yankees teether, the baby indoctrinated into Bruce Springsteen by daddy, the aftermath of her puking right as I went in for a kiss—*wamp wamp*. In response: *Awww* or *Hahaha*. Each time, I was briefly soothed to be seen all over again as adorable, offended that no one had asked if I was okay.

It's hard to pinpoint exactly when fathers became funny. I don't even mean *funny*, because at the heart of the *dad joke* concept is the idea that he's fun to laugh at, not with. I'm wondering more when the cultural imagination of a father opened up to the possibility for, then expectation of, attempted humor. In the history of American literature up through the twentieth century, there's no more reliably *unfunny* archetype—think of one of Faulkner's fathers conveying any sort of wink within the menace, Atticus Finch slipping in a punch line mid-lecture. In classic movies, too, a father is a hero or a monster, either way looming outside the gag. But I grew up laughing at dads because the medium that demystified, then mocked, the simple fact of their presence was the American sitcom. TV, that most domesticated way of consuming art—a perfect symbiosis in which the family gathers to watch family reflected, distorted, absorbing the reflection, returning.

That dynamic is long gone, of course, but the current boom of internet dad humor ever cycling through my algorithm is rooted in the famous sitcom dads that the internet dads grew up on, stoking nostalgia the way those sitcom dads were once stoking nostalgia for an idea of some baseline middle-class American comfort that was already a myth. Before I was born, there was Archie Bunker and Redd Foxx; in the nineties, I watched Cosby, Bob Saget, Al Bundy; later, in high school, I spaced out to *Everybody Loves Raymond* and *The King of Queens*. To encounter a funny dad Instagram reel or tweet feels like the next tiptoe forward in what has been over half a century of incremental character development.

The scenario remains static: the dad is a stranger doing his best in a strange land (contemporary domesticity). The differentiation in punch line, then, lies in the dad's perspective, and more specifically, I think, in the dad's relationship to resentment. How much, how overtly, does he mourn a before time (in his mythology of his own life, and in his mythology of society) when things would have been easier, and no one would have laughed at him? The family man, anchored by job, by mortgage, by mouths to feed, loyal to a wife who no longer sees anything remarkable in him, increasingly sexless, bankrolling children less grateful than *he* had been for the food on the table—the misery of that condition is a foundational concept in postwar American humor. His response changes not in core feeling, just in the intensity of its expression. So Al Bundy sits on the couch, cowed by life, and responds by calling Peg ugly, then a decade later, the King of Queens says, *Sometimes I just want to run away from you*, but only after his wife says something similar, and they hug at the end of the scene. The joke lies, either way, in the valley between the threat and the result: guaranteed ineffectualness and the knowledge that, even at the edge of unacceptable misanthropy, he might still be kind. Now, grudging, bumbling kindness is the dad character's default, rage is rendered down to performed exhaustion and wimpy complaint. But the conceit remains.

The end point of this trajectory, I think, is the specific subgenre of the *dad joke*—blank, vaguely cheerful, a closed loop of corny. It's a depiction of absolute harmlessness, but there's still something fundamentally hostile in its refusal to engage beyond the level of the pun. In 2018, searching for the origins of the dad joke, *Atlantic* writer Ashley Fetters traced a history of American dad identity that moved from power toward participation. She quotes the historian E. Anthony Rotundo, who says that postwar, as (white, middle-class) women first entered the workforce, fathers had to look for value and identity beyond simply *provider*, so they *tried to befriend their children and take a place in the main currents of home life*.

Rotundo wrote this in 1985. To me, it embodies perfectly a bizarre tension that I feel in modern fatherhood, where any sentiment can seem so embarrassingly dated and also . . . not. Fetters goes on to quote Natasha Cabrera, a professor in the University of Maryland's Department of Human Development, about the current status quo in the limited definition of hetero, two-parent households: *Dad is the worker, but he gets home and plays. Mom also has to work, and has to have dinner on the table, and has the emotional role. Mom is everything else.*

Here, the power and the limits of humor are revealed in equal measure. The dad joke, the dad *joking*, is both a sign of engagement and a stand-in for the full emotional spectrum born from true responsibility. Cabrera points out that this assumed dynamic implies that mothers can't be funny, too busy doing everything else. Obviously, that's absurd, but I do think this says something about why dad humor is defined as its own, explicitly formulaic genre. There's no subtlety or struggle to it, no urgency or critique. That's the point: it's not just a joke but the easiest possible joke.

Years after the fact, my wife is comfortable telling people that she probably had postpartum depression. If we're together, I jump in and say, *Me too!* I like to think that, with proper timing and delivery, this is funny; maybe it's even a nice gesture, diffusing the tension around what she had been willing to reveal by being the eager buffoon. Or maybe it's annoying. Either way, easier than the truth: I was desperately depressed, perhaps more so because it felt unearned, an affront to my wife's suffering rather than a chance to empathize.

The pain she experienced breastfeeding—both the literal, blistered-nipple variety and the shame of feeling unable to easily do the thing everyone had claimed to be innate—was so vivid. Our lives revolved around it; whenever the baby was hungry, the air in our home felt like a high school on the morning of the SATs. I was there with the bottle ready, which often the baby rejected as though I was hurting her. It was not the shame of failing at the role I was supposed to be born to perform. Instead, it was the opposite: confirmation of a uselessness that was supposed to be inborn in me.

Little baby howling around the nipple of the bottle; big, doofy dad saying, *I'm not even doing anything wrong!*

We went to a second lactation specialist a week before my wife was supposed to return to work, worried that either her career would be stunted or the baby would starve. In an observation room, I attempted to bottle-feed. The baby hit her most operatic protest yet, wailing for an hour, hunger and rage and fear combining into some new super emotion. The specialists were chuckling because, wow, they'd never seen anything quite like this. They said they admired how I kept trying in a tone meant for a child or a dog.

Later, we met friends. The baby napped in the stroller, completely exhausted, while I did a whole bit: *They'd never seen anyone this bad! No dad has ever been more useless! No baby has ever been more of an asshole! Look, sorry, I said it: she's an asshole, she gets it from me!*

The most seductive part of self-deprecation is that it can feel like hard honesty, even allyship.

The bottle-feeding settled down eventually; we survived. Then my anxiety shifted to the naps she wasn't taking on my watch, calculating in my mind the moment I woke up how much sleep she would need, tracing failure across each day. Then it was the fact that she wouldn't walk. Then it was something else. For the first two years of my daughter's life, between my parental leave and COVID, when my wife still had to go into the office, I was alone with her for nearly half of it. (I'm compelled to add: not saying that's special, not a hero, millions do it, my wife was *way* more involved than many working fathers would have been, I genuinely think we coparented well, etc., etc.). These remain the most emotionally intense years of my life, the ones I value most when thinking about who I've become as a person and who I want to be. That still feels ridiculous to say; immersion into the realities of caregiving should not be a revelation. But it was. The long, slow arc of each day, the way the baby evolved in front of me from something so unknowable into the most familiar person: her smell, her sudden, terrifying, ecstatic bursts of movement and emotion. I've never felt more joy or more despair, often within the same day. I've never felt prouder or more ashamed, often within the same day. I was too full of fear, too easily disappointed, and I still regret the degree to which despair outweighed joy and shame outweighed pride. I'm so glad to no longer be in that place; sometimes I miss it in a way that makes my breath catch.

Every day, I'd flee our home with her, as a form of respite— to coffee shops or libraries, or, in lockdown, literally any place outdoors where she might be able to toddle up to someone and make their face soften behind the mask, no matter the weather. She's always been at ease around people, even strangers, a quality that fills me with an evergreen, affirming type of awe. I look at her with this awe, and she looks back at me in a way that seems so generous, so loving, finally free from restlessness. These moments have felt like a matter of survival for both of us, but they're also a repeated performance. A chance to be seen fathering with no context beyond our twin smiles, and know that a stranger would never consider the shame and anxiety always thrumming in the background of my lived experience.

Still, sometimes, my daughter will cling to my knee as we walk; she'll look up from her smoothie and coo, *My Daddy.* I like watching people watch her as she dawdles across a restaurant to bus our table. They look to her, then their eyes scan the room to land on me waving, nodding her forward. I lean into performed ease. Once, a woman came up to me at a busy coffee shop and said, *I think you're amazing.* Which is so silly, I know. As soon as she walked away, I was blushing, embarrassed, but also I wanted to look around and see who might have heard. It felt so *good* and then instantly like a lie, loneliness smuggled in under validation.

When my wife and I were together in those early days, I often found myself living vicariously through the emotional register available to (or forced upon) her. In merciful bouts of late-night quiet, I'd be looking over her shoulder at the various mom accounts that the algorithm shoved in her face. At the recommendation of many friends, she started subscribing to a weekly newsletter called *Evil Witches,* and that shaped our conversations during the hardest months. These mothers wrote all the thoughts we had so much trouble getting out.

When our daughter still tolerated long stretches in her stroller, we'd make evenings move faster with a fifteen-minute walk to the grocery store. We could be with her but talking over her, in the adult world, in motion, like people, ourselves. During these walks, my wife recapped *Evil Witches*—posts about regretting motherhood, about kids who never seemed to have the desire to be loved, all the taboos. The posts were, in the cathartic darkness of their honesty, often hilarious, that most satisfying form of humor that makes your body tense and your eyes dart.

Sometimes, I did feel like an interloper as I laughed and nod-ded. The best mom content, after all, is actively flexing against the weight of expectations foisted upon only mothers, the frus-tration and loneliness of invisibility or never-ending critique, and in many cases the lack of support from men who are theoretically partners. I felt seen by, buoyed by, the rueful darkness of this writing, but also, there I was, or someone like me, at the outskirts of each anecdote: a minor character or a foil.

One newsletter was dedicated to moms who regretted having a second child, who hadn't been honest with themselves in terms of how much they resented caregiving, or whose first kid was nice until they got a sibling and then turned intolerable. Some-one wrote about watching their husband, who'd wanted a second, lose interest, and the *rage* she felt, tricked into loving this being she never had space to love. We were talking a lot then about not wanting a second and how weirdly betrayed we felt by parent friends who, after seeming miserable for a year, were all cheer-fully checking ovulation windows again. *What the fuck? What was* wrong *with them?* Really, we were asking, *What's wrong with us?* And *Evil Witches* was saying, *Nothing.* That felt good. It felt unlike any other conversation I was having, possibly because I wasn't having *any* conversations beyond these ones, devouring the CliffsNotes of my wife's reading material, never clicking sub-scribe for myself.

My daughter was so beautiful as we talked above her, hum-ming to herself to match the murmur of our voices, smiling at passing strangers—this pure, open being that filled our life more than we could have imagined, and weren't we assholes for ever thinking differently? *No*, we promised one another. We loved her, and we never wanted to deal with this shit again. My wife read one particularly dark missive aloud and muttered *Jesus* at the end, and we laughed, and I touched her shoulder with my non-stroller hand.

On the other side of the mom content spectrum, though, was the endless, often contradictory loop of advice, these voices that claimed solidarity but, more and more, felt like pressure. Most present in our home were the sleep-training influencers, particularly this one who later, to the great chagrin of many liberal parents worshipping at her altar, was outed as a Trump donor.

Her voice filled our lives; she loomed over my shoulder when it was my turn to stand in the dark with the screaming baby and move through her patented steps. Without this woman, I would have had no inkling of how to behave as my baby refused to sleep, but I still grew to despise her gentle, *You got this, Mama, trust the steps.* It became important to me that she was a fraud, though I had no real justification to believe so, and honestly, her not being a fraud would make my life way better. When my wife cried, I would try and fail to console her, then get frustrated and say, *She's making you feel worse!*

What did I want this Instagram influencer to do? Acknowledge that it wouldn't get better, so why try? At a certain point, my wife said, *Please stop making me defend her, I don't even like her. If there's a better method, go fucking find it.* The look on her face when she said it—righteousness at the front of the emotion but desperation behind it.

There's a clichéd joke here, I know. A family on a road trip: everyone's hungry and upset; they're lost. Dad's at the wheel, of course. The kids are starting to whine. Mom says, *Pull over, let's ask this person, maybe they can help.* And what does Dad say?

To take it from The Dad's mission statement:

The Dad is not a person—The Dad is a lifestyle. . . . We don't tell dads what to do or how to do it. We help them escape the craziness and take a break.

When I speak to Joel Willis, the man who started The Dad and, up until a few months ago, helmed its explosion of growth, he says, "From the beginning, we knew dads don't want to be told how to parent. They just want a chance to laugh, a chance to be seen. I know for me, if you're saying, 'Next up, we've got a parenting expert,' that's when I tune out."

Willis, who many others I spoke to in the *dad space* refer to as *the OG*, started as a nobody, with no great plans. He had a corporate job and a pretty regular dad life in Cincinnati. He started tweeting little jokes, silly domestic humor—nothing blue, that's not his style. Then he started writing freelance. The venues were all mom-facing, and he ended up writing for Scary Mommy, which, like many now huge online parenting communities, began as one stay-at-home-mother's blog. Twitter and Instagram were relatively new, suddenly spaces where caregivers could be content consumers—and sometimes producers—all day long. It was Jill Smokler, founder of Scary Mommy, who had the idea to bring dad humor under a larger parent-content umbrella; she tapped Willis as dad number one.

"We had to think: what would dads be looking for?" Willis says. "We had a specific breakdown of what our content would do. If I'm remembering right, it was sixty percent make you laugh, or just about. And there were other things—you know, build ad partnerships, all that—but then it was five percent make you feel feelings. I like to think we bumped that up a bit in the end."

He's responding to my very vague question about the vibe present when scrolling though The Dad's feed. Sometimes I imagine the tonal shifts like the heart monitor of a near dead patient at the climax of a movie—a flat line until this exaggerated spike of life. Graze through different versions of the same topical or seasonal joke, and then, every once in a while, these heartstring explosions that mimic the experience of watching a game with your father when there's a rain delay, and suddenly you're looking at a kid with sunken eyes and a shaved head talking about his one wish, and then you're like, *Dad, are you* crying?

The past month of The Dad's Instagram feed, at the moment of writing, includes these headlines:

- *Heroes: Dad Makes a Wrong Turn and Ends Up Saving Three Kids from a Fire*
- *Good News: Three Dads Livestream Cannonball Run, Raising $156,000 for Their Kids' Rare Condition*
- *Adventure: 8-Year-Old (with His Dad) Just Became the Youngest Person to Climb El Capitan in Yosemite*
- *Sports: Coal Miner Dad Rushes from Work to Experience His Son's First Basketball Game*

These are nestled between memes about how, when the kids are at Grandma's, dads try to have sex with their wives, or dads eating all the Halloween candy and calling it *the dad tax*, or a dad and a son laughing at the word *balls* while a mom remains unamused, or the amount of candles women buy in the fall, or the difficulty of admitting when it's time to turn up the thermostat.

I know this extreme polarity of tone—either *ha ha ha* or *wah wah wah*—is central to the algorithm gods keeping attention, but to bob in The Dad's waters does conjure more of a sitcom experience for me, which is probably why I return to it. The gags will always find purchase at the end in a big bear hug, a sense of preordained safety and triumph. It sticks out from the rest of my feed, which, until I clicked on The Dad, was entirely devoid of parenthood, even as my wife's was instantly transformed by it—just sports hot takes, jacked entrepreneurs talking about blasting away belly fat, a blond bro asking strangers how much is in their bank accounts, blurry fights outside a club somewhere, bestselling writers unboxing galleys, Drake. A racked, teenaged consciousness frozen in the cloud. Against that, dad humor is both a gesture toward my actual reality *and* a safe space in the most literal sense—too benign to provoke anxiety. A fantasy already (sort of) achieved.

When I tell Willis that I've enjoyed the product for a while now, he leans back in his gaming chair and gives the smile of someone used to hearing that. At this point, it's fair to call him an internet celebrity. He'll be out with his kids, who are older and more aware now, and someone will come up like, *You're* the *dad!* That's cool. It's not just that his kids, who of course think he's corny, have to reconcile with the fact that strangers think he's cool; the strangers think he's cool *for the very corniness*, and he had a large hand in that corny-to-cool pipeline. Last year, the Biden administration invited his family to the annual White House Easter Egg Roll; a secret service agent asked for a selfie together.

"It's wild to me that we're talking about The Dad as some cultural inflection point," he says. "When we started, I thought it was impossible for a parent site to have a following of mostly men. That was the challenge."

It took a long time to get there. Even now, if the scales of followers have tipped toward majority men, it's not by a lot. That's a central secret in the dad content space," Willis tells me. Even when something is by a dad, or specifically branded as a father thing, you have to assume that the bulk of people it's actually appealing to are women. Fatherly, for example, which is owned by the same parent company as The Dad, and remains the most notable hub for father-focused essays and reportage, promising to *empower men to raise great kids and lead more fulfilling adult lives,* has never had a majority readership of men. As I've talked to dad content creators, from the obscure to the famous, they've all reported their metrics as 20 to 30 percent male followers *tops.* This is not, of course, scientifically gathered or sorted data; none of these creators know how many of their followers are from single-parent households or queer families or are nonparents who simply find comfort in the character. But no matter how you look at it, the implication is that these public depictions of engaged fatherhood are not sustained by fathers engaging. On the other hand, when I asked how many of a prominent mom site's eight hundred thousand followers were men, they reported two percent.

"Everything in the parenting space feels too gendered," Willis tells me. "We always wanted to get around that—not masculine bro humor but something else. We were portraying the image of 'Hey, caring, involved dads are cool.' Now you've got Ryan Reynolds and The Rock painting their nails with their daughters."

But what is that particular fantasy of nontoxic masculinity doing if even just the image of a normie dad engaging online is propped up by an audience of women? It's a tension that permeates the whole industry: of *course,* a parenting conversation shouldn't exist along a strictly defined gender binary, but also, it's hard for me to imagine a version of the conversation where gender isn't, if not the main focus, the underlying structure on which the whole industry is built. So most everyone has absorbed some language of equality, a universal commiseration of *parenthood*, a gesture toward shared household work, but also, the site had to be called The Dad, and it's succeeded through a combination of caricature and the novelty of that caricature participating at all in the conversation.

In hopeful moments, fatherhood has felt to me like this chance to imagine something new. This rupture in life when you see expectations burned down and something better, richer, rise to fill the empty space. But then, in the face of that possibility, identity, family, community, gender, sex, all of it, has often never felt so present and rigidly defined. There's the eye contact stranger dads make at the playground, as though something notable is happening. Or the way I hold back on my instinct to hover near my daughter at certain parties, not because I should just let her play but because the men are watching the game and the women are taking their turns checking on the kids, and I feel extra neurotic, ashamed to break a code that no one in the room would acknowledge exists. Or my awkwardness as my daughter happily explores her body in the bath, like *Maybe this is a moment for Mama, maybe it's time for Daddy to go poop in the other bathroom!*

There's another classic meme concept: Dad just sitting on the toilet until someone notices he's gone.

The joke becomes the anchor of the identity—this particular voice, this particular way of framing the world. You can feel love like a dad or frustration like a dad or hope like a dad. On a vacation with family friends, when my daughter and her little pal painted my nails, did I rush to post a picture, holding a White Claw in my newly pastel hand, challenging gender norms (just like The Rock!) in the most toothless way, while also reinforcing them? Of course I did.

In 2021, The Dad put out a *Survey for Dads That Will Solve the Mysteries of Dadkind.* Of course, it moved from jokes into the mushy stuff. Start with *Which way should the toilet paper roll be put on?* Or *Is a gas grill or a charcoal grill better?*

"Then, at the end," Willis remembers, "we asked, 'How much do you love being a dad?'"

He leans back in his gaming chair and smiles.

"The answer was something like 98 percent loved it. And that's what it's all about."

There's a constellation of dudes whose work finds its way onto The Dad's feed, who I now follow. They come from Nashville, from Kansas City, from Florida, from Toronto, from Brooklyn. Some of them, I only know their time zone or area code. On Zoom, some look like their avatar and some not at all. Some say I'm the first person who doesn't know them in *real* life to whom they've shown their face. They have names like Kevin and Mike and Chris. A few just got started in the content game and are lingering around ten thousand followers across platforms, some have eclipsed fifty thousand, some are over two hundred thousand. Simon Holland, a graying man in a blue button-down shirt in his home office outside Atlanta, has seven hundred thousand followers on Instagram.

"My kids are old enough now," he tells me, "that they'll run up with their phones and show me the account of some celebrity, like, look you've got more followers than this person!"

He laughs and raises his eyebrows.

You, the general *you*, would probably recognize Holland's avatar if it flashed by—white guy, sunglasses, stubble, close-cropped hair, maybe he's on a boat? Hard to tell. Could be a particular kind of anyone.

"I'll admit I have a hard time keeping the dad accounts straight," says Tara Clark, the woman behind Modern Mom Probs, another frank, funny site that began as a stay-at-home blog and has turned into an empire. "There's the one with long hair; I remember him. But you know, it's lot of white guys with short hair and the one-syllable name talking about their lawns."

She's quick to say that this isn't a dig. Tropes exist, everyone plays into them because that's what people expect, and in the content game, rule number one is to meet expectations, which, again, when it comes to parent humor, stick close to the comfort of the sitcom playbook. Suburban, staunchly middle-class; though not universal or explicit, the implication is straight and cisgender, often white. There are many popular accounts featuring the lives of queer dads, dads celebrating various racial and cultural identities, single dads, disabled dads, but the lack of crossover they have with the parent joke hubs is conspicuous. The joke is embedded in, dependent upon, a pretty static definition of the norm.

"I've been doing this long enough to know that's not going to change," Clark says. "Moms like wine, moms like Starbucks. Dads, you know, have their football, the cargo shorts, the grilling. It's not the whole story, obviously, but people know what they like."

Joel Willis, for instance, told me he owns a single pair of cargo shorts, only ever worn for video content.

The dads I talk to do begin to run together, if only in name: The Dad Briefs, Kevin The Dad, Dad and Buried, McDad, Dad Man Walking. Some slight variations on the theme: Henpecked Hal, for example. I've got messages unanswered from Dad at Law, Matt the Dad, A Bearer of Dad News, Dad V Girls, Diary of a Dad. Each dad who responded was thoughtful, helpful, cheerful. Each seemed bemused by my curiosity. Each spoke to me from his home office in the middle of a corporate workday. Each described his foray into the content world as an outlet for a creative self otherwise stymied by real life. Almost all said their decision to start posting, and sometimes even their account names, were their wives' ideas.

"She said, 'You have a way of telling stories about the kids,'" a man named Shane tells me. "She said, 'People will laugh at this.' She came up with the name, bugged me for a year. Finally, I was bored enough at work. I didn't want anyone to know at first—like what's this gonna mean to have strangers reading about my life?"

The name Shane's wife coined in 2019 was Dad Man Walking. He has over fifty thousand Twitter followers now, and after the necessary pivot toward Instagram in the past couple of years, he's got that number nearing that magic fifty mark, too. Just starting out on TikTok, but it's going well. Yesterday, he went semi-viral on a tweet that said, *Apparently after your wife finishes a pint of ice cream, the correct response is not "holy shit I've never been able to finish a whole pint."* The day before, I watched a reel of him eating a pickle and a Snickers at the same time, wearing a T-shirt with a picture of a cassette tape that says *Rad Dad Mix: Not Old, Vintage* on the label. The day before, he posted a TikTok combining a popular sound clip of a comedian mocking a short guy with the caption *When my 7yo gets smart with me*. His persona is gruff and bearded; his arms are covered with enough tattoos to hint at a former life.

"You know it's viral when you can't keep up with the notifications," he says.

These days, it's hard not to get overwhelmed. Shane is sort of underwater at the moment. Work is a lot. His wife homeschools their three kids; every single member of the family is trapped together. They had to move out to the exurbs for more room.

The rise of Shane's creative productivity and popularity coincided with the pandemic and a new life of remote work. While there's no way to track the analytic trends of accounts with dad pun names, everyone I've spoken to agrees that it's probably not a coincidence that fatherhood content has exploded during a worldwide shift away from office work. Good parenting material, after all, is born from the trenches of constant contact, the sense that each little missive is fired off by a fellow sufferer/chronicler hidden behind the couch, reaching into the void for confirmation of life. Even as studies show that the burden of pandemic childcare and the potential career consequences have fallen overwhelmingly on mothers' shoulders, simple presence among the responsibility (and content) of life trapped with kids has become the purview of all parents more than ever before.

Kevin The Dad, a quiet, thoughtful Australian living in Toronto, says it's amazing to think of what he missed at the office, these fleeting moments of the everyday, the real *stuff* of parenting.

"I never had the opportunity to take paternity leave," he tells me, perched in a brightly colored room, kid art on the walls, yanking his head around periodically at the sound of a screech or mewl.

When I give what I hope comes off as a knowing chuckle, he says, "Right, so now I'm trying to do this with you, but I've got him over there who's going to need a snack soon. Maybe it's silly, but that's not the experience I had before. This is a different lens for me. There's more that I see that I want to record because, you know, all this stuff he's doing now, it will be gone in a week."

It's exhausting. Every time his kid says something funny, he has to write it down; when he and his wife are watching TV at night, he has to keep track of what images could become memes if juxtaposed with a child crying over a juice box. *Has to* is, of course, a debatable phrase. This isn't his *job*, but . . . maybe someday he'll be able to monetize? That's not even the main goal; the main goal is something he can't quite articulate. Kevin is like every other Dad™ who I've spoken to, in that, before creating dad content, he wasn't much of a social media guy at all. So there's some particular nerve struck with this experience, never struck before—repeated, public validation, all of it centered on one facet of his identity. When talking to these men, I never manage to offer up my own posting compulsions. I don't describe the feeling of holding out my phone when my daughter is saying something ridiculous and hoping to catch it clearly—how often does she call pepperoni *macaroni* and why do I still have no *proof*? I'm not trying to brand my *dad*ness, or at least not exclusively, but . . . I mean, kind of. It's the center of my life, this black hole of consciousness into which all other parts of me are inevitably sucked, but also, if I'm honest, I think it's the most likable thing about me.

I get *way* less traction than these dudes, and still the selective broadcasting of my day-to-day dad musings has grown to feel essential, a valve that needs to be opened often, or else the pressure of life unshared might explode. Here's another morsel: my daughter telling me not to come with her as she goes to play with older neighbors—*lol embarrassing dad already.* Buried in the gag is the proof that it happened and I was there, that she feels safe and confident in herself, and maybe I had something to do with that, and maybe I need everyone to know.

At the advice of some larger accounts, Shane's got a merch store set up with some slogans from his most viral posts. He's putting as much as he can into TikToks and Instagram reels. At first, Instagram incentivized views to the point that he'd clear four hundred extra dollars a month, but now that he's proven reliable, then plateaued, it's back to peanuts. He's happy to shill the odd product if he believes in it, but . . . he shrugs.

Eventually, they all come to the same realization: dad content is harder than it looks. It's not innate in their funny dad selves; it's work, poorly compensated and potentially cannibalizing time from actual work, or from the families whose silly little exploits they document. But when you've got fifty thousand people who love (or at least *know of*) you for variations on the joke, what are you supposed to do? Stop? I know I wouldn't.

"Sometimes, in the rooms," Shane says, "we'll joke around, like, 'Man my kids are giving me nothing lately, when did they get so boring?'"

He laughs, then leans toward the camera. "Kidding, kidding," he says.

We should talk about *the rooms.* Everything, it seems, happens in *the rooms*—it's a phrase tossed around by parent content creators the way an AA'er might use it: offhand but full of genuine appreciation. The place where one does the real work.

In truth, they're just private DM rooms on each platform, that, if you post parent content long enough, well enough, someone invites you into. This goes way back. When I talk to Mike Julianelle, the man behind the juggernaut Dad and Buried (almost 250,000 followers on Instagram), he remembers that, in what he describes as peak blog era, he was in a closed Facebook group just for dad bloggers that must have had a thousand members (maybe five, he adds, that he'd actually want to hang out with). At its worst, Julianelle says, especially when it's only dads, these become spaces where everyone wants attention for what they're doing but don't want to listen.

More often than not, though, discussion of the rooms is only positive. They bring together really big accounts and those just starting out; mentorship springs up among people who have never met, maybe haven't seen one another's faces, couldn't give you a last name. Shane was one of a couple guys who told me he was helped along by Henpecked Hal (another account that, if you're at all online, you've probably come across—avatar is a picture of Al Bundy, tone is one of matching crankiness; his posts have achieved that semi-fame of unattributed ubiquity). So a star like that will be in a room, but also a newbie with three hundred followers who just got noticed. They're all trying out bits, giving advice, mobilizing to aid one of their own being attacked in the comments.

It's the hallowed shoptalk table at the back of a comedy club, except virtual and on a Tuesday afternoon, as people are slogging through IT jobs or half watching on the sidelines at soccer practice, and a lot of the time is spent commiserating about earaches. They're all hovering in some stage of the purgatory between novice and willing to call themselves at least a *type* of comedian.

They're all working in a subgenre so narrow in its dictums, its need for brevity and instantly recognizable universality—how many ways can you say, *If I wasn't a parent, I'd probably be happier, but not really*? Or *Women have expectations that men fail to live up to*? Or *I need caffeine in the morning, booze at night*? They help each other through it.

Simon Holland tells me there's joke formats within the space that he—not to be bigheaded, just honest—considers *his*, and they've now become repeat viral moments for everyone else.

I ask for an example, and he says, "Okay, so you know the one where it's like, 'Let's get married and have kids, so instead of [insert cool thing] we can [insert awful thing]'?"

Of course I do. A classic.

Well, that's his from way back. And it's not like he minds it being public property; it's just interesting how some people use it so well, find new things in it, whereas most just make it seem, in his words, "kind of mid and played out."

Every dad in the space is cultivating a voice *just enough* his own. And yet, despite the repeat character within these jokes— somewhat emotionally stunted, often wanting nothing more than to be left alone, feeling in petty, compulsive competition with his peers (another Simon Holland banger is the *rival dad* joke format)—their relationships behind the scenes subvert the stereotype more than perhaps any they've ever known.

Henpecked Hal, who offers me only that his name is Chris and claims that his Zoom camera isn't working, says, "In the rooms, we're as close as you can be without really knowing each other."

He laughs but says, while it's weird to acknowledge, he means it. You come in thinking you just want to make your little jokes, get your likes, but eventually, if you stick around, it has to be something more. You're in these spaces every day with people going through the same stuff, who begin to resemble friends.

He describes the moment he understood the true power of parent jokes online, from way back in the infancy of his posting (2016). He'd begun a list of all the shit that made his toddler cry over the course of two months. He did it, he tells me, because "sometimes I could barely stop laughing, this stuff was so stupid."

He fit the funniest examples into a tweet, posted, and was shocked when it shot above four hundred thousand likes.

"The thing I realized," he says, "is I didn't matter at all. My jokes, the actual shit my kid said—that wasn't what made it popular. I could see when people were retweeting it, they weren't saying, 'Hey this guy's hilarious,' they were saying, 'Check out the replies.'"

All these strangers were bringing their own lives to the bit, their frustrations that either resembled or one-upped Chris's, or the little oddities they'd forgotten in their own kids and realized they missed. There were a lot of older parents, he says, pining for that particular hysteria of toddlerhood. In the rooms, everyone was chiming in, too, cheering him on.

"It became an open forum," Chris says. "I just started that forum."

He describes parent content as a closed loop—any gesture toward specificity is only in service of the invitation for recognition. I guess, in some ways, that's the concept of all humor, of all art. But there's something particular to these constraints. I know I'm often still amazed by the tension between how overwhelmingly important I find every detail of my daughter's life and how they instantly resemble every other parent's anecdotes. Is that a disappointment? A relief?

For Shane at Dad Man Walking, his popularity escalated during the hardest period of his life. His wife was diagnosed with breast cancer. He was trying to not get fired while handling the homeschooling, while caring for her, while attempting to sublimate his own fear and grief. He was posting through it; he was in the rooms.

"You know," he says, gesturing to me through the screen, "it's hard for us guys to say what we're feeling. I've had more guys express what they're really feeling, I've expressed more, in these rooms, than in the entire rest of my life."

He says this without judgment; it's plain fact. He was, still is, loath to complain (well, unless it's for a joke) and even more unwilling to ask for money, but when he unburdened himself in the rooms, he was encouraged to set up a GoFundMe. People shared their own stories and shared the GoFundMe nestled within their jokes. The speed with which the money came in stunned Shane, as did the amount of men he'd never met in his replies and DMs, offering vulnerability along with solidarity. He wrote back.

"Maybe it's easier," he says, "if the person you're talking to doesn't really know you."

I'll admit that part of me is tempted to frame this all as an easy joke. It fits snugly into the cartoon dichotomy of how a dad story can be told: either stubborn stoicism or the biggest, most obvious emotion. It's the curated ratio of the The Dad—giggle, giggle, giggle, weep. A dude doesn't think he needs kindness until it smothers him and refuses to relent—Robin Williams whispering *It's not your fault* into Matt Damon's ear in *Good Will Hunting*.

But, as always, recognizing the joke doesn't mean I'm not in it. I want to tell Shane that I haven't found what he has yet. That it's still enormously difficult for me to be honest with other men, particularly about parenting, like if I'm honest I will have lost at some undefined competition constantly running through my mind. I'm thinking about the first time my dad groupchat approached honesty and how it felt like a revelation. We'd existed mostly as a repository for tepid laughter. I spent paternity leave sending near daily pictures of me at a bookstore/bar, holding a beer, the baby just visible over my shoulder. Everyone smashed the *haha* response. We competed unofficially for the best way to describe the grossness of a diarrhea diaper. We complained about new aches and pains, the flabbiness born from the world's most exhausting type of inertia. Then, one night my friend Jon wrote, *Does this ever get better?* He was in the hell of failed sleep training, sending a lonely missive. Of course, there was a flurry of response. Of course, we'd all been waiting for the chance to say it gets better, which really meant a chance to say, *It was hard for me, too.*

That was three years ago and I still remember it. Sometimes, I feel our conversations nibbling at the edges of that same tone, restless, someone needing something they won't articulate. Often, that person is me.

The problem with parental solidarity is that it's both an introductory necessity and a myth. Helping keep a kid alive shouldn't be, isn't, enough to foster a coherent collective point of view. Parents who love their own children are doing very cruel things to other people's children every day. But in this moment when a cultural conversation around the aims, stresses, and responsibilities of parenthood (as always, read *motherhood*) is unavoidably political, the world of the online dad, for the most part, just isn't.

Meanwhile, any time a mom posts about being a mom, a bunch

of guys who look like my cousin Dave want to make them pay for the sin of being a woman in public. This is no revelation, I know, but I find it particularly weird that the tropes the dad joke persona embodies create a picture of a man who looks a lot like the cousin Daves of the world: white dude, straight, short-cropped hair, worried about inflation, possessing a lawn and interested in caring for it, annoyed at the various sensitivities, privileges, and complexities of today's youth. These implications go unspoken. A crucial part of the bit, performing and consuming, is that the *dad*ness defangs this idea of a man. A dad can make the world as narrow as he likes, craft a joke that attempts to hit no nerves.

Here's how Joel Willis put it to me: "I'm not a political person. I have opinions, but it doesn't interest me. Whereas with Scary Mommy, Jill has strong political opinions and the site takes that on, which is great. It's important."

When I talk to these dads, there's near universal agreement that motherhood, especially public motherhood, is a political act, if only for the pressures foisted onto moms. When big mom accounts take a stand, the dads support it in that particular tone that so many of us fall into when discussing our wives' experiences in parenthood alongside ours: helpless reverence.

A few of the dads say versions of this: that in real life, if anyone cared to ask what they think, they probably agree with the Scary Mommies of the world. We're speaking, I assume, about the right to choose, parental leave, universal childcare, maybe even gun control, though we don't say it. They do the thing that I hear myself doing whenever I talk parenting, the quick list of acknowledgments of various privileges as a caveat to whatever opinion is about to be offered, like the side effects at the end of a pharmaceutical commercial—a requirement sped through; at this point, you hardly register it.

Simon Holland tells me, "I know the privileges I have as a straight white dad guy, right? Like, I get it. But I've never been of the thought that once someone's got a certain number of followers, they suddenly have a responsibility to weigh in. I didn't do this to be a beacon of truth or hope; I did it to make you chuckle for five seconds. I'll say it like this—to me it's the same as not cussing much. Why am I going to cut out whatever percentage of my audience if I don't have to?"

The last thing a dad account wants to do is come off as preachy. If there's an agreement that fathers don't like being told what to do, well then they certainly don't want to be preached to. A dad will make fun of how much he sucks, yes of course, but it's not exactly cool when some other guy thinks he's better.

"I haven't been scared to write about having daughters and all that, changing the diapers, making dinner," Holland says. "But it's not like I have this woke self-importance to tell other dads, 'You should do this.' I just happen to do it."

There is, I suppose, something hopeful in the idea of cook-the-dinner, change-the-diaper fatherhood posted, shared, and reshared as something apolitical. That even the guy in your mind who's angry at taxes and participation trophies loves his kids, tires himself out with all that love, and needs a chuckle break. In Ashley Fetters's *Atlantic* piece, she quotes a linguist saying that dad humor online stands as an oasis in what is otherwise the desert of *a new age of nastiness* within political and cultural discourse. (The linguist was also a dad, and it's unclear which expert point of view he was speaking from.)

"There wasn't a lot of talk about masking, vaccines, all that, in the rooms," Vinod Chhaproo tells me. "I have my opinions, I'm sure others do."

Chhaproo works on Wall Street and raises his kids in New

York City. He was born in India, and his extended family is still there. He's also a dad making jokes online, a beloved member of many rooms, and now has a burgeoning stand-up career. That's the thing with parenting, he says. It can be so universal. Putting the kids to bed, cleaning up after them—you can always find a place to commiserate. But on the other hand, you're working within parameters that everyone *knows* but most don't live. He wasn't raised here, he doesn't have a lawn or a car or a set of memories about how it supposedly used to be.

Sometimes the reality of the world can't *not* force its way into the rooms. After the Uvalde school shooting, Chhaproo found himself commiserating about his sadness, his anger, his fear—these were fellow fathers he was talking to, after all.

"I was talking about being afraid of taking my kids to school the next day," he tells me. "And one pretty popular account is former military, I think—knows more than me anyway. He was sending me links to these backpacks you can buy that are bulletproof. That was nice."

I can't tell if Chhaproo is poking fun at this exchange or not. I don't think so. Either way, the possibility to not think so is key. Ultimately, a lot of the conversations I have with the dadfluencers come down to this central equation: the degree of self-awareness they feel in their joking dad personas, the degree to which the audience acknowledges it, and the degree to which it matters at all. How much of one's self does a dad see in the bit?

Simon Holland puts it like this: "With my Rival Dad thing, I think probably seventy percent of the audience is laughing at how silly it is, this toxic masculinity, competitive thing. And then thirty percent are like, 'Wooo yeah, I'm gonna kick this rival dad's ass!'"

Holland is thoughtful about his work and why it's funny and

all the subtleties of fatherhood talk, sometimes even as he's claiming that it ain't that deep. The bit wouldn't hold up, he says, if there wasn't truth to it. Like he's got friends who mean a lot to him, and that's beautiful, but he still wants nicer shit than they have. Even if he knows it's silly, even if he doesn't like it in himself, he feels it. He notices that, of the people who recognize his name and come up to him, there's a subset of men who can only respond by tossing ideas at him like they're doing him a favor, unaware that they're fully embodying the joke.

The other side of the interpretation risk is not when macho dudes identify with something you mean to critique, but when an audience assumes *you* aren't in on your own joke. For Chris at Henpecked Hal, his biggest hit (and a tweet I genuinely love) was also a chance for people to call him a misogynist asshole. It's a simple conceit: *My wife left me home alone with the kids to go out drinking with her friends. A lesser man might whine and complain, but instead I'm just playing Chumbawamba's 1997 hit "Tubthumping" over and over and over. On the jukebox at their bar. Using the TouchTunes app.*

"I had all these people in my mentions," Chris says, "like, 'You piece of shit, your wife gets one night to have fun, and you have to stay home with the kids, and you're going to wreck it?'"

So, there he was, climbing up toward half a million likes and also debating whether to respond to all the haters, just to say, Hey, *obviously* I didn't ruin my wife's night, *obviously* I just did this for a few minutes and she thought it was hilarious. He says, "The funny thing is my wife likes to go out and I don't as much. If anything, I'm more often the one at home putting the kids to bed—not saying that as like, wow, look at me; that's just how it is in our house."

He sometimes regrets his Al Bundy avatar—no matter what,

hundreds of thousands of people are going to read his jokes in that voice. But it's not just the avatar. Nearly every dad I speak to has the stories of feeling willfully misread as the replies seize upon a bit about telling his wife she didn't finish the dishes or complaining about his kids in a way that seems too . . . mean. Like actually mean.

"For a dad joke to work," Chris says, "You can think you're the hero in the story for a while, play it up, but in the end you have to know you're the fool."

Yet that's the problem: the dad is an inscrutable foil; it's up for debate what he knows. I cannot help but think here of Bean Dad, the name given the man who went horrifically viral for an anecdote that he definitely thought was cute. He tweeted through the experience of realizing that his nine-year-old daughter had never had to open a can, then making her learn self-reliance by not letting her satiate her hunger with baked beans until she could get them open herself. He slow-played it into a now infamous twenty-three-tweet thread, documenting a six-hour odyssey of her failing and quitting and complaining, and him doing a jigsaw puzzle while otherwise being a classic self-reliance-stick-in-the-mud-grump. He was labeled an abuser, a narcissist, dangerous, ableist toward his daughter (who, in the assumption of these tweeters, was differently abled, I guess). In his apology, Bean Dad told the world that his daughter had been snacking the whole time, they'd been laughing together. He hadn't mentioned it in the tweets because . . . that's not the bit. And the bit sucked— don't get me wrong! I'm sure there's a great chance the guy *is* a narcissist, but he also isn't the dad in the joke, not exactly. He's a guy who didn't consider that he could be thought of as someone not defined by good intentions. As a cruel man. As a bad father.

That's the worst thing you can be, right? In all its dopiness, the dad character exists to own an identity that feels better than anything previous, that has come to dominate self-conception. The joke says, I'm fine being lame and old and out of shape and a shell of my former self and just as corny as I said I'd never be, because I'm *this*. Dadness is gentle, absolving, until it isn't. Part of the joke is that you can screw up in all these ways and still be lovable, still be *good*, but then the line between good and bad gets pretty thin, and then a joke becomes unforgivable.

One of my first conversations was with an account I don't want to name. We were talking about how sometimes dad memes can feel like a man referencing his own father as much as himself. He said his dad was funny, a real character, just not . . . present, in the ways he has learned to be.

"But I think part of the comfort," he said, "is you realize everyone's dad was the same. Every dad is the same. Now *I'm* the one telling my daughter I'll be there with a shotgun when she brings a boy home."

He laughed; I didn't.

The question nagging at each individual dad creator is *What's next?* I think you can ask that for the whole genre—is there a certain point when fathers look for more? Or when the idea of a funny father as this blunt, fixed entity might dissolve?

In the summer of 2022, shortly after the Scary Mommy umbrella was bought for 150 million dollars by Bustle Digital Group and added to an enormous portfolio ranging from *Nylon* to *Gawker*, Joel Willis quit The Dad. He says he got tired of waiting to see if it would be prioritized, allowed to evolve. We talked in the fall of 2022, and he said that The Dad's actual website hadn't been updated since early spring—indeed, the current lead piece is his own essay about taking his kids to the White House Easter Egg Roll. Right below is a post about the rift between The Rock and Vin Diesel that's almost a year old.

Media consolidation is always rough; Willis knows that. But his tiny team had built this underdog into *huge* brand awareness, seemingly limitless potential. They had the memes, yes, and flourishing video content, but they'd also moved into some more long-form writing that he says was working. They ran a weekly personal essay series, highlighting the experiences of fathers from all sorts of places and backgrounds, queer dads, single dads—an at least somewhat representative chorus of what American fatherhood might really look like. It's stalled, at least for now, while the memes chug along as an almost uniform portrayal of hetero, middle-class, suburban id. If Willis hadn't told me the website was dormant, I wouldn't have known.

All the men I talked to have had their work shared by The Dad's feed since I began this essay; their followers continue to tick up. Do they fantasize about a future in which they could become full-time creatives? Of course. But it doesn't seem realistic. Real money comes from leaning heavy into TikTok, which means having their kids on camera performing the bit for whatever brands pay most, like that insufferable clan with their music videos, dancing around in matching pj's. It's a different genre.

Still, there are hustles to be had. A man named Slade Wentworth, who goes by The Dad Briefs, has a book on the way called *New Dad, Same Bad Jokes*—a combo of life advice and quips for any occasion. He's working on another, specifically contracted by the discount retailer Five Below, that will only be sold at their stores. Simon Holland tells me he's collaborating with some folks toward a TV idea, and we'll see. Chhaproo is doing his stand-up, and that's something that many of the dads I spoke to fantasize about, maybe even have a little tight five they're working on for . . . someday. But there are routines and responsibilities to live up to—that's the whole genesis of the material.

When I first started working on this essay, the *New York Times* reporter Kashmir Hill wrote a piece about spending twenty-four hours in the nascent Metaverse. She stumbled into a virtual comedy club and began talking to a father of two young kids who'd been gaming with his friends late into the night and then couldn't bring himself to take off his headset after they went to bed. So he ended up on a virtual stage telling *an extended joke about how having children changes you, because of the way they lock eyes with you while they poop.* This was the first Metaverse depiction that made sense to me, a clear distillation of an already throbbing impulse: the dad who needs validation, in some form or another, while his kids are asleep; a fantasy from which he can—must—unplug.

Chris tells me that, yes, sometimes the tiny frame of social media dad jokes can feel stifling. He has more to say. Some of the dads talk to me with great candor about what they wish was said. One hasn't yet figured out whether he can discuss his wife's postpartum depression and how that changed the whole family's world and how they've worked to get back to themselves. Simon Holland says that fathers need real supportive communities more akin to what he sees from his wife and her friends. He has an idea for a bit: a spin-off of the Rival Dad conceit, evolved into

Rival Dad Groupchat. Still funny, but more toward solidarity—not just comparing but sharing. Tending to the grill, coveting the greenest lawn, but also . . . realer?

Is that something men actually would seek out? He doesn't know.

The other day, on Instagram, he posted, *Helping in the kitchen this morning. So far I've used 467 paper towels.* I laughed and laughed. Me too! I'm messy enough to take out a whole old-growth forest!

My wife has been away for a work thing with a quarantine tacked on after an exposure. There's a running bit about what happens to my daughter's hair when my wife is away, like tracing a movie character from before a plane crash to a month stranded on a desert island. She's working with me now, at least, and expressing pity in a big, exaggerated way. She said to me, *Awww, it's okay, you're bad at this, I forgive you.* She patted my arm, an impression of me patting hers. Isn't that the funniest thing? I sent my wife a picture of slapdash pigtails, then told her what our daughter had said. Sent the same exact combo to the dad group chat. I tweeted it. Funny is funny.

I do need to get better at doing her hair, though.

An Inspirational Collective Reflection on Joy, Love, and Responsibility from Some Famous Fathers of Daughters, Both Real and Imagined

The greatest gift a parent can give a child is unconditional love. And many of us believe a father's love, even imperfectly, like a mother's love, mirrors divine love.[1] Try to be supportive, and not steer them one way or the other.[2] Allowing children to be children might turn out to be the best education of all.[3] Fatherhood, after all, is about childhood. Fatherhood is walking the floor at midnight with a sick baby who cannot sleep; fatherhood is an arm around the shoulders of a child crying because a balloon is lost.[4] It's chaos and it's a joy.[5] It's a dark continent, and no one really knows anything. You just need a lot of love and luck— and, of course, courage.[6]

I remember thinking to myself, *I just became immortal.* This is what I've dreamed of being all my life—not immortal, really, but a father.[7] Anything up until then was kind of an illusion, existing without living. My daughter, the birth of my daughter, gave me life.[8] How wonderful, how sane, how beautifully difficult, and therefore true. The joy of responsibility for the first time.[9] My daughter is going to know me better than anyone. I don't just want her to love me like the world loves me.[10] I refuse to settle for becoming a *Disney Dad*, one whose role is nothing more than outings to theme parks once or twice a month. I want to share the joys and responsibilities.[11] We'll live, and pray, and sing, and tell old tales, and laugh at gilded butterflies.[12] Remember how we picked the daffodils? Nobody remembers, but I remember.[13]

I have a three-year-old daughter. She knows nothing, and it's our job to raise her the right way. She's been a blessing. She's taken something that could've seemed so bad for me, but it turned out to be so good. I get to take my daughter to school.[14] One day, I hope to be able to tell my daughter a story about a dark time, the dark days before she was born, and how her coming was a ray of light.[15] There's a lot of violence in me for sure, I don't know if it was genetic, if it was learned. My daughter, she's me in female form—without the anger, as much. She's got a loving house and everything like that.[16] She knows when I'm joking. I take gun safety serious (the gun was not loaded and had no clip in).[17] A man adopts a role called Being a Father so that his child could have something mythical and infinitely important: A protector.[18] One of the things a woman hates more than anything is weakness in a man.[19] Strong men also cry. Strong men also cry.[20]

You feel those feelings. You feel possessive and protective, but I refuse to be one of those disapproving dads.[21] I am powerless with her. I love all my children equally—of course—but with the boys I can be a little stricter.[22] Having a daughter makes you see things differently.[23] People always told me, if you ever have a girl she'll change you. And not only did she change me, she made me, I guess, a more sensitive person that realized I have so much more of a responsibility to women in general.[24] I finally became a good and real man once I had my daughter.[25] She helped me think about God in a different light, which years later developed into my own personal belief about Him, or Her.[26] I'm glad I'm raising a girl because boys are . . . I don't like boys. I don't think women are better than men, but I do think men are worse than women.[27] I used to operate under the assumption that us guys had a chance, but then I realized I was wrapped around my two-year-old's finger, and she knew it.[28] The father of a daughter is nothing more than a high class hostage.[29] We are all better for the strong women in our lives.[30]

Like all families, ours is not perfect, but it has been wonderful. Its flaws are mostly mine, and its continuing promise is grounded in her love.[31] My children love me, but they don't understand.[32] At first, you want to love them, but you don't, and faking that feeling makes you wonder if your father did the same thing. And then one day, you see them do something, and you feel that feeling you were pretending to have, and it feels like your heart is going to explode.[33] It fills up like a balloon that's about to burst, and then I remember to relax, and stop trying to hold on to it, and then it flows through me like rain and I can't feel anything but gratitude.[34] I tell my daughters I love them all the time. They say, *Dad, we know*, but I tell them over and over.[35] There is no consolation like a daughter.[36] Holding her in my arms is the best drug in the world.[37] There have been times in my life that I've figured, *I've had a good run—why not just do this stupid thing, this selfish thing*. I don't know that I would do that today—now that I'm a dad and reasonably happy.[38]

Kids are awesome! I don't see mine enough.[39] I want to make sure the days I'm away are the days I absolutely have to be.[40] I love you, okay? I love you. Daddy's got to go back to work.[41] We own a piece of America. I couldn't be happier if I tried.[42] You want to see what your daddy did for you? Come here, I'll show you. That's right, daddy did that for you.[43] I use my daughter for strength. I'm thinking about *her*, when I want to be successful it's for *her*. She knows who I am. She's my biggest inspiration.[44] Children teach you that you can still be humbled by life, that you learn something new all the time. That's the secret to life:

never stop learning. It's the secret to career.[45] Like arrows in the hand of the warrior are the children. Blessed is the man who fills his quiver with them![46] Nobody enjoys being equal.[47] Someday, I'll win.[48]

For an hour, I have walked and prayed because of the great gloom that is in my mind.[49] That's the trouble with caring about anybody, you begin to feel overprotective. Then you begin to feel crowded.[50] Why would you think you make me sad? No. No. You're wrong. Being your dad makes me so, so happy. You don't know.[51] But nothing inspires more shame than being a father.[52] It is the thankless position in the family—the provider for all, and the enemy of all.[53] A good father is one of the most unsung, unpraised, unnoticed, and yet one of the most valuable, assets in our society.[54] A fatherless child thinks all things are possible, and nothing is safe.[55] Without the encouragement of your father, the world is a dismal place. It's very difficult to be a courageous person unless you have your father, in body and spirit, behind you.[56]

Even the fact that one would suggest that I was like *my* father—I find that greatly offensive.[57] I'm a good person. I've led a good life. I've tried to do a lot of good for a lot of people. I'm not perfect, I know that.[58] There's no such thing as a perfect parent, and it's so easy to mess up. But hopefully I've messed up less than most.[59] You know that I love you, right? Your mother doesn't think I love you enough.[60] Baby girl, I'm sorry. I fucking hate when you hurt.[61] I just wanted my kids to know me.[62]

Countless times I beat myself up thinking about all I could have done to be a better father. But I look at my girls and I know I did everything right here. They truly are perfection.[63] So, my advice? Relax. It's worked out for dads forever, it'll work out for you.[64]

NOTES

1. George W. Bush, speaking at the 2001 National Summit on Fatherhood.
2. Bill Belichick in an *NBC Sports* segment about how all of his children, even and especially his daughter, followed him into coaching.
3. Mike Huckabee in his book, *God, Guns, Grits, and Gravy: and the Dad-Gummed Gummint That Wants to Take Them Away.*
4. Ronald Reagan in his "Father's Day Address," signing the holiday into law.
5. Brad Pitt.
6. Bill Cosby, from his book *Fatherhood.*
7. Matthew McConaughey.
8. Johnny Depp.
9. J. D. Salinger in 1955's *Raise High the Roof Beam, Carpenters.* In his daughter Margaret's memoir, *Dream Catcher,* she writes, "My father, a writer of fiction, is a dreamer who can barely tie his own shoelaces in the real world, let alone warn his daughter she might stumble and fall."
10. Ed Sheeran in a 2021 interview shortly after his wife gave birth, about to leave on tour.
11. Alec Baldwin in his memoir *A Promise to Ourselves: A Journey Through Fatherhood and Divorce,* describing the way family law is prejudiced against men, as evidenced by him losing custody of his daughter Ireland, who later became famous as the recipient of his voice message calling her a "rude, thoughtless little pig."
12. *King Lear,* act 5, scene 3, as Lear and Cordelia are being taken away, and he finally sees his error.
13. Ted Hughes's poem "Daffodils," written shortly after Sylvia Plath's suicide, describing a brief, happy scene with their daughter.
14. Ray Rice, in an interview two years after he was suspended from the NFL when a video surfaced of him knocking his daughter's mother unconscious in a hotel elevator.
15. Nick Flynn's memoir, *The Ticking is the Bomb.*
16. Joe Rogan.
17. Former NFL player Jay Feely on X (then Twitter) responding to

backlash against a picture of him holding a handgun next to his daughter and her prom date.

18. From Tom Wolfe's *Bonfire of the Vanities*, after Sherman commits vehicular manslaughter on his way back to his wife and daughter from his mistress's apartment.

19. Tucker Carlson in a radio interview during which he also called women "primitive beings," recorded when his daughters were seventeen, twelve, and nine.

20. The other Jeff Lebowski in *The Big Lebowski*.

21. Jerry Seinfeld talking to *People* magazine about accepting his seventeen-year-old daughter's high school boyfriend; Seinfeld, himself, dated a seventeen-year-old high school student when he was thirty-eight.

22. David Beckham in an *Entertainment Tonight* segment—#2 in a list of "5 Reasons We Love David!"

23. Tracy Morgan, whose youngest child is his first daughter. Two years before her birth, he drew criticism for saying in a comedy routine that if he found out one of his sons was gay he'd stab him.

24. LeBron James, holding his daughter at the podium to accept his Harlem Row Fashion 360 Award.

25. Mark Wahlberg.

26. Norman Mailer, quoted in the memoir *In Another Place: With and Without My Father, Norman Mailer*, by his daughter, Susan Mailer.

27. Louis C.K., in an *SNL* monologue, one year before the first allegations against him surfaced.

28. Matt Damon, who in a later interview credited this daughter for having the conviction to get him to stop using homophobic slurs.

29. Garrison Keillor.

30. Mark Zuckerberg, telling *People* magazine why he hoped for only daughters.

31. Bill Clinton in the prologue of his memoir, *My Life*, a book dedicated to his mother, his wife, and his daughter.

32. Johnny Cash in the song "Drive On."

33. Don Draper, *Mad Men*, season 6, episode 5, asking his new wife to talk to his daughter because he's too drunk.

34. Lester Burnham from *American Beauty*, right after he nearly sleeps with his daughter's best friend.

35. Brett Favre.
36. From Chekhov's "The Father," one of his few prominent stories or plays that feature a present, alive father, though the story takes place with him drunk outside the door, begging to finally be let back in.
37. Kurt Cobain, on his daughter Frances Bean, referencing his well-publicized heroin addiction.
38. Anthony Bourdain in his last interview.
39. Elon Musk in his keynote address at SXSW in 2013.
40. Kobe Bryant.
41. A receiver on the Los Angeles Rams in the HBO docuseries *Hard Knocks*, holding his daughter, who has toddled onto the field.
42. Seymour "Swede" Levov, in Philip Roth's *American Pastoral*.
43. Walter White in *Breaking Bad*, season 2, episode 12, holding his infant daughter and showing her the drug money hidden in the insulation of the garage.
44. Hafþór Björnsson, the world's strongest man, in a self-produced documentary about his life, discussing the daughter he hasn't seen since the girl's mother filed a protection order.
45. Clint Eastwood, father of six daughters, in a 2008 *Esquire* interview called "What I've learned," in which he also denounces the new *pussy generation* of men.
46. Chris Pratt quoting Psalm 127:3–4 to announce the birth of his daughter on Instagram.
47. David Mamet.
48. Bernard Malamud, quoted by his daughter, Jana Malamud Smith, in her memoir *My Father Is a Book*, in a scene in which he stands in the bathroom shaving, preparing for a day of work, speaking to himself but loudly enough for his wife and children to hear. The memoir also uses the metaphor of her father as a hot air balloon: *At once lifting the family and consuming all our heat to fire his updraft.*
49. From Yeats's classic "A Prayer for My Daughter," in which, on a stormy night, while his daughter sleeps, he prays for her life to be filled with innocence, safety, and someday a kind husband.
50. John Updike's *Rabbit Redux*—Harry "Rabbit" Angstrom gets a four-novel arc, ending on a deathbed scene when his wife and children forgive him.
51. The father in the 2018 film *Eighth Grade*, sitting next to his daughter as she puts a box *full of her hopes and dreams* into the fire.

52. Jonathan Safran Foer in *Eating Animals*, about raising his kids vegetarian.
53. J. August Strindberg in his final and most autobiographical novel, *Son of a Servant*.
54. Rev. Billy Graham.
55. Howard Stern.
56. Jordan Peterson in a collection of clips from his lectures and interviews called "Things You Must Know as a Father."
57. Tom Cruise in his deposition for a libel suit against two magazines that claimed he'd "abandoned" his daughter.
58. Brett Kavanaugh in his first interview on Fox News following the sexual assault allegations brought against him after his nomination to the Supreme Court.
59. Mel Gibson after the birth of his ninth child with three different women.
60. Tony Soprano to Meadow Soprano, *The Sopranos*, season 2, episode 10—he's drunk; she's trying to go to bed.
61. Eminem to his daughter Hailie, in the song "Arose," after his overdose.
62. Steve Jobs, when, at the end of his life, his biographer asked him if he had any regrets, and he spoke only of his relationship with his daughters.
63. Joe Giudice, from *The Real Housewives of New Jersey*, in an Instagram post from when his daughters visited him in the Bahamas after his fraud conviction and deportation.
64. Mark Cuban in an interview with Life of Dad, a media group whose "creative and video teams work with brands to craft original campaigns, activating a community of 3.5+ million Facebook followers."

A Fan's Notes from the Domestic Future

I bought my daughter a LeBron James T-shirt. It was way too big at first, which was cute in its own way, and now it fits just right. In so many of the pictures I've taken in the past couple of years, his image is there: a vivid screen print, post-dunk, flexing, screaming, the yellow of his jersey popping against the black background. I spent . . . a lot of time on Etsy looking for the right one, and I'm proud to say I made the perfect choice. The image of the two of them together is always a pleasure for me: her soft body, her bright round face on top of his muscle, his scowl. She got obsessed with the idea of wearing a necklace like her mom, so we let her pick out a hand-me-down gold chain from the jewelry box, and she wore it over her ballooning LeBron shirt with black tights and sneakers, her hair slicked back in a ponytail. She looked cool as hell, or not really, because toddlers can't look cool, only like an incongruous, miniature version of a cool adult, which is its own pleasure. My wife talked me off the ledge when I wanted to spend a not insignificant amount of money on little Air Force 1's or even—I cringe now just thinking of it—Timberlands. My too-long white-kid-in-Timbs-and-a-flat-brim-hat phase is over, but that's a nice thing about having your own kid: there's a blank slate not freighted with all the cultural baggage accumulated in a life, and nobody can really say shit to them or, by extension, you.

Anyway. She studied herself in this outfit, standing in the full-length mirror, tugging her chain, running her fingers along

LeBron's raised outline, puffing out her chest. In all the *many* photos, she's got her particular smile that suggests she believes she's gotten away with something—wearing what she wanted to wear, even though we told her the necklace was fragile and the weather was too chilly for a T-shirt, and in the end getting praise for it. Now she says his name like it's one long word, and calls it her *LebronJames shirt*, sometimes shortening it to, *My LeBron-James*. In the car, in her booster seat: *The buckle is covering my LeBronJames!* Or if I'm overcome with the desire to snuggle her as she's watching a movie: *Get off my LeBronJames!* I could write about the goofy joy of her voice chirping out his name forever. I tagged LeBron once in one of the pictures I posted. No response, of course. It's not like I thought there would be, but still, it was nice to imagine. LeBron has been known to retweet randoms that he finds inspiring or adorable; that *could* be her (me).

I got the shirt during a quarantine shopping spree—yada yada, we all know that game. Long, restless days with my daughter, watching her outgrow her clothes in real time. Everything was stained and stretched and sad. I replenished with a Yankees jersey, a Knicks jersey, plus some swag to show the occasional passing stranger her (my) good politics (*Abolish ICE*, written in cheerful *Sesame Street* font). Then, for myself—I guess I wanted to look young again, though I never dressed like this when I was—tank tops, band T-shirts, those big, intentionally ugly sneakers, lots of tie-dye. A bandana around my lengthening hair that I hoped was a Bjorn Borg vibe, but I think read more David Foster Wallace cosplay. I was doing a lot of low-impact cardio while listening to basketball podcasts during naptime; when I picked my daughter up out of the crib, she crinkled her nose at the smell of sweat. As the weather changed, we were out in the neighborhood every day, fleeing our claustrophobia, me in too-short shorts because I thought my quads popped, a backward hat, a vintage Knicks Jersey, her in her LeBron shirt, a chain, some shades, holding my hand. For a while, this felt hopeful. It felt like the opposite of attrition, and everything else about life then was attrition.

At the end of the summer, the NBA playoffs resumed at the otherwise deserted Disney World Resort campus. I got obsessed with all the reporting about what the players were doing to pass the hours: cards, golf, pool time, wine club, karaoke. It was the most believable portrayal of rah-rah-team shit I'd ever seen. A dream! *The* dream! In interviews, the players spoke about the pain of missing their families right alongside the joy of getting to know each other in a way the normal world wouldn't allow—I imagined summer camp secrets way past bedtime, giggling whispers among the world's tallest superrich. It made me feel happy for them, sad for me, that axis of prime pathos in fandom.

LeBron was transcendent throughout the playoffs. And in the footage off the court, he appeared even more as a benevolent god than usual, hopping into other players' interview sessions with jokes, a man entirely at ease. He seemed like the happiest person on earth, but not in a frivolous way. Happy for everyone else's sake; Atlas carrying the need to fill our long hopeless days with something remarkable. He and the other players had debated even continuing after Jacob Blake's murder at the hands of police, and there were stories of how he'd called Obama to talk about protest, power, solidarity. Never before had the binaries of responsibility and play, capitalism and activism, frivolity and dire importance, felt more blurred. To revere athletes as something far greater than the parameters of their job seemed rational; for someone like me, who'd done this my whole life, there was a weird, unearned thrill of *I told you so.*

When the Lakers won, LeBron gleamed with sweat, his body hung exhausted, confetti rained in a near empty building and he appeared like a man on top of a mountain in a snowstorm. Then he was smoking a cigar, chin tilted up, shrouded in smoke. Then he was FaceTiming his family as chaos swirled around him; the scope of the drama shifted—he was the hero, battle won, ready to go home.

We never have the TV on in front of my daughter, unless it's her stuff. (I swear, this wasn't some grand, morally superior plan; it just sort of happened.) So, my fandom is solitary, only nocturnal, nothing resembling my regular life there to intervene. I enjoy the compartmentalization. Still, the morning after LeBron's victory, I put her shirt on her. I said, *Yayyyy, LeBron,* so she did, too, happy, hopefully not surprised, to see the big smile on my face.

Frederick Exley opens his classic autobiographical novel *A Fan's Notes* with his narrator's heart attack, as well as his anticipation for a big Sunday Night Football matchup between the Giants and Cowboys, after *a weekend of foodless, nearly heroic drinking.* That's all in the first sentence. Throughout the first chapter, he introduces an unflinching portrait of his own dissolution—his self-loathing existence as an English teacher; the addled passivity he's content to live with, alternately a decrepit old man and a child in his own eyes, never a functional adult. He and a friend take a woman back to a motel from the bar where he watched football, and in the motel, he chooses to lie on one bed and listen to the noises of other peoples' exertions in the other, waiting for the greater thrill of the morning paper. He saves the sports section for last, a treat. He describes football against the hazy backdrop of his life like this:

> An island of directness in a world of circumspection. . . . It had that kind of power over me, drawing me back with the force of something known, scarcely remembered, elusive as integrity—perhaps it was no more than the force of a childhood forgotten. Whatever it was, I gave myself up . . . entirely. The recompense I gained was the feeling of being alive.

Exley's book is about the underbelly of a life that is remarkably recognizable in the speculations anyone may make about men they know and where they go within themselves, and also even in the worst versions that some of us might imagine about ourselves. His was the first depiction of obsession with an athlete, in his case Frank Gifford, as something that, even in its commonness, could be destructive. It was realism and caricature at the same time, which feels right. Interest becomes adoration, becomes fantasy, which becomes comparison to the fantasy, which becomes another chance at self-sabotage, even self-erasure— always teetering right on the edge of pleasure, where it can topple over into the grotesque.

Maybe that's a bit dramatic. But the register of sports discourse is inherently dramatic, that's the point: you get to make really grandiose statements about life and its meaning, and they feel sort of appropriate. Almost nothing is too ridiculous. Those who speak most bombastically about athletes, the Stephen A. Smiths and Skip Baylesses, have perfected a type of straight-guy camp: lavish soap opera emotion directed at this one arbitrary arena, the full palate of a macho feelingscape.

To tone it down a bit: loving sports, first playing and then watching them, has been the longest-tenured pastime in my life and by far the most weirdly intense. I know that isn't unique, but in a life otherwise ruled by a smug, near puritanical fidelity to the remove of self-awareness, it stands out. There's the obvious stuff: the staggering investment I've made (financial, emotional, timewise) into cataloging and deriving meaning from the successes and failures of strangers. Lately, though, as I find myself a person-with-child perhaps more obsessed than I've been since I *was* a child, I'm most taken aback by the way fandom alters time and how I'm stoking that sensation as much as any. Years collapse and expand as I remember single games or one player's entire career, a pace at odds with how I experience my reality. With the players I love, especially, memories of their exploits and my investment have begun to function like hiker's cairns in a life suddenly moving too fast—I was in that place then watching that game with that friend, and how long has it been since I saw that friend, and how different was my life then? Not so much, maybe? Or a lot? It depends on the day.

Then there's the enormous significance I find myself placing on the simple *ages* of these strangers and their relationship to my own age, which, like Exley's narrator, never seems to fit how I feel. It's the most basic human data point, the second one a child learns after *What's your name?* When my daughter stands with a group of new friends, they're all just shifting on the balls of their feet and forgetting to modulate their voices as they either scream or whisper, *I'm three! You're four! He's two! I'm three!* That's me facing down the Wikipedia page of a basketball player who's somehow only thirty-one, though I cannot remember life without him.

It's a cliché, I know, and I suppose it makes sense—sports *always* allow us to foist enormous emotional significance onto raw data: a one-point lead, an extra inch moved, the fraction of a second elapsed. As a boy, these numbers functioned as an invitation into emotion, then imagination, then narrative. It wasn't just that sports dominated my feelings; it's that they were the only space in which I let myself explore fully feeling. I was not a particularly creative or engaged kid. I had a hard time with anything that wasn't concretely provable and therefore—in my warped, exacting definition—just. I didn't do the arts and crafts thing; I didn't give myself over to the stories of cartoon heroes. But I had two imaginary friends that meant a lot to me. Both were on the Yankees; one was a defensive specialist shortstop who batted eighth (five foot ten, 175 pounds), the other a solid-hitting first-baseman (six foot one, 205 pounds), who topped out one season at nineteen home runs, nineteen being my favorite number—big but not . . . ostentatious. I kept their pretend exploits reasonable because in my fantasies, they were training me, and it seemed statistically improbable, and therefore delegitimizing, to think my own stats would surpass a professional journeyman's. It all felt less vulnerable that way, not naked, unbridled fantasy, which was an important trick to play on myself.

Often, I was giddy with expectation for what heroics or grand failures might await them in a scenario I hadn't yet invented. I merged the fantasy with the actual Yankees lineup once I got old enough to demand the sports section each morning to inspect box scores. Then the Jets and the Knicks, too. Then focus narrowed onto players that I deemed—through some intense, cosmic yoking—mine. The anticipation I felt between waking up and the paper arriving lingers at the base of all anticipation for me still, the foundational sensation of tender optimism mixed with dread.

If you're good enough at sports as a child to fantasize about playing as an adult, there's a clear line of demarcation in your life: youth, when you played and believed, then the chasm when you stopped and a certain percentage of the optimism you ever felt about yourself died instantly, then . . . I don't know, the rest. I say this as someone who was never actually that good, so I can only imagine the hollowness felt when a real athlete becomes just a person. It's my favorite genre; I'll always be down to watch a tearful thirtysomething titan retire, describing the past fifteen years as a lifelong epic, already lodged in times of yore. Most recently, I watched Roger Federer, my favorite non-LeBron athlete, retire, and this most stoic competitor was hyperventilating through his tears. He had to put his hands on his knees. He sputtered out, *It was just . . . so incredible. My God.* His family watched him, proud and inconsolable. What could be more beautiful than that?

I was sixteen when I began to suspect that I was more fan than athlete. I'd made it onto a travel baseball team with players who were slightly older and much better. I could have been the oldest player on the younger team, maybe still the worst or maybe not, but I'd gravitated toward the satisfaction of being the baby, the enigma, as though more important than success were the six months separating me and these future major league draft picks. It was dawning on me that I wasn't good, didn't have much motivation to get better, but you couldn't say for *certain* that there wasn't some potential latent, ready to develop the moment I matured. A coach called me *clay*—not exactly a compliment, but I loved it. To be included in that basic metaphor, this body that *could be* deserving of someone's disappointment, then eventually, in some great future, pride. Even being a waste of talent was seductive, the *drama* of it. Not a regular, plodding life; instead, one swaddled in regret.

There was a racial component, too, that I didn't articulate to myself, because a lot of sports engagement has to do with fraught racial dynamics and an unwillingness to interrogate them—a swirling set of assumptions about manhood, who gets to take that mantle and for what reasons. The best players on this team were Afro Dominican, students at a school in Washington Heights known only for producing athletes. Their lives were (I assumed) much harder than mine, and therefore so were their bodies and their resolve. We didn't feel like peers; I didn't see them as children, the way I saw myself. Our best pitcher threw ninety-five miles per hour and was dating a cop who would show up in uniform to cheer for him. In the dugout, he told stories about using her handcuffs on her. Our best hitter was the most muscled teenager I'd ever seen. At tournaments, when suburban parents questioned his age or whether that body was natural, he'd smile, wink, say, *Pushups*, and then demonstrate, though he was later caught for steroids as a minor leaguer, torpedoing his career. Our right fielder had a baby; his girlfriend would sit in the stands and talk to my parents about what their life would be like when he made it. All these stories are true, but the truth didn't make it feel less like legend in the moment, and doesn't make it feel less fraught and stereotypical to look back upon now.

I viewed these teammates with the intensity and distance of a fan. I was a wide-eyed boy whose life was more interesting, more impressive, simply for watching them. I could fear them, worship them, pity them, all at the same time.

In my sophomore year of college, I finally quit. I do think of that period as a definitional moment in my life. There was the person before it and then what came next, which involved long hair, cigarettes, thrifted blazers, and suddenly becoming a 4.0 student who showed up to office hours looking for a new authority figure to mete out praise. Even now, if someone throws me the what-made-you-become-a-writer softball (lame sports metaphor intended!), I go back to this story of quitting, like the man I am now couldn't have been unlocked without the death of that boy, when—Jesus Christ—it was nearly two decades ago and it was a Division III team at a liberal arts college that cared more about its Quidditch club.

A bookend nearly a decade later:

The last time I played pickup basketball, I was twenty-eight. There were teenagers on the court, and though they were kicking my ass, I remember thinking, *Maybe once I come into my body, I'll be able to hang with them.* I didn't even register this thought as absurd in the moment—if anything, these kids were looking at me and trying to discern what might have been so long ago. But every time I play a sport, I'm returned to the consciousness of a boy still waiting to bloom. I remember all over again that pre-blooming is the best of all feelings, one harder and harder to find. I got tangled up going for a rebound; my shoulder separated. I felt hot shame as everyone watched me walk to my car, arm limp at my side. An orthopedist told me I'd stumbled into my first chronic health issue. At best, he said, I was shooting for slowest possible decline. I swear to God, he actually said, *I know it feels like a metaphor.* Even now, if I get a shoulder twinge during an otherwise lovely afternoon with my family, I smell decay.

All of this to say:

An athlete, a real one, is forever both younger and older than a regular person. We can see an entire lifetime in them, bask in the magnitude of that idea. How could it have happened so fast? We saw them, after all, when they were just a baby, though a baby like Hercules in the myth; we watched their first coltish televised steps. It's the bizarre combination of paternalism and reverence. These are the people we want to be when we grow up, while maintaining to ourselves that they never had to.

LeBron is thirty-eight now; I'm thirty-six. I've been obsessed with him since we were both in high school, and his games (against starstruck, peach-fuzzed kids, while announcers crowed, *That's a man*) were shown nationally on ESPN. Other than my wife and daughter, he may still be the person whose victories mean the most to me, and whose setbacks give me the longest lingering unhappiness. Like I'll be in a sour, fatalistic mood, yet when I run through the circumstances of my day, I realize that things are fine, except, oh yeah, LeBron was passive in the fourth quarter of a loss, and people are saying Jordan would never do that. This feeling is nearly as intense now as it was when I was sixteen, which, in my experience, is pretty rare for feelings.

When he beat the Warriors in 2016, I was in England with my wife and couldn't watch the game, but stayed up into the early hours of the morning refreshing the box score on my phone, absolutely racked until the end, when I woke her up whispering,

He did it! Everything else that happened on that trip is filtered through the prism of the joy, or really *relief,* of LeBron's victory. Standing in front of Jasper Johns's *Two Flags* at the Tate Modern the day after LeBron won, a wild poppy field in the Cotswolds, and three days earlier LeBron beat the fucking Warriors. Brexit passed while we were there; I viewed it mostly as something I had to talk about instead of LeBron.

I'd assumed that in the aftermath of his win, I'd be most satisfied by images of him dominating, then taunting. And those *were* thrilling—his famous block stretched out in midair, his sneer at Steph Curry and how small Curry looked, how ordinary in LeBron's shadow. It was the familiar thrill of temporary vicarious swagger. But quickly, what meant the most to me, and what I rewatched until I remembered every second of it, was LeBron at the podium post-win, MVP trophy on a table in front of him, flanked by his sons, his toddler daughter perched on his bent arm. He was exactly himself, as I'd come to define him: a mixture of Sisyphean exhaustion and regal invincibility. His voice had its usual timbre—all diaphragm, engineered to swallow a room. On normal-sized chairs, at a normal-sized table, he was so large. His daughter was so small. She was cradled in the crook of his elbow, which showed no sign of feeling her weight. In the video, she required nothing of him, only his body holding hers as she sat soothed by the familiar vibrations of his voice. What a gift. It was like, for her, maybe for him, they could've been alone. But they weren't.

In the video, his daughter and his trophy are about the same size. He chose, for that moment, to hold her, not it. You could imagine a version of him that definitely would not happen that night, still holding her as she went from sleepy glaze into manic frustration, then back, laying her gently in a crib, and what an intimate image to conjure: this man who made all motions better than anyone making that one. My wife and I were about to start trying for a kid; the world was only potential. There's that sense of invincibility when you're first considering parenthood; for a blissful moment you feel so *good*, so certain in your goodness, just for being the person who wants it. It's like—and I know this is a theme here—you're at an apex, young and old at the same time.

So maybe I felt the need for my own evolution and therefore the need for something else in him to ogle. But also, Steph Curry, his rival, the wholesome *team guy* who grew up with money, was heavy into family-man content, too. His daughter was already perma-viral, interrupting his pressers all season to be precocious, and he was such a patient, sweet dad, and now here was LeBron after snarling him off the court, *also* a patient, sweet dad—no cracks in his greatness, no holes to poke in the righteousness of loving him.

The scope of fandom shifted; a fantasy of physical domination comingled and drew extra power from a twin fantasy of elite domesticity, almost incongruous, and that made it all the more compelling. There was this beautiful new public dimension to the greatest stars in basketball, but to consume it still meant heaping meaning onto your favorite stranger's performance of unbothered excellence, grasping at allegiance. The very real power of these iconic Black men bringing fatherhood into the frame, refusing to separate caretaking from the image of their success, mixed into the familiar blur of voyeurism and imagined solidarity.

I watched the video again, basked in his happiness and mine.

And did I close my eyes? Did I imagine myself loved like that, loving like that, as the cameras flashed? Of course I did.

That postgame moment now bleeds into thousands that LeBron and other superstar jock dads are willing to reveal, broadcast, fold into their brands. Regardless of the commonness, the occasional staged stiffness, or even clear self-promotion, I'm drawn in all over again to the image of these hardest men doing the simple act of fathering softly, which really means fathering at all. *Hardest* is a loaded term, one of so many examples within the sports lexicon where racism, misogyny, and homophobia can be laundered through compliment. Even as the NBA has eagerly embraced T-shirt slogan liberalism, you still watch a game and see a player do something transcendent, and the language on the tip of the tongue to express awe is something along the lines of *That's a man.* Anything defined as weakness gets the opposite metaphor—as I write this sentence, literally yesterday, a beloved NFL announcer excoriated someone with the phrase *It's time to take the dress off.*

As a boy, when various sensitivities hindered my development as an athlete, a coach would always prod me toward *manhood*, and if I continued to fail, I knew I hadn't reached it. At a baseball camp, a coach called one player a homophobic slur, then asked the rest of us, *Any of you men have a problem with that?* I stayed silent. The only player who spoke up was made to run laps as the coaches jeered, *Pick those feet up, sweetie.* To be anything gentle was terrifying.

Around that same age, I remember looking at early pictures of LeBron's high school fame—these were pre-memes, I guess—and there was always an emphasis on a shot of him postgame, standing with his arms out over the shoulders of two or three tiny girls from the opposing fan section to give a sense of how larger-than-life he was, both literally and in the specter of his celebrity. The girls in these pictures were often white and blond, beaming. They were peers, maybe friends, but that seemed so incongruous in these images; that was the point—his remarkableness, but also his Blackness, which prevented him from ever being seen as a child, and their whiteness, which was all wrapped up in pure, innocent youth, and then you thought of their desire to be touching him, this child like them, but not really.

Twenty years into my LeBron fandom, all these memories co-mingle. When you watch someone as long as I've watched him, that one-sided relationship holds the shifting context—all the bad or good vicarious thrill one can derive from a fantasy of someone else. I'm a man now watching him, wanting to feel righteous for doing so; I was a boy then watching him, awash in angst and a nebulous yearning to feel powerful, to feel desirable. It seems so long ago, but sometimes it doesn't; he's been there the whole time. For me, for a lot of people, I think, sports is where we put the gross stuff. It's the arena that recalls, emboldens, justifies the basest impulses. So you can grow up, the way you view games and players and yourself, can evolve, or you want it to, but there's a twisted foundation underneath.

In the mid-nineties, three decades after *A Fan's Notes*, another great writer / tortured fan, David Shields, wrote *Black Planet*, about a Seattle Supersonics team that garnered all the coded terms that would soon be used to exceptionalize and denigrate LeBron—*brash, cocky, naturally gifted*. As a kid, I remember their two best players, Shawn Kemp and Gary Payton, were the pair everyone wanted to play as in video games. I also remember a joke from the time about Christmas presents, and the punch line was a reference to how many children Kemp was rumored to have fathered.

If Exley was the first to explore the connection between fandom and addiction, Shields turned the exercise into an investigation of a more insidious pathology—not just sad men obsessing over exemplary bodies; sad white men obsessing over exemplary Black bodies. Still, adoration wrapped up in disconnect. About Gary Payton, Shields writes: *I'm not him. I'm really not him. I wish I were him. I love him—this phantasm of him—to death.* Then, later: *It's a safe love, this love, this semi-self love, this fandom.*

Shields shrinks into himself; the figures of Kemp and Payton loom larger and larger, though the portrayal of them never changes. No matter the cultural critique, fandom overwhelms, as it always will. The book becomes about the show of looking outward when you're really looking back at yourself. Payton and Kemp are a frame through which to see the cloistered, neurotic reality of Shields's life that *must* not, for the fantasy to work, have any relationship to theirs.

Shields writes about his time with his young daughter in the book. The insularity of parenting is as all-encompassing for him as it is for me, or anyone; the internal fight about whether this new life is a miracle or a burden is all over his pages. The act of watching the players he loves stands in opposition to his real life watching his daughter, cannibalizing it—illicit non-domestication. At one point, he's so overcome with love putting her to bed that he feels like *an imbecilic monster for expending energy on the exploits of these aggressive men who are strangers.*

Then he leaves the room to check the score. In another, she's on her trampoline, jumping higher and higher, and he's briefly so proud, but he's thinking of Gary Payton jumping the whole time. In the most controversial scene of the book, his daughter finally asleep, he's having hushed new-parent sex with his wife, and he imagines his body as Payton's until he comes.

Near the end, Shields listens to Payton discuss a rare slump in a postgame interview, suddenly vulnerable, and only here does his interest falter because *the macho mask has slipped so low you can almost see his face.* It's the culmination of a relationship always meant to be one-sided—what Shields wants from Payton, the fraught pleasure of deciding where someone else's authenticity lies.

I've reread both Exley and Shields for this essay. Both feel appropriately dated but still profoundly relevant, which, in the face of the datedness, creates a discomfort typical of modern sports fandom. I keep thinking about the limits of self-awareness. How many different ways can you say, *This obsession of mine is fucked up, stunted,* while still obsessing? You can read *Black Planet* now, thirty years later, and say there's nothing interesting anymore about the guilt of the white gaze, certainly nothing productive, but also, thirty years later, the sensation isn't much different. There's no romance left in a man obsessed with his own demons screaming at the TV, and yet there are the demons, there's the TV, and when my daughter is asleep and my wife is scrolling, sometimes I have to remind myself to muffle my screams.

Whatever you think about an athlete is already a trope that has been held up as gospel, then critiqued, then reintroduced as something new, with a contemporary morality attached to it, then critiqued again. Like art, I suppose. To get worked up about an athlete now feels very similar to having a passionate reaction to a piece of art—the overwhelming subjectivity of the feeling fighting instantly with all the knowledge of what could or should or will be or has been said to contextualize that sensation, and then the worry: *What does this say about me?*

Some scenes off the top of my head:

LeBron and his wife, Savannah, sitting courtside at their son's game with the same jittery pride as any other parent, necks craned, ignoring the cameras.

LeBron, back home after winning the championship, annoying his daughter Zhuri in her palatial playhouse as she tries to do homework.

LeBron, on the grass, letting Zhuri style his famously thinning hair, side-eyeing the camera in mock protest.

Lebron, one arm around each son, pulling them in close while they do that performative kid squirm but never break away.

LeBron and Zhuri in the back seat lip-synching to *Frozen* until he belts out the chorus in a terrible falsetto, and she watches, tenderly ashamed.

He is big; they're small but getting bigger. Sometimes they're dressed fancy and sometimes they're in sweats, on a couch, or in the garden, or eating dinner on Taco Tuesday. Bronny is old enough for prom. For Zhuri's third birthday, she got a tiara that said, *Young, wild & 3*. Bryce does a good impression of his father; everyone laughs. When LeBron is in the shot, his smile swoops low and stretches across his whole face, a different expression, I think, than any other in his arsenal, reserved just for them (and everyone watching).

I know the evolution of his children's faces, the millennial-rich-person greige of their living room. It brings me great joy to believe in the importance of the images of his family life, which becomes an extension of believing in his goodness, his worthiness, how he always makes his teammates better, *Unlike fucking Michael Jordan, who just made everyone afraid, and that's not leadership.* I root for this part of LeBron now as much as I do his play. It's become so important to me that he means it all. That being the greatest of all time (again, fuck Jordan) is all the greater because it disappears in the face of what's really important—those kids on his Instagram who walk with him unfazed through the crush of paparazzi; domestic bliss, domestic presence framed over and over as his greatest accomplishment. It's a measly counterpart to that contemporary motherhood cliché, the question of whether powerful women can have it all. Instead, it's whether this great man chooses to, and look, he does. Look, his sons adore him, even as teens. Look, his daughter feels supported as her true loud self.

This is a moment for the athlete as a human being. Or rather, whether or not a fan agrees that they should be treated as humans has become a line in the sand. Either you recognize that, often, the athlete is depressed, has trouble sleeping, needs a day off, misses his family, or you maintain that we shouldn't consider the feelings of people bigger, stronger, richer, more beloved than the rest of us. It's a seismic shift that happened fast, certainly within my adulthood. The writer Hua Hsu put it beautifully in the *New Yorker* in an essay about the boom of intimate jock podcasts: *Growing up, an athlete like Michael Jordan could feel ubiquitous yet totally unknowable. . . . Controlling one's image meant withholding any sign of weakness or vulnerability.*

I do, though, think vulnerability, at least a certain fetishizing of athletes deemed vulnerable, has always been part of the love for fans like me. If Jordan's face never betrayed anything but cruel, capitalist confidence, you could find enigmas to root for in juxtaposition, log your allegiance with what you assumed to be their pain among all the brilliance. The first athlete I loved outside of local rooting interest was Allen Iverson—the anti-Jordan, recruited while unjustly imprisoned for fighting racists in a bowling alley brawl, always maligned and dissected, full of breathtaking grace on the court. There was a quiver to his voice, even when he was at his most brash. He felt like greatness and inevitable tragedy coexisting in equal measure. Andre Agassi was this way, too, flashy yet always seeming near tears. There was pain internalized into Iverson's narrow frame, captured in Agassi's lonely little shuffle between points. If Jordan was impenetrable, these men were tortured, which did seem more human. I could love what it felt like to root for them, choosing only to see their wounds.

LeBron ushered in a shift. To love him feels like I've had a front-row seat to his multi-decade battle demanding control over the story of his own humanity. Fatherhood is the final, strongest, most inarguable proof. He and Tom Brady (who I hate with the force of a thousand suns but must acknowledge here) and Serena Williams and Roger Federer have—through sheer longevity, wealth, and excellence—refused to succumb to any tropes other than the ones they want to occupy. They aren't capitulating to the spectacle of the used-up racehorse metaphor; if there's a glue factory, they've purchased it and converted it into part of a lifestyle brand. They're telling the exact story they want to—here is their kitchen; here they are showing off a self-deprecating side; here (always) is a little clip of them training their children, or their children helping them train—this image of perfect circularity, the excellence we love them for, but with all the hard edges sanded down, no love sacrificed.

Especially for athletes like LeBron and Serena, who have endured every predictable version of racism in their careers, to see them through the images they want to broadcast, to watch them consolidate ownership of themselves, is a triumph. The fan can bask in vicarious triumph, as always, but this is the most satisfying kind, gesturing ever closer to connection, since the myth is being told by its hero. It's not, of course, that a fan like me believes everything on a superstar's Instagram or in a superstar's self-produced documentary. It's that it feels better to choose fidelity to their version, almost participatory—tending to their story until it begins to feel like your own.

At the end of his essay, Hsu writes, *If . . . the internet makes us feel that we might be understood, then athletes are still avatars, but for our real selves, rather than our fantasies of greatness.*

I love this sentence, but I don't think *real selves* and *fantasies* are separate things here. What makes a fantasy of greatness most compelling is when, if you squint, you might be able to see your real self in it. If both broadcasting and consuming on the internet has done anything for day-to-day consciousness, I think it's brought our fantasies and our lives as close together as we can possibly make them through sheer will and delusion. With parenthood, especially when it's hardest, when I feel worst at it, the fantasy becomes most important. The fantasy I mean, here, is the one adjacent to my life, the one that my life is believable as, that someone else might even consider my life to be, that I consider a fantasy when I see it in someone else, like LeBron James. If Exley and Shields were driven by love of the unattainable, the self-flagellating mantra that nothing about the athlete could resemble their pathetic humanness, this is the opposite. This is fandom propped up on an even more thrilling lie: that their lives might just resemble ours, and therefore we might be a little closer to exceptional.

My daughter is forceful and stubborn, the way Zhuri appears to be. LeBron is good-humored in the face of it. He's happy that she isn't thinking about who he is to the world; she behaves as though she's the totality of it, the only thing that matters.

She is, right? I want to ask LeBron that. She's the only thing that matters?

And to myself: She is, right? She's the only thing that matters, and you're okay with that?

I've hardly ever worked in front of my daughter. The truth is, there hasn't been much pressing for me to do—almost all the time, if I'm ignoring her, it's a choice. Sometimes, at the playground, I see a parent trying to hold a professional tone on the phone while also keeping their eyes gentle for a kid demanding acknowledgment of monkey bar achievements, and I'm filled with envy, and I find it so beautiful when their eyes do stay on their kid. Or I'll witness a parent swoop into view who has been, and is often, called away, and their children run to them with a joy reserved for special occasions, totally obedient, eyes wide at the opportunity for shared time.

I flip the second quesadilla of the day; I try to call another dreary walk with the dog an adventure. When I'm on the phone, she starts screaming at me to hang it up. If she hears my fingers clacking on the keyboard, she comes to close my laptop like it's a game, and she's laughing, laughing, as I try to keep her away with my forearm, and sometimes I have to yell, *This isn't a joke!* She's good at acknowledging when we tell her something matters, but she'll get a last little jab in—*Is it a joke?*

Sometimes, before bed, I'm overcome with the need to tell her how much I love her, like if I don't capture the fullness of the feeling, and she doesn't hear me and understand before sleep, there's a chance she'll go to bed unaware. There's a chance that the day will have not provided her with that knowledge or me with that knowledge or at least the chance to hear myself say it, and that would be a failure, a day wasted, a zero on my imaginary scoreboard. I'll ask her, *Did you have fun today? Was it a good day? Were you happy? What did we do today?*

Last season was terrible for LeBron's Lakers. By the end, he was injured, like the universe was reminding us that all bodies, even his, eventually break down. But he had a great game against the Warriors on a Sunday afternoon, nationally televised. He scored fifty-six points and was his vintage self: prowling, flying. A couple hours after the game, he posted a photo of Zhuri facing down a big bowl of pasta at a restaurant. He wrote, *She asked if I could take her to dinner after the game.* He put little sad-face emojis, but the kind that suggest being more overcome by the beauty of the world than anything. My daughter was next to me asking me to read her another book, her elbow pressing down on my thigh, her face twisting up to see mine. I was filled with vicarious heartwarmth at the beauty of this dad and daughter, and also, I didn't want to read another book; I wanted to look at LeBron's Instagram.

I've got a tab open for a YouTube video of Tim Duncan's Hall of Fame acceptance speech. I watched it again this morning. Duncan has become a more compelling subject post-career—a little wink in the eye amid his stoicism, a searcher's salt-and-pepper stubble, fantastic hair. The vibes of a scuba instructor / bad poet / generous lover, when I spent my teens and twenties viewing him as drone, demystifying basketball stardom and relegating it to something more like middle management. When I did mushrooms in college, one friend freaked out, ran away, and we found him hours later in the dorm basement watching a Spurs game because Duncan was so predictable in his excellence that he provided grounding in reality. To find affection for Duncan now is recognition that his framing as anti-cool had little to do with him and everything to do with a certain type of fan's desire to celebrate *humility*, which then allows a fan like me to define myself in opposition to that type of fan. It's also recognition of my age. The quiet contentedness of his affect seems hard-won, something to yearn for.

Imagine: excellence, but more than that, happiness. Or maybe he's miserable; I don't know. He looks content to me onstage, and he never had to sacrifice excellence to get there. That's how LeBron seems now, too. Since having a kid, I've often felt like those are diametrically opposed options—either be a person who allows himself to feel content *or* forgo contentedness for the familiarity of self-imposed anguish, the churn, and at the end of that maybe triumph. I can feel gears catching in the recalibration of ambitions I once considered to be a straight line, the sense that I like myself and my life better now, but still wonder if this is really who I am.

When Duncan speaks about his daughters, he manages to talk in a way that suggests he's not still just speaking about himself. He says, *I'm so excited to see what comes next.* He says, *I cannot wait to see who you become.* From the crowd, quiet reverence for the part of him that isn't what's being celebrated, but also, everyone would agree, is the most important thing—that old chestnut, which feels like bullshit, until a moment like this, when you remember why it exists.

One of the other stars inducted that night was Kobe Bryant, though posthumously. There's no athlete more associated with fatherhood, particularly fatherhood of girls. (I'm pretty sure the #GirlDad phrase can be traced back to him, and now it's so ubiquitous that a stranger said it while high-fiving me in a men's room after we'd both cajoled our daughters into peeing.) Bryant was the first athlete whose public fatherhood made the entire world see him differently. It's a key pillar in the duality of his brand-turned-legend: revere him for his ferociousness as a player, tell tales of his single-minded pursuit of excellence and cruelty to anyone who got in the way, then juxtapose that with gentleness, selflessness, patience—those words so easy to associate with a dad and his girls. As though he reserved all his kindness for them, and that's somehow a more powerful gesture than just . . . being kind.

This is further complicated by the fact that the first act of Bryant's fame involved a rape trial. His oldest daughter was six months at the time. A nineteen-year-old hotel concierge was with Bryant in his room for five minutes; when she left she had blood on her underwear, Byrant had blood on his shirt, and she immediately told a friend she'd been assaulted. In an article for *ThinkProgress*, Lindsay Gibbs called it *one of the most high-profile rape cases of all time*. I remember it being that, but still, to read the article is jarring. It had all been very public, nobody had exactly forgotten, yet it came from a different time with a different Kobe Bryant, one unrecognizable in the shadow of the wise, vigilant #GirlDad. His lawyers were merciless with his accuser, told the world she was promiscuous, suicidal, hoped to be famous. Bryant looked on unmoved.

Neither the victim-blaming nor the fact that a powerful man rebounded while his accuser's life was ruined is unique to Bryant's case, but I do think that the very public display of embracing fatherhood helped bury the memory faster and with more finality. It's the enduring idea of fatherhood as the end of one life and the beginning of another, a clean slate. How could a man who cares so much for his little girls be bad? It's easy to scoff at the contours of this cliché, but it still works.

When he died alongside his daughter, a tragedy so enormous that it can't *not* foster hagiography, they were in a helicopter on the way to one of her basketball games. There's a viral clip from a late interview with Bryant when he discusses the origins of his helicopter use. He details his late-career daily routine, and it becomes a story of how to stay an efficiently excellent athlete while also an efficiently excellent father. He wanted to work out at four a.m., take the kids to school, go to practice, then another workout, and always make sure to pick them up from school before heading to a game; he incorporated helicopters so this schedule wouldn't be spoiled by traffic. He streamlined his world into the two things that mattered—work for self, work for them, no fat of inconvenience.

The first time I watched the clip of Kobe going through his helicopter logic, I started to cry, which, even as I was doing it, felt ridiculous. He was just so *purposeful*; I guess that's what got me. That was always his bit, and it had never compelled me, but this time I bought that his Randian self-optimization was, in fact, a feat of selflessness. It didn't feel like I could understand that level of dedication to either my family or my craft; working on one exhausted any resources I had for the other, and even then, I wasn't working *that* hard. I was pining for the sensation of exhausting myself in a way that felt productive, powerful, not merely survival. And of course that wasn't parenthood I was thinking about. Or love.

A few weeks earlier, I'd told my wife that when our daughter grew up, I wanted her to see me as someone to be proud of. As though that was something I wished *for her*. We'd taken her to visit my parents. In their bathroom, there's a cutout from the *Boston Globe*, now embarrassingly yellowed, with my face and a review of my first book that was all about my promise. I'd taken my daughter in there to wash her hands after touching every gross thing she could at the park. She was sitting up on the sink, giggling because it tickles her sometimes when I rub soap on her palms, and then she stopped and stared at this picture of me, a different version of me from a newspaper in a frame. She didn't say anything, but I told myself I saw recognition, then confusion. I said, *That's Daddy*, and a wave of self-pity caught me off guard. I hadn't thought of myself as the person in that picture in a long time, hadn't written a word in even longer, and had gotten most of the way to a fabrication of my personality in which I would disappear professionally, dedicate my life only to her care, and be fine with it. In an instant, that was gone. All it took to make it disappear was this passing thought that my daughter would consider me a loser and that I might resent her for making me one.

She woke up early the next morning, and it was my turn to wake with her. I had to go to the bathroom, so I brought her in with me, sat her down with as many objects to hold as possible. For a while, I talked to her; sometimes she responded, sometimes she didn't. It felt like we were there for hours, but not much time was passing. Her cheeks bore the deceptively adorable glow that means the cusp of sickness. Her eyes were bright, looking to me. I knew I wouldn't move until she got upset, my elbows reddening a little circle on each thigh. I could hear a clock ticking on the wall outside.

What I'm trying to say is that the idea of father-as-model remains so seductive. That a father's love is most powerfully expressed through pride—his pride for his kid, theirs for him, creating a template of a life worth living, then guiding them through it. The older my daughter gets, the faster time passes, which is both nice and terrifying. The days don't creep, they gallop along with tenderness and frustration, always a conversation. She asks questions that aren't answerable and watches me contort myself to try to make sense of them, and grins at that, and a whole morning has gone by. When she thinks I'm telling her what to do or trying to push her out of the conversation she wants to be having, she's enraged. We negotiate, settle, continue. Sometimes, this is the furthest I've ever felt from restlessness, but then I think about how nothing has progressed, we've done nothing beyond pass the time together nicely. Anyone can do that.

After Roger Federer's farewell address, cameras stayed on him as he consoled his daughters, who were weeping, presumably because he couldn't stop himself from weeping, and they didn't know what to do with that. As the crowd stood and cheered for him, he leaned into them, and the audio picked up the most beautiful semi-convincing line: *I'm so happy. I'm not sad, okay?*

In the last televised moment of Kobe Bryant and his daughter together before the unthinkable tragedy, they're in the front row at a Lakers game. He gets his ovation, gives a little wave, but then he's whispering advice to her, their faces mirrors, almost touching, looking out at the action as she absorbs his wisdom. There is no more compelling final image. He's pointing to the court, to his world, now hers, and her eyes are following his. They're surrounded and observed by thousands, but they seem to believe themselves to be alone.

Exley ends *A Fan's Notes* fittingly, on a recurring dream. His beloved dog is dying, and every day he's holding his dying dog, trapped, imagining that this next night, *I will find the strength to turn and walk on about my business. But then evening comes, and sleep, and then the dream, and then that shuttering of heavy blackness. And when again the vision comes, I find that, ready to do battle, I am running; obsessively, running.*

That's the last clause of the book: *obsessively, running.*

It's an image of endless exhaustion, even in grief, even when nothing is happening, even in a dream, which is such a close relative of a fantasy.

In the first two years of my daughter's life, I was so consumed with caring for her, both in time and new emotional weight, that if I ever stopped to think about it, I could identify a blank space in my consciousness where there ordinarily would be all the usual anxieties: about my accomplishments, my future, my body, the sense that no one would remember me. I'd get to bedtime free of thoughts about anything other than the task at hand, which in a weird way felt like the closest I'd ever come to an athlete's zone, that place where only the moment exists, and nothing is theoretical or metaphorical, you just *do*. I could still feel the space where all my old shit should have been, had always been, like a phantom limb. We shared an HVAC vent with her bedroom, so any sound she made woke me up. We sleep-trained her with such vigilance that eventually she didn't cry, but that didn't make her a better sleeper; reliably, at three in the morning, she'd be chirping, singing to herself, scraping her nails against the lacquer of the crib.

We decided if she wasn't asking for us, we wouldn't go in, so I'd be awake with her, yet with no obligation to her. Only then would my familiar consciousness return: that churn, that fear of anything I could define as a loss. I never went back to sleep. Often, I'd go into the living room and do pushups while watching all the sports clips I'd missed or whatever indistinguishable docuseries about striving prospects Netflix had to offer. In the shows, young athletes were as dutiful as they were remarkable; their fathers were stern and proud.

Everything about these lonely hours was the antithesis of the person I wanted to be. Maybe that was the point; again, the place to put the parts of ourselves that we wish we outgrew. I could turn on the monitor and watch her in night vision, eyes wide open, all alone, this ever-present specter, and try to manifest the next day, just a couple hours away, when I would become a better caretaker—smiling, grateful—and she would become a toddler willing to even gesture at an interest in learning to walk at an age-appropriate time. I'd be crouching, telling her to trust me, and she would, tumbling forward: only shared pride.

So much of the access my jock-dad idols provide into their lives now revolves around the hard stuff—the pain of losing, the toll taken on their bodies, the pressure of fame. The only thing that's never hard, never fraught, is fatherhood. Instead, it's a metronome of joy, the reward they've been waiting for through the tedium of their remarkable days. Absent from the portrayal is . . . well, everything else: their partners doing most of the childcare, the staffs working in their homes, all of it. And that's an obvious point, I don't even mean it to be damning. Nobody's public portrayal of family life reflects reality, but usually I roll my eyes. When someone you worship begins to resemble someone you could know, the depiction is more seductive. I'm already conditioned to look to them as a fan, full of enough awe that it feels intimate. So I choose this performance of excellence, happiness, life—one that has nothing to do with me—and find in it a chance for hope or self-scorn. The act of caring, then, becomes another thing to be competitive about, another way to measure up.

My daughter doesn't have any recognizable characteristics of an athlete. Despite the enormous force of her emotion and will, it doesn't occur to her to direct those things toward victory, certainly not when pushed, or for anyone else's approval. They explode forth only when she's being asked to do whatever it is that she doesn't feel like doing and is aghast at the interruption from the little world she's created for herself in a given moment. It's the quality in her that I recognize least and am most regularly awed by. We were on a beach this summer, me and her and my brother, along with some friends and their kids. A boy spent an hour maniacally trying to control a skimboard. My daughter asked for a turn and within ten seconds was puzzled, then bored, then went to look for shells. There were two boys, one her age and one slightly older, and they glued themselves to each other in competition; that upset my daughter, the way she gets upset when we try to have a conversation over her head. She clung to me for a bit and I her—still, after all this time, unsure what to do next—but then she drifted away.

The parents did the thing where we huddled around some booze and tried to offer as much information as possible about our pre-kid lives while watching our kids and letting things get as close to the edge as possible before intervening. These friends were meeting my brother for the first time and asking about me as a kid, since he's much older—if he was hard on me, roughed me up. I shared a memory about him pitching a baseball at me as hard as he could when I was young, splintering my wooden bat, and me crying with rage, demanding that he throw again. *Hahaha*—classic me! But we were both a little sheepish. Sometimes I think I overplay just how competitive and jockish I was as a kid to emphasize to myself that there's been some change, a hard-earned valley between my adult self, affable enough, and the memory of a racked lunatic beating a tennis racket into the ground until it broke.

The little boys wanted to race. One of their dads drew a thick line in the sand with his heel, and they mimicked a sprinter's stance, which somehow both had seen enough times in their short lives to approximate. They were adorable in their seriousness. Someone yelled for my daughter to join, and she sauntered over. We all asked them to pose for as long as they'd tolerate so we could film them, these little people acting so intentionally like *people*, a scenario someone may have captured in our childhoods, all those years ago, with a giant camcorder. A dad yelled *Go*, and the boys took off. They were sincere blurs in the same direction, as my daughter decided to make sure she traced the entirety of the starting line with her toe before casually following them. Everyone was yelling, *Go! Go! Go!* She looked up to see our line of faces, and what did she think? How goofy were we? How suddenly resembling children, so distant from any pose of rationality or authority? She kept her eyes on us as she trotted in the direction the boys had gone, grinning, yelling, *Yaaaaaay!* Everyone thought this was hilarious and said, *Yaaaaaay!* back at her. The boys returned breathless, one very pleased and one very sad. The moment passed, nothing important, but it felt huge to me, like this crystallization of what I love yet cannot access about her, maybe what I love *because* I can't access it.

My mother didn't care about sports at all, and was indifferent, then annoyed, when I showed interest, then obsession. She described to me once the sensation of watching me on the field in some all-star game as a kid where I was supposed to be—or at least it was very important for me to think of myself as—the best player. I was off, rattled by the pressure of my own expectations. She watched me from an excruciating distance—close enough to see my emotion, too far away to have any effect on it. She saw me start to cry and pull my hat down to try to hide it, then force myself to keep going. I remember this, too. To be honest, the vast majority of the moments I remember from childhood are sports failures. Even the memories of a victory center on the anxiety leading up to it, then quick relief that I might not have to hate myself at the end. It cannot have been as bad as I remember it, or I would've stopped caring or at least stopped receiving positive reinforcement. Of all the types of person I was or wanted to be for the first half of my life, this version feels most central to my self-conception and also most distant. I just want it on the record, like, otherwise what was the point?

I like to think I'd be relieved if my daughter never played a sport. I like to think I'd be happy if she never mastered anything and lived a life of dabbling and vibes, free from the self-imposed trap of constant competition that I remember. Watching her, accepting that, I might also be free. When kids are racing and she's dawdling in her own world, with her soft, open face, her eyes glinting with what I see as kind mischief, it's very easy to want that. But then at swim class at the Y, when she has the exact same expression as the teacher begs her to kick, and she's frozen while the rest of the pool churns with the exertions of her peers, their progress, and then the teacher is looking up at me like I should have some right thing to say to make my daughter change, I am instantly panicked, which can so easily fester into shame.

My wife and I lean against the damp tile wall and keep smiles on our faces as we whisper, *She . . . really isn't good at this?* And then, *Should we . . . worry?* We assure each other: *No, who gives a shit?* She's four and she's happy, but there's the nag of imagining what lovingly diligent documented achievement, hers and ours, might look like. I see that mom giggling with joy every time her daughter leaps into the water, snatches up a kickboard, and swims away; that jacked dad pantomiming the breaststroke along the side of the pool as his son watches, then copies. It's all such a cliché—there are those parenting moments that crop up that are so basic, so referential, that you see yourself from above as the cartoon you were dead set on not becoming.

At the end of the class, my daughter chirps *thank you* to the teacher, fumbles on her Crocs, nuzzles into the big towel I'm holding, and says, *I did great!*

I match her tone: *You did great! Let's get brunch!*

We put her LeBron shirt on her in the locker room. She reeks of too much chlorine, a smell as instantly transporting to one's own childhood as graham crackers or Play-Doh. We go to the same spot for brunch every week after swim, and the server says, *I know you*, to my daughter, which makes her beam and also makes me beam. *She is*, I whisper to my wife as my daughter trots to our table, *objectively perfect*. She's into the word *routine*, so we talk at the table about how much we all appreciate this routine, how lucky we are to do it every week.

Once, in an interview on Father's Day, LeBron said, *The best part of fatherhood is seeing your kids in you.*

I'm pretty sure he just misspoke with what was meant to be another cliché. Maybe not. Either way, I like the line as he said it and choose to believe it: not looking to them for the confirmation of what you've provided, but rather the opposite. I guess that's its own cliché. Parenthood is the greatest cliché factory I know of beyond sports, the biggest feelings reduced so easily into a few general categories of realization. You choose which ones to believe in which moments, or really you choose who to believe when they say them and whether one of those people is yourself.

The Lakers lost their first four games this year. LeBron seems old and tired on the court, just about ready to check out. In the midst of it, a few days ago, he celebrated Zhuri's birthday. She's bigger now, but still small on his lap in a photo on Instagram. They're posing in front of a sculpture made of crowns—he's King James, she his princess—wearing matching tan overall sets and Timberlands. In the caption, he writes, *Love you*, five times, all in a row. They are spectacularly ordinary, kind of. I really mean it when I say I hope he's as happy as he looks.

Gratitude Is Just Math

She looked like a rag doll in a purple jacket, flying from the platform leading to the biggest slide.

When she landed, the air was thick and crackling with something new.

I put away my phone.

When I held her and she cried for real, the kid who pushed her said, She fell.

He looked afraid of me.

He had red hair like his father, who said, loud enough for everyone to hear, What a sad accident, I hope she's okay.

A week later, the boy and his father were back; all of us remembered, but none of us acknowledged it.

My daughter said to the boy, Chase me, and ran away laughing.

I was so proud.

The father stood next to me in work boots and a sweatshirt that used to fit.

He said, She's beautiful.

I didn't say, He's beautiful, but I should have.

He said, She in school? I said, Yeah.

He said, Mine's never been, my wife stays home, she's scared with COVID.

I didn't say, I'm scared, too, but I should have.

Dark clouds spackled the sky.

We didn't exchange names, but he told me that the birth was early, that there was a hole in the amniotic sac.

He told me the boy loved everyone, he just didn't know how to do it right.

The boy was pushing my daughter on a swing.

They both had those frozen kid smiles, where they're trying so hard to show you happiness, but also they feel it.

I'm not young, the man said. We waited a long time for this.

When it started to rain, my daughter looked at me and said, Why is it raining?

Isn't that the funniest thing?

We left without saying goodbye.

Once, my daughter was on a ladder that swooped up from gradual to steep.

I was far away, pretending to be the kind of parent who doesn't hover.

I think she was trying to yell something at me, and then she fell from the very top.

She landed on her back, across the horizontal bars below; the metal left bruises like grill marks on a hot dog.

When I rushed to her, another parent said, Oh, that one's gonna cause some damage.

When I held her, weeping, another little girl was in her grandfather's arms weeping.

He said, She feels bad, she wants to know it's okay.

My daughter and this girl stared at each other while weeping, and I said, She's okay, I promise, aren't you the sweetest thing?

My wife held my daughter on her lap and tried to comfort her.

She said, We can go home, it's okay, let's go home.

My daughter went from sad to angry; she screamed, No!

She climbed the ladder again, not looking at anyone until she got to the top.

We felt such awe; I started to cry at the crowded playground, which was embarrassing.

She is the kind of person who will get in trouble, who will allow the world to hurt her, and I was never that.

She only wants to be friends with the boys that hit her now.

About her friends, she will say, Sometimes he's nice and sometimes he's mean.

When I watch her try to hug someone who doesn't reciprocate, I have to look away.

Sometimes, she seems loved out there in the crowd; sometimes she seems so lonely.

How is that possible?

Someone hung himself overnight on the climbing structure.

All we saw was the police tape on the way to school.

When I found out what happened, my first thought was, I hope no child saw it, in the park as the sun rose, after an early wake-up, the way we have been so many times.

As though worse than a person feeling that much pain is a child knowing that much pain exists.

I didn't like that thought, but it was the one I had.

The playground was open that afternoon.

My daughter came tumbling out the bottom of the twisty slide between two strangers, their bodies a tangle.

Before I saw her, I could hear her howling as they moved through the tube, a sound so joyous you could confuse it with despair.

Once, I was at a party, like a whole other person.

I smelled like cigarettes.

I was drinking mystery punch and staining my lips.

There was a fat yellow moon, like from a book I read her before bed.

This guy who was even drunker than me got real close to my face.

He yelled, over the music, How do you raise a child in this country?

I thought about how much more often I felt safe than in danger, full of love than bereft, content than restless.

Like at least two-thirds of the time.

I screamed, Gratitude is just math! into the music, but he couldn't hear me.

I found a corner and stood and watched like I was at a playground, bodies dancing in a tangle, sharp smiles glinting.

For some reason, I held my breath.

I was on a big deck; there was a cool wind on my face: miraculous.

Sometimes I think I'm easy.

I find meaning anywhere.

I held still as long as I could.

Anything can happen, you know?

On the Fantasies of Various Apocalypses

We were watching a show that was fine, I think. Or good—it was probably good. It looked nice, famousish people were in it, there was a tone that was both jokey and hugely emotive, the combination of which created a path for the viewer to feel in big, uncomplicated ways without any challenging buildup to that feeling or discomfort or self-critique. In other words, it was a show like a lot of shows. The first episode centered a father and his son alone at the end of the world. It never says where they are; there's a forest thick enough to hide in, a climate verdant and temperate enough to allow them to farm vegetables and raise a flock of gleaming white ducks, whose origin is unaddressed. I'm snarky about it in retrospect because it did make me feel very deeply in the hour I spent with it, and I resent how easily I'm made a mark by B+ content, despite the pleasure I take in turning myself over to that experience each evening, between when my daughter goes to sleep and I do.

I'm working on a grand unified theory of what we don't actively look for in a book or movie or TV show or poem or song or Instagram post—anything that might occupy 50 to 75 percent of attention for a given span of time—but that we demand in some unarticulated way. It's four words, so maybe not that grand: pity, envy, recognition, surprise. I'm not a visual thinker, and I was never good enough at math to understand graphs, but in my head it looks something like this:

Envy

Recognition   Surprise

Pity

I find it alternately comforting and depressing to think that what I'm feeling when engaging with a novel or a Muriel Rukeyser poem made newly viral or the season 3 slog of *Schitt's Creek* can be tidily converted into a dot on this graph that I just made up. But here we are. Anything great, by which I mean it provides an experience that nags at me and burrows into my consciousness as a distinct entity, sits exactly in the middle: absolute zero. That's the pleasure of tension—whenever you feel yourself pulling toward one particular sensation, you're yanked back into depth, which means uncertainty.

Most of the time, though, I'm seeking out the nice scratch of a single emotional itch. Sometimes, I'll be scrolling through Instagram reels while my wife is scrolling through TikToks in a different corner of the same room with my daughter's stomping and babbling, finally mewling, bouncing around the distance between us. A flood of ambient pattern-making, the brief rush of a new face onscreen resembling the previous one, doing the same dance to the same song, a slight tweak to the expression of faux bashfulness, staged surprise, then onto the next. The feeling is one of ear pressure building, almost daring myself to see how long I can go before I hold my nose and blow, clear out space for the noise of the world to rush back in. Scroll on—recognizable envy, recognizable pity, some kids in a car yelling along to Olivia Rodrigo. I yell along to Olivia Rodrigo, too. I have no problem with how derivative her work is of songs that came out before she was born; I loved those songs and now I love her songs. She allows the listener twice her age (me, *ugh*) to experience the joy of recognition without feeling static, and also there's that sense of victory when an aesthetic that once resonated resonates again, plus the weird stab of pleasurable pain at watching younger people *feel* at the level I once felt, still at the stage when every emotion is like an audition monologue for personhood, the same sensation as watching my daughter vamp in front of the mirror in her mother's clothes. I play "Driver's License" on the piano while my daughter watches and bangs her wooden drum, and I sing along and I feel like a teenager, full of petulance and heartbreak, a spigot of emotion left running. I envy anyone who isn't yet as old as me, and that makes me care.

Back to this Netflix show I can't even remember the name of. Whenever I see anything about a dad in an important moment who isn't a monster, or honestly even who is but is at least very loudly present in that moment, a tide of feeling swells from my stomach up into my throat, finally pooling in my eyes. And this forgettable show is all *that*, in particular one climactic scene when the father is gripping his son's shoulders after he tries to leave and explore the ruined world. He's yelling at his son in a way that's more of a plea, eyes wet and desperate. I know this will stay lodged in my emotional memory, along with a million similar scenes, organized together around reminding me of a sensation that, if I haven't achieved exactly, I at least want to achieve, probably because I've seen it rendered so often. It's stuck in this space made for the same depiction of fatherhood, over and over, a groove hollowed out in my expectations for character development otherwise not concerned with the domestic. His face—full of rage but also sorrow, the inability to convey what he needs to convey with words, everything justified by true desperation, and all that feeling channeled into big hands on a small, fragile body.

It strips away any context, even and especially whether I felt the scene was good. It's just that tone: instant, continued crescendo. Now, in a pandemic, hurtling toward environmental collapse, these scenes feel omnipresent. There's always another narrative to build around a reason to flee, tiptoeing a frightened child through the husk of what was once the world while an enemy stalks or a sickness infects or a fire, real or metaphorical, burns closer. These stories forgo the boredom, ambiguity, nuance of common life, live in the emotional register of perma-crisis, all while inviting the audience to say that such a story is now at least adjacent to lived experience.

But no matter the particular apocalyptic melodrama of the setting, it all bleeds in my mind into a long-established continuum of fatherhood fantasy: catastrophe. I think of Tony Soprano in the pool trying to rip the plastic bag off his son's head, free him from the cinder blocks tied around his ankles. Tony is so large and graceless splashing around, but he's strong enough to be useful enough to prevent his kid from dying in this moment, which is extremely poignant to me as a large and graceless man who likes to think of himself as at least strong. When he drags the boy out of the pool, they're alone together. He sits there holding him from behind like a giant sopping baby and screams, *What's wrong with you?* It's a sound in a different register than anything James Gandolfini conjures over six seasons in a performance as nuanced as any I've ever seen. He isn't funny or menacing or sexy; he's just out of control and sad, though even that is tinged with menace. His sadness is anger, and somehow that conveys decency. As though anger is the baseline, but when the anger is born from the desire to save—*Why can't you feel better when it's important to me that you feel better, when I'm telling you that I don't want you to die*—we're invited to find love. If the father is so sad that the world might hurt you, or you might hurt yourself, that it seems like he wants to hurt you, then he means it.

My daughter has been hitting at school. Her daily report sheet comes headed with the phrase, *Today I was:* fairly *behaved,* which, in the sunny parlance of early childhood education, I have come to realize is as close as you can get to, *What a little fuckhead.* My wife has a round angry bruise on her elbow from a bite that occurred on the sidewalk when we were trying to prevent the child from uprooting the sharp metal ladybugs staked in a neighbor's tree pit. Sometimes she bites to get free, but other times, it's as though she needs to create a physical manifestation of what she feels inside to make us understand.

Her violence, when it explodes, still shocks me. Up close, I can see a little cloud pass over her, a reprieve from who we tell her she needs to be, like she's slipping out of too-tight shoes and wiggling her toes. When she lashes out, there's relief on her face before there's fear and then sometimes contrition, though the contrition is wrapped up in knowing it will make *us* feel good, make *our* faces soften. I got a call from school one day, and when I heard her teacher's voice, I tensed up in anticipation of the embarrassment of what she might have done. But this time she was the victim; a new kid lost it and got a grip on her cheek with untrimmed nails. He didn't catch an eye, the teacher assured me, but did gouge her face as they pulled him off. It was an uncomplicated pleasure to hug her tight at pickup, to dote on her all evening, to ask her again and again if she hurt. When she snuggled into me, I cried. She asked me why, and I told her because I loved her, which was true. I vowed to never succumb to anything less than this crescendo of affection, but the next day, she was herself again and so was I.

Often, especially when alone with my daughter, I've felt the overwhelming need to hear *Sorry* when she's wronged someone, or *Please* when she's screaming her desires. She's so frequently out of control, or careening toward it, and that's the feeling I've hated most in my own life. When she's getting there, I feel myself getting there through her, and these words become a heavy blanket to throw on the blaze. Sometimes I hear myself say this phrase: *It's okay to feel whatever you want to feel, but you have to be kind.* I know this confuses her, and by confuses her, I mean she's calling bullshit. She screams back, *Daddy doesn't want me to cry!* Or *Daddy doesn't want me to feel sad!* Or *Daddy says I can't be frustrated!* I say, *No no no, baby!* My voice gets panicky and defensive. I feel the intense desire to put my hands on her shoulders, to know that she can't wriggle away from me toward danger, which really means uncertainty, which really means the fullness of herself. I say, *Look at me, please; listen to me, please.* My *please* is exactly as forced and contemptuous as hers. Like I demand of her, I'm conditioning the intensity of the feeling with the banality of the word.

My wife got COVID early, before the vaccines, the same day we got alerts on our phones that there were no more hospital beds available in our state. She left to quarantine in her boss's empty attic apartment while my daughter was napping; too soon after, my daughter woke with an unexplained howl and wriggled in her sleep sack against my grasp. I decided to focus my many unreconcilable feelings into a goal of having something to show when my wife returned, to make this moment of desperation an opportunity for growth, maybe even transcendence. This is a stupid reflex I've noticed in myself—a desire to separate the type of *dadness* that I practice from that of beer-commercial fodder, the adorably lenient chill-bro stopgap killing time until Mom comes home and says, *Why is she choking on a Pop-Tart while you watch football?* The desire to not be assumed the lesser parent, the parent who does less, means less, and therefore is bothered by less. The flip side of not wanting fatherhood to be a joke is having no sense of humor about it at all.

Every day felt so quotidian—string cheese, tantrum, book, yogurt, tantrum, park her in front of *Moana* while I teach over Zoom, blowout diaper, book, clock check, repeat. But it also felt monumental, like something we had to *survive*, and I didn't want to admit that I was overwhelmed until the strain of trying to repress the embarrassing feeling became the predominant feeling, both unnecessarily effortful and familiar. I forced my daughter out into nature on cold days, limited screen time more than usual, tried to introduce the scales on her tinny, tuneless xylophone.

I'm always amazed by how fast the world fades away when I'm alone with her. Scope narrows and narrows onto her face, and I forget other people, imagine they've forgotten me. In my mind, so fast, my daughter and I are high up in a tower, we're huddled against a blinding snowdrift, we're on a boat, and I no longer know if anyone can see us from shore. So, we were bobbing through our quarantine days, as everything seemed too real and also like a giant metaphor. I was foggy and frightened. We kept our distance. She rode on my shoulders through the background of other people's photos at the park or on the pedestrian bridge over the river, squinting into hard November wind. It was so easy to think that this was it. My wife was texting about a burning in her chest; my daughter seemed symptomatic, too, so every day I took her to the parking lot of a minor league hockey stadium where a military kid in hazmat gear swabbed our noses, while I pinned her arms to her side and screamed, *We have to, baby, we have to!* over her howls.

It did feel like a TV show, one that I'd call trash but that would move me to tears. There was a sense of beauty, purpose, self-importance among the awfulness, the grim yet galvanizing gravitas of COVID terror, just like climate terror: it's not that you're ambivalent about parenting; it's that you're ambivalent about parenting *in this doomed world*. The martyr fantasies, the symphonic tragedy of what we've brought our kids into, and the sense that society at large won't save them, so we must trust our own vigilance—it's all supported by science! I'm not trying to make light of the dynamic, and it never feels light as I live it; that's the whole point: nothing chill, no extreme unnecessary.

At home, my daughter whined and whined, demanded and demanded, like a regular kid in regular times, and I demanded a *please* before I gave her anything. The worst part about a little scene in which I'm growling, *Say the magic word*, at a confused, cooped-up two-year-old like an ogre guarding a bridge is that it didn't occur to me *at all* in the moment that I might be ridiculous. She's her best (herself) when she's feral, free and silly as she rattles the cages put up around her; I know this about her and love it in an academic sense. I recognize it to be true all over again each night when I think about the best parts of the day and rue all the boldness and wildness and weirdness I failed to appreciate.

On one of the last days of quarantine, we were fighting over whether she'd let me change her diaper before nap, which was right on the heels of fighting over her need to nap in the first place. She was so tired, waking up at five every morning, and I said to her, *Baby, you're so tired, can we just do the thing that your body needs*, to which she screamed, *No body!* These little moments of accruing friction, each unremarkable on its own, steadily fraying the rope that tethered us, my body extra exhausted from carrying her through the hikes she didn't want to go on in the first place. She was trying to run away and I was holding on to the waist of her leggings—again, with proper distance: funny, like the little girl with the dog pulling at her bathing suit on a sunscreen bottle. But her tug became a writhe, and I wasn't giving in because I was thinking about how I was failing to execute this most basic thing, and why couldn't she just let me be competent? Why couldn't she let me be the kind of father she needed right then, which really meant the kind of father I wanted to see myself being? She tried to turn herself so she could hit, then bite me, and I pulled my body away. She slipped on socked feet and hit the floor hard, a dull crunch then a quick exhalation. For a flash, I felt only annoyance—if she had just *obeyed*—then some stirring that what I should have been feeling was concern. There was a pocket of silence that portended real pain, then she exploded into sound. She had blood in her mouth as she screamed, which added a gargling quality. She looked up

at me, face full of blood and mucus and tears, distraught in a
singular way that we lose as we get older.

What I want to articulate is the small sense of relief I felt—
finally, a moment both terrible and significant, a change in tone.
I picked my daughter up and held her tight as she screamed
through blood. She was, I think, still furious at me, the only person available to blame for this shock of pain, but also the only
person available for comfort. The claustrophobia of that moment
for both of us. Of course, she went from being the biggest, most
unmovable object in the world to the smallest, most helpless.
She fit to my body, every part of her stuck on my torso, my little
tumor. Her heartbeat, hummingbird fast, her hot, wet, trem-
bling breaths—such tropes that I almost thought I was projecting them. My own breath, too, loud and ragged, my own heart
beating so close to hers. Again, a scroll of scenes in my mind:
Tony and his doomed son in *The Sopranos*; Jimmy Stewart in
It's a Wonderful Life when he sees his children at the top of the
stairs and clutches onto them; John Wayne picking Natalie Wood
up out of the dirt, holding her to the sky as she balls her fists to
fight him, then finally relents, the smoke of gunfire behind them,
the strings swelling.

My daughter pressed her face into my shoulder and wiped
bloody mucus onto my shirt. Very quickly, she was docile. She
needed me; she loved me. I was needed; I loved her. She let me
take a wet compress and run it across her face. She let me put
her down for a nap, limp and warm in my arms as I sang to her,
then curling in on herself as I set her in the crib, wished her the
sweetest dreams.

When I first read *The Road*, I was blown away, but this coincided with a time when I'd just been shown the spare wonder of Carver and done the whole what's-Hemingway-really-saying-in-"Hills-Like-White-Elephants" thing. It felt like capital-L literature because it most resembled what I was learning in capital-L literature classes. It's not a particularly enjoyable reread—dark to the point where the only thing to do is laugh, which is the last thing it wants. There's one note hit over and over: love is expressed, then instantly deepened by circumstances outside that love. The man keeps his boy alive in a world entirely ruined, which is the opposite of the innocence of the boy. Pathos is manufactured through conceit instead of interaction.

A semi-related memory: around the same time in college, I went to see *I Am Legend* with some friends, and one of my friend's childhood dog had just died. The movie follows Will Smith and his sweet old dog against the backdrop of a world full of zombies with hollowed-out eyes that only emphasize the fullness and soul of Will Smith's, as well as the dog's. Of course, he tries to save the dog and he can't. Of course, he has to smother the dog with his big loving lethal arms. We all looked over at our friend as he wept.

Now another: at the movies on Christmas, months after my brother's overdose. We were watching Tom Hanks in *Cast Away*, a film different from *I Am Legend* in all specifics but very much the same at heart. A man is alone in responsibility. A man feels afraid. A man is trying his best in the face of impossible difficulty. In *Cast Away*, Hanks finds a washed-up volleyball, paints a face on it in his own blood, loves it and tries to protect it because everybody needs something to care for. Late in the movie, Hanks and Wilson, the volleyball, are escaping on a raft. Wilson falls off and floats away; Hanks reaches out for him, weighing his own survival against the chance to save the volleyball. He's left screaming the volleyball's name into a storm. In the theater next to me, my father wept. When I looked over at him, not even thinking to hide his tears, he was the most sympathetic version of himself I'd ever seen, all the texture smoothed out into the clean lines of a father meant to protect against the world, who had lost, and the losing made the effort clear.

Kids aren't dogs. Obviously. Nor are they volleyballs with sweet little faces drawn in a smudge of blood. They are more complex, more assertive, often less blameless, and that's the problem. Still, there are the same notes to play, lodged in the same space in my emotional memory. Small, beloved creature silent or near silent, the father doing his best to prevent the worst. Everything has broken down, often everyone else has disappeared, certainly any maternal figure has disappeared, and then, with no guardrails of recognizable society, a depiction of faithful paternal love can blossom.

In a rare interview on the occasion of *The Road* being turned into a movie, McCarthy was asked about the fact that, in a love story between father and son, they never say that word to one another. He responded, *I didn't think that would add anything to the story at all.* He said the dialogue that did appear in the book was often stuff he and his son had actually said to each other in real life, just set in the world of the novel. So the famous conversation in the terrifying pitch-black before sleep, when the son asks what the father would do if he died and the father says flatly that he'd want to die, too—that was more natural than, *I love you, good night.* I remember reading that scene the first time and being so moved by the clipped, somber finality of it, the drama of the sentiment made stoic and somehow dignified by the danger of the plot, the idea that they *would* die, that without the son, there literally would be no world left for the father. McCarthy calls it *just a conversation that two guys would have.* It's hard to know if he's fucking with the interviewer.

In the novel, the man says of his son, *If he is not the word of God, God never spoke.* He says of himself, *If only my heart were stone.*

It's a book of almost peerless melodrama, because it's entirely climax. Every sentence is a deathbed confession, a scenario in which feeling cannot be tawdry or self-serving, only profound. Interdependence, the mundane, annoying hum of it, becomes biblical sacrifice. There is no other good in the world—nothing at all in the world—so look at how beautiful care can be.

I went back to give a reading at my undergrad institution. I was on the bill with a former professor, the one who showed me "Hills Like White Elephants" and Carver, out of whose tutelage I emerged with a story about a disaffected bookish young man clumsily losing his virginity at a party (my wheelhouse), but then visiting his Holocaust-survivor grandmother in the nursing home, mercy-smothering her when nobody else had the courage to, and finally slitting his own wrists to lie down next to her and bleed out.

I hadn't realized how prominent a short story writer this professor was then because college students don't understand those things, though he often spoke with what I now recognize as a great deal of pain about a novelist friend who was so famous that even we students had heard of him, and the stupidity of the market generally, Oprah in particular, and once had us practice workshopping by going through a story he had forthcoming in *Harper's* that, if memory serves, was about two boys who crucified another boy for reasons buried too deep in language for me to access.

Luckily, the writer didn't recognize me—I wasn't memorably awful, just forgettable. After we read, we went out to dinner with some other professors, and I was fully cloud-nining it, texting under the table to college friends, like, *Holy shit, look at me now.* Conversation turned to how I should start a family, as I'd achieved the other things these men had in their first acts: book, job, marriage. The writer began to discuss when his children were babies—*Twins*, he said, *can you imagine?* I couldn't, still can't.

He grew animated at the table, describing a moment when he was sitting on the floor comforting one twin who was sick, but then the other was ignored long enough that she got hungry. He had one in the crook of each elbow, trying to reach a bottle into one screaming mouth while holding a pacifier to another. Both slipped off him onto the floor. He stared down at their misery that he was unable to make go away. They screamed so loudly, so endlessly. He left them there and called his father, and then *he* was crying, but he was still watching them as he cried, always an eye on them, the way it would be forever. It was, he said, the most honest he'd ever been with his father. The *helplessness*, he told the table. His father shared his own memories, for the first time, and this was an act of kindness. I'm not selling it right, but it was sort of ecstatic the way he described this moment.

I was awed by the story, and the way he told it, and the fact that it had never occurred to me that it might be a story this man would have to tell. What that means, I think, is partially that, until I was a father, I simply didn't see fatherhood as central to the identity of men I admired. But also, it means that this wasn't a story I could conceive of him writing or teaching if someone else had written it. This man wrote and taught about violence, PTSD, addiction, arson that didn't have a reason but on some molecular tight-lipped trauma level made sense. Vietnam stuff— even if it wasn't directly related to Vietnam, it carried that vibe, another *type* of story so ubiquitous that it creates its own little brain groove for similar narratives to fall into: men broken by the world, hurt boys looking at those broken men and breaking themselves. Characters I wanted to emulate, or at least inhabit in art, because their pain *had to be* interesting—either little boys failed by their fathers or men still too awash in inherited pain to be responsible for anyone.

I didn't remember this until our dinner, but over a break from college, I heard about a reading series on the Lower East Side where the story writer was featured. I made a few friends go with me, stood in the back, and heard him riff on what it was like to teach *kids these days*, or really a certain kind of kid— Northeast, liberal arts, etc. In retrospect, fair: we must have been insufferable. He said he read so many stories that pushed so desperately to find hardship, but we didn't know war or the fallout from it, though we were right in the heart of the Iraq and Afghanistan occupations then, so maybe the argument was there was no draft?

I'm not writing this to settle scores, though at the time I was really hurt and never took another class with the writer or made eye contact with him on our tiny campus. What I'm struck by, looking back, is this creative instinct taught to and by men to reach for a darkness that feels ancient, mythic, something absorbed from an idea of what our fathers or grandfathers endured. Art defined by suffering; suffering defined as something greater than the daily responsibilities of common, comfortable life, and the shame buried underneath about that comfort. A sick twin and a hungry twin, the fear that you cannot feed or placate them, and then what? Most likely nothing dire, just the clock inching forward, more care and your loneliness within it, then the feeble phone call—*Please help.*

In a documentary about her album *Blue*, Joni Mitchell described the desire for her music *to strike against the very nerves* of her life, hoping that the strike would then resonate on the nerves of the listener. I like that this makes what is otherwise an easy-to-dismiss sentiment—*relatability*—a physical sensation. More tonguing a toothache than a treatise on empathy. Forget telling a story or raising the stakes; just a flash of excruciating consciousness. I felt that when this writer spoke—a raw, open nerve of life lived, ongoing, that would never appear in the grim fantasies of his art, where every man is too broken to hold a bottle to a baby's lips.

When I think back now, though, the story told at that dinner full of professional storytellers, all straight cis men with partners and children, still fit fatherhood into the tone of grim fantasy. It was a domestic scene with no markers of common life. No television in the background of the retelling, no stroller or car seat referenced that might provide a portal to an outside world. No wife to share the burden of parenthood or to stand witness, potentially judge. Nothing beyond the babies' most desperate needs and the lone man suffering to provide them, finding some revelation at rock bottom. Extreme care. And isn't that the story I'm so often gravitating toward, as well? The moment when no detail resembles the safety and community of everyday existence.

From the same two-week period of my wife's quarantine that I can't shut up about, this image: Thanksgiving, walking the dog and the kid together. We were waiting on her test results, and I was assuming the worst. Every window of every apartment we passed was lit up, it seemed, with people very much not alone; I could smell a bonfire in a big backyard, hear laughter. My daughter choked on a sniffle and when I wiped her nose acted like that made her choke even more. I stopped to watch a family in a first-floor apartment, post-meal, a grandmother flitting around an ovular living room with a pot of coffee. It felt unreal, or like a memory. I didn't point for her to look because I thought it might remind her that her mother existed and make her sad, and I didn't want to deal with that before bedtime. It started to rain on us, and both dog and kid hated the rain. I put the dog in the bottom of the stroller and huddled my body above them both, feeling the water on my back. I thought of myself then as a literal shelter, a building that leaked but never broke, and that made me feel better than human, not less than. At home, she was shivering. I wrapped her in a big towel and held her to me. I sang into her ear, and we watched the rain streak our windows.

What unsettles me is how fast this story becomes the only language suitable to express my life with her in a way that feels . . . earned? Artful? Worthy of recording? Something lonely and enormous but with an endpoint, satisfaction. With no resemblance to the joy, shame, silliness, interdependence, complexity, *ceaselessness* of real life, even though I did live it.

In Kate Zambreno's stunning novel *Drifts*, she begins with a discussion of Rilke trying to capture the present tense, a day lived and recorded unfiltered, or, as she quotes Sontag saying later, *dynamic contemplation*. Rilke is alone as he attempts this. He's writing about trying to write about existence to his wife, the sculptor Clara Westhoff, who is with their infant daughter, suddenly unable to, as Zambreno puts it, *be the peripatetic artist*. Rilke writes home to her: *One lives so badly because one always comes into the present unfinished, unable, distracted*. The irony is that *unfinished, unable, distracted* is a condition of living heightened to a hysterical and/or unmanageable degree when existence involves caring for an infant, which Rilke has chosen to avoid in his quest to better understand and record the distracted condition of living.

He's full of regret in his letter, not for missing the shared existence with his wife in that moment, but for not fully taking in the existence they'd shared before. There is something so poignantly misguided and also very understandable to me about this: to flee and then, from safety and solitude, mourn the past as the present ticks by and the future demands something new of you. The quest for the unattainable (I think this can refer to both the act of nostalgia and the act of making art) renders you helpless, which, for me anyway, is its own kind of pleasure.

This makes me think back further, to Plutarch's letter to his wife upon the death of their child. In it, he's the official chronicler of pain, but the pain is hers. Or that's not fair, there are different pains—hers is that of burying the child that she cared for in every moment of its truncated life; his is that of absence, the inability to access the lived experience of the love until it was too late. The saddest part of the letter is that, by the time he's writing it, he's pretty sure the funeral has already happened, and that when the letter reaches his wife, he may have already returned to her. Imagine that scene—Plutarch there watching his wife read the letter that was supposed to be a comfort or some attempt at solidarity in a moment already long past. An exercise in complete futility or the instructions for his wife's grief that she'll never read, so really the instructions for his own.

Only, my dear wife, in your emotion keep me as well as yourself within bounds. This is his only reference to his own grief, smuggled into a warning to his wife that she cannot become submerged by it.

There are two ways to read the letter, or at least two ways it's been discussed in every classroom I've ever heard it discussed—he's heartless or he's tragic. It depends on whether or not you take him at his word. Has the text survived as a brutal historical testament to the commonness of infant death in ancient Greek society? Or is it an early example of correspondence as an attempt to work through something, an essay about grief, even if it doesn't have the language to say it yet, something raw and profound leaking out in the subtext? I went to a reading once where a translator performed a version of it that aimed to mimic the feeling he assumed was embedded in language that was unavoidably formal. I was surprised that by the end I was weeping. Why? Why was it that easy, that affecting, and also weirdly kind of a relief to imagine softness in a text that didn't provide it? Why is the possibility of care so seductive when it comes from a source that doesn't know how to, or maybe doesn't want to, express it?

I've got another little visual aid, this time for the polarity of emotional register present in the vast majority of fatherhood portrayals:

Boredom/Apathy/Repression   Hugely intense feeling of any kind

I loved Max Porter's slim, staccato novel, *Grief Is the Thing with Feathers*. I read it on the heels of Hanya Yanigihara's *A Little Life*, which I also liked, but its sprawling maximalism of pain made the concision with which Porter did pain even more appealing. They were opposite books, at least in form, but they played the same note at their cores—establish the worst possible thing, tip the emotional register until it's spilling, then have at it. In Porter's novel, a young father, known only as *Dad*, faces life after the sudden death of his wife. Obviously I'm not doing it justice here, but a giant bird-metaphor-thing arrives and helps him move from numbness to grief to something resembling hope.

The father's perspective in the novel is introduced like this:

> *I drank. I smoked roll-ups out the window. I felt that perhaps the main result of her being gone would be that I would permanently become this organizer, this list-making trader in clichés of gratitude, machine-like architect of routine for small children with no Mum. Grief felt fourth-dimensional, abstract, faintly familiar. I was cold.*

It's all the sitcom clichés but with no *Laugh* sign, filtered through the beginning of a hero's journey. We're set up not just for the triumph of his emotional recovery but also his birth into a life of . . . participation? Parenting in a way that previously seemed both annoying and like his wife's job? The implication, as I reread the novel now, is that the fullness of his life with his children, and his own emotional access to it, could only be born after his wife was dead.

At the end of the book, spreading the mother's ashes, the father is loud, finally full of feeling, and that's the point. Into the wind on a beach, he and his sons scream, *I LOVE YOU I LOVE YOU I LOVE YOU!*

We've been watching a lot of *Coco* (amazing! I could literally watch it every day and find something new to appreciate!), and now when I think about this climactic scene from the novel, I'm mostly imagining a cartoon skeleton and a cartoon live boy who he's learned to love howling up from a sinkhole: *I'M PROUD TO BE HIS FAMILY!* And then I'm thinking about *Garden State*, which I watched not as a dad but as an angsty teen, when sad, numb Zach Braff is also standing in the middle of a giant hole, next to Natalie Portman, whose manic-pixie-dream-girlness has saved him from himself, screaming—this time, no words; the volume alone is catharsis!

We're back to that feeling I have so often now that every emotion stirred by a text is a stick poking an already existing sensation of that emotion being poked so many times, reaggravating what hasn't yet healed. That docile pleasure of familiarity—there it is again, and it still works. The final gesture in the story arc that takes us from numb, from nothing, to an explosion of

feeling, and finally, only then, presence. He—whoever the he is—
has emerged triumphant into full personhood. I'm being unfair.
What I mean is that it I find it hard to separate depictions of
fatherhood from those of boyhood or young manhood. Everything is a coming-of-age story, the saga of accepting presence
in a world of people, responsibility to some of them—the basic
human contract made myth. I distrust these stories; they're the
ones that move me most, that's why. I return to them—briefly
placated, weirdly envious, squinting so I might see myself, still
unmade.

I have often found fatherhood to be lonely, but it's hard to parse
how much of that is a choice. Any invitation for connection,
any reminder that there are those embodying a role identical to
mine, makes me recede back into myself. I was sitting outside
at a street fair with my daughter strapped to my chest—she was
young enough that I was worried she might slip out; I remember
that. We were at a folding table next to a food truck with people
who were supposed to become our core group of friends because
we all had babies and almost nothing else in common. There
was steady chatter, but I didn't know what to contribute, so I
just listened and nodded. Or I may have been talking constantly,
straining to latch on to each anecdote shared by anyone else with
one of my own, while refusing to let myself acknowledge that as
it happened—I really don't know. Like so much from that time,
I remember the shell of circumstance, fill it in with what I'd like
to be true.

Either way, this guy was talking about starting a group called
Rad Dads for those of us at home with the babies while our wives

returned to work so that we might find solidarity on this grand new adventure. I was like, *Oh yeah, cool, for sure*, but never got the guy's number and only ever saw him again at baby brunches or first birthdays. For years now, when I'm around other adults and a little drunk, I might tell the Rad Dad anecdote for laughs, which usually works and always leaves me feeling like a bully. Rhyming aside, it was a nice idea. One that would have been often awkward, sometimes its own burden, but still: nice. Community, intimacy, through all the small, repeated actions of each day, a mutual witnessing that might diffuse the weight of it all, but also dull the satisfaction of carrying that weight because, look, it's nothing special.

The last times I saw Rad Dad's face came during a pandemic stretch when a bunch of parents started doing a weekly Zoom trivia as an homage to bar trivia in the *before times*. He was silent, lurking in the back of the image as his wife gave smiles effortful enough for both of them. Sometimes she'd ask him to chime in, and he'd shrug or audibly scoff; she'd frantically fill the silence with more cheer, the skin on her face tight. Again, I'm being unfair. I don't know their lives, and we were all a bit strained on those nights. a bunch of cooped-up toddler parents already dreading the next day's hangover. But there *was* a distinctly malignant shadow to how he seemed to feel that was discussed in side chats, with the particular satisfaction that occurs when someone who'd been relentlessly jazzed for the concept of parenthood, or the joy of this pure, newborn clay made in their image, then so quickly resents the practice of caring for an actual human with opinions. I wanted to reach out to him, but I didn't. Of course. He seemed so pained and also so silly—easier to focus on the latter.

He was the kind of guy who'd spoken of fatherhood as a clean break in his life, the opposite of any disappointment that had led up to it, the chance to transcend into an identity that felt worthy of him and he it—he would take his baby into the woods, he would hold his baby to his chest, as his father never had, he would serve this greater purpose, this blood purpose, finally. Another famous line from *The Road*: *He knew only that the child was his warrant*—that sort of vibe. If life can be a protracted, excruciating act of becoming, fatherhood glistens as a place to reach, then rejoice. And I did relate to this, watching Rad Dad's detachment on these Zooms, his unwillingness to participate in the download of medium-cute life updates. The sense that there must be something more. I hardly ever feel that way anymore, which amazes me, which I love, but that desire for some future transcendence, for the *real* story to begin, like I'm still tragically, blissfully unmade—it's so silly to acknowledge, but it's always just under the surface.

The meanest thing I ever said to my daughter came right after she got her first vaccine shot. I'd pulled her from school early. We waited together for the nurse to call us in; I told her that her body was going to be so strong, even stronger than it already was, and she liked that. She made a muscle, and I tried to get a good picture. As they swabbed her and prepared the needle, it all felt like less than I thought it would. Had I been expecting balloons and unanimous tears? Maybe. *Something*, anyway, to reflect the magnitude of what had been, what was ongoing. When the needle went in, my daughter just watched it, she didn't cry. I said, *My big, brave girl.* When it was over, I hugged her on the toilet so she didn't fall in while she peed. She smelled so much like herself.

I could feel her shoulder blades, the space between them the span of my fingertips. I took a deep breath, and she asked me in the sweetest voice if I was okay.

We had time to kill. She was feeling fine, and she said she'd go on a little nature walk with me to this spot overlooking the river, where we've taken her since she was a tiny baby, strapped to my chest, her drool hot on my shirt. It's the place where I've most indulged in the fantasy of fatherhood while also living it. When we got there, though, something switched in her. She whined and stamped. She wanted to go home and watch something. She said she didn't want to be with me; she didn't want to tell me why. She started to scream, *No!* before I could finish any sentence. I sat on a rock and asked her to sit next to me, and of course she refused. She was tired, bored, wanted to go home. Was Mamma off work yet? Why wasn't she with Mamma? Why wasn't she watching a movie? Why didn't I have cookies? Why was I talking to her? I heard my voice spit out, *Shut up! Think of everything I do for you! I could be doing what I want to do, but I'm here doing this, and you don't even fucking deserve it.*

I was aware enough of what I said that I looked around right away to make sure we were alone, so much of fatherhood in public is being constantly observed with only generous eyes, but also the anxiety of how fast that can change and what it would feel like to know that any contempt received has been earned. I spend most of my days saying kind things to her, not out of responsibility but because her presence has made the awareness and expression of joy, of care, of contentedness, natural in my life, which I'm so grateful for—the opportunity to say, *I love you I love you I love you*, like it's breathing. But right then, it seemed like those words disappeared. I turned everything that felt so easily true into a lie, as though this grotesque version bubbling up was the real me, or that's what she'd think.

I did a turn in tone without even pausing, like if I landed on a singsongy *All I'm saying is that if we agree to something, it's fair to follow through,* she might not notice the hardness of my eyes, the ridiculous, low, villain timbre that was just seconds before present in my voice, my menace. It was a mirror of the moments when she moves from her own rage into instant, performed contrition; she has, of course, learned this from me—how to tamp yourself down, how to reach for, or at least feign, control, because the alternative feels worse. She sees me as well as I see her. From a distance, I am so grateful for that: she sees me, she knows me, she is always looking. She cried and pushed at me, but I hugged her and apologized until I heard my voice crack. I offered her a snack as a truce. We sat next to each other, each pouty, each still afraid of me, and the only sound was the crunch of apples. I pointed to a squirrel, and our eyes followed it together up a tree. It was heavy summer heat, the grass hard and dry, the air quivering like a puddle. From a distance, we must have looked like the most beautiful thing.

I read an essay recently by Janet Manley on the literature of fatherhood. Really, it's about the blank spaces in the literature of fatherhood that are so richly occupied in the literature of motherhood. She identifies a moment of good dad writing that *hits on what I understand as the key themes of writing about motherhood: the figurative death that takes place, the invisible work of care, the confrontation of your own shadow in your child's personality, the knowledge that you aren't writing the story in the end.*

What I see as the tension in thinking about, let alone express-ing, fatherhood, is the way it sometimes seems like an inverse of these expectations. While the motherhood literature Manley references explicitly fights against assumed invisibility, figura-tive death, a body broken open and then cannibalized, claiming visibility, claiming life, for fathers it's sometimes the desire to feel pulled under, the desire for the completeness of a death, if only for the promise of rebirth and therefore absolution. The bind comes when you want so badly to be seen for your invisibility, you want total control over the process of your lack of control. *I'm drowning! I'm on fire! Hello?*

The result is survivalism of the most disappointing kind—caring turned into an apocalypse, every apocalypse just a meta-phor. Another polarity of emotion, never filled in with the or-ganic growth born from steady, ceaseless experience, which is another way to say *life*:

Suffering   Catharsis

There was a long period of time during which my wife and I tried and failed to get pregnant. Not as long as it felt, but still long enough emotionally that it lives in my memory as a dis-tinct era: college years, Brooklyn, graduate school, disposable income but still young, infertility. Long enough, as well, to cre-ate a sense of the act of simply becoming a parent as this grand mountain to climb—we were exhausted on our journey before ever reaching the path we hoped to follow. For many years, our lives had seemed, if not exactly brimming with purpose, pur-poseful enough, but suddenly they were small. Suitable only as the *before* to a life story.

I was going to the movies a lot, sometimes with my wife but often alone. I always did this, pre-kid—in any periods of unrest (or in some cases literal panic attack onset), I'd flee to the darkness, with the single glowing image, and also, I suppose, the nostalgia of sitting in a movie theater, which as a setting and corresponding way of being recalls every other time I've sat at the movies, feeling vividly myself, a continuity that grounds me. This was early Trump era, when every white liberal was either forced or allowed (depending on how you want to look at it) to see themselves in a world that felt dystopian, pitted against forces that you could call *evil* with a straight face, and you could think about all your little life decisions in the context of survival.

I don't remember how closely together I watched them, but first I watched Viggo Mortensen in *Captain Fantastic* and then Ben Foster in *Leave No Trace*. Each movie centers on a father who is broken but brilliant, whose narcissism is entirely wrapped up in the totality and depth of his care for his child or children, who has created a world outside the normal one into which no other person can enter. He's actively endangering his kids, but also he alone is protecting them. Each movie, of course, removes a mother from the very beginning of the plot, lost to tragedy, not conflict. The fathers mourn as they protect as they care; the three actions are inseparable. They suffer, so they feel love; everything else is gone, which is convenient in narratives about stubborn, egomaniacal white men. In these worlds, there's no complicating grotesquerie of their racial privilege, for instance—the cartoonish whiteness of their particular convictions doesn't bump up against anyone nonwhite, because they're either in middle of nowhere, Alaska, or Portland.

I don't think it's an accident that the most compelling, or at least well-received, portrayals of contemporary white people across forms embody worlds in which we aren't asked to think much about whiteness—like how Sally Rooney appeals to white American audiences in part because her Dublin reminds them of Brooklyn, except the sadness and ambition of these young white people never has to contend with the displacement of communities of color all around their fantasies. It's the same creative instinct fueling the marooned father genre—providing license to feel fully for a character who, when surrounded by other characters, is probably more perpetrator than victim.

When I watched these movies, I was growing more certain of my desire for a child and also probing the depths of my ambivalence about the whole concept of bringing a theoretical child into this world. I know this is not at all unique. The personal and the political circle and nip at one another; the baby is the most personal thing, then immediately a reflection of what you believe or wish you did or want them to. What was most striking about these movies, back to back, was the clarity of the father's vision and the belief of the children in the vision. The fathers are allowed to be both wrong and heroic, harming their children but maybe less so than the society they shield them from. In both movies, the children break away in the end but do so making sure the father knows he wasn't *bad*, that they appreciate him. They realize he couldn't bear having his feelings hurt.

After my daughter's birth, there were no movie theaters, and also nothing solitary or nostalgic—everything was uncharted experience, crowded with new life. The TV hummed in the background. A big sleep-training show for my wife and me was *Naked and Afraid*. Against the sounds of our daughter's wails, we'd sit with the visuals of absolute desolation: two humans curled like dying bugs under the shade of a lone tree or around the warmth of their feeble fire as thunder boomed above the tundra. The show had—and this was a nice thing—way less action then we'd expected. Mostly, the people just starved, scratched at bug bites, shivered, opened their mouths when it rained.

Often, it played out as a drama (or even broad comedy) about gender—a man frantic in his self-appointed destiny of keeping them both alive; a woman rolling her eyes. The producers were clearly aware of this dynamic and stoked it, pairing a vegan Earth-mother type with a Mormon bow hunter, etc. So much recognizable bickering, but also they could die. They suffered by choice, unwilling to acknowledge the choice, only the suffering. Many had a family at home, and they spoke of this survival challenge as a part of their role as caretakers. They were marooned naked with a stranger and a television crew to provide an example for their children, or to show themselves and the world that they *could* do this. If everything crumbled, they would keep their loved ones safe. The only way to explore the full extent of their care for their families was to leave and risk their lives for good TV.

We were watching some episode, and a newly gaunt middle-aged man sat on a rock with a blurry rectangle over his genitals. He said, in a voice that suggested the onset of delirium, *I want my kids to see me and know they can do anything.* I remember being very moved as I watched; I was like, *Wow, what if these were his last words,* before the shot of a medical helicopter extracting him too late, thinking of his children so far away, trying to survive for them? I was in sweatpants, exchanging vicious whispers with my wife about whether our infant deserved comfort, bemoaning her inability to just fucking fall asleep.

These weren't the man's last words. If I remember correctly, he and his partner won, shared a chaste hug, took home twenty-five thousand dollars each to—I don't know—retile a bathroom? The show leaves no time for a where-are-they-now, because how depressing would that be? How small? Sometimes when we watched, I'd imagine these men eagerly answering the door for the camera crew, their children safe, noisy, and ungrateful in the living room behind them, missing the jungle or the desert, still survivors in their own minds.

Finally, silence from my daughter's room. My wife and I exhaled, let our bodies settle, touched each other again. We had a last quick bout of disagreement over whether it was worth it to flip her pillow over as she slept, since we knew the one side was drenched in snot and tears, but we didn't have the energy to sustain it. My wife made a little half joke, and I responded with a little half laugh. We gave each other necessary reassurances that we didn't fully believe—*It's getting a little easier, right?*

We had her fourth birthday party at a local pizza place with a tatted-up, gauge-earring waitstaff and a bunch of vintage pinball machines—hipster Chuck E. Cheese. In the weeks leading up to it, she seemed both shockingly old and shockingly young to me, sometimes within the same ten-minute span. The nonlinear quality of how her body and mind and personality progress is always jarring, even if I've known it to be true for so long. She is exactly herself, then she seems to be fighting something, unsure, unsatisfied, so quick to panic, and then one morning, I realize she's evolved, all of a sudden, even as I watched her, thinking that nothing was changing. This is intoxicating but also terrifying. Then another few weeks pass, and I can't remember how she used to be.

My parents came up for her birthday, and she did what she

always does with my mother now, which is nestle against her and let her read books until her voice is shot. My wife and I still have this ingrained worry that even when my parents are around, our daughter will look for us, like we can't not be *on* or that would bait disaster. But she's at ease without us; she's at ease in so many places. I like watching her when she isn't thinking to look at me, moving confidently through her expanding world. When she does look up, she seems surprised to see me there, where I've always been.

But a few weeks earlier, her teacher had mentioned prolonged bouts of sadness, how sometimes she couldn't express herself when she needed to, how she could be so fragile. She said it casually, like of course we knew, but that was the opposite of how we'd been experiencing our daughter lately; it felt like a report on a former kid. So now there was this new anxiety to stoke, a nagging sensation of not trusting ourselves or the version of our daughter that we saw.

My wife kept wondering if she was *too* comfortable with us, too attuned to the equilibrium of our house, or if we hovered too much, always ready to help put her boot on *before* she got frustrated. We asked each other if we were hoverers, like if we saw ourselves at the park, would we say, *Damn, look at those hoverers?* We didn't know.

I shut down for a few days, my own regression. Like I'd been promised some triumphant emergence out of toddlerhood, a particular mountain of intensity and worry summitted, and now that fantasy was gone, so I'd been betrayed and deserved to sulk about it. My wife asked me what was up enough times for me to finally spit out that I was dreading the birthday party that we'd been planning for months. She raised an eyebrow and said,

Dreading? She was right—the word was just a showy stand-in for the truth: I was afraid that this day that should make her feel so good, so proud, would career into something out of control where she was crying, how children often cry at parties, and all these faces would be closing in on her, saying, *What's wrong?* she should be happy, and maybe some older kid would laugh at her, and in that moment, all I would want to do is snatch her and flee and hold her outside in the cold until she stopped fighting it, and tell her she was loved, which would feel good for me but rob her of this messy, wild party with her little school friends who she screamed at and received black eyes from and wept over and returned to each morning with the brightest face, arms reaching for a hug she'd been planning since she woke up.

Sometimes, I can't think of anything more daunting than the mundane enormous terror of watching a child grow. The alternating jolts of happiness and pain, the pressure, the looming specter of a pizza restaurant filled with screaming, often mean, children and their stranger parents and my daughter, who I think I know until those moments when she's a mystery, newly distorted, before she snaps back into focus as herself.

On her birthday morning, we all took the dog for a walk. She helped me hold the leash and reminded me what I usually remind her: that we go at the dog's pace, let her sniff. She looked up at me, one eye squinting against the sun. She said, *I'm helping you!* I said, *We're doing it together!* She said, *I love you, too—* she's been doing this lately, suddenly filled with the urge to express her love, but still conditioning it with *too*, since she learned the phrase by us saying it until she finally responded. She went around our little group: she loved me, she loved her mother, she loved her grandmother, her grandfather, the dog.

Her party was chaos but good. The parents seemed grateful to be at a place with booze; we talked about the funny ways our children said each other's names. At a certain point, my daughter and her friends started chasing each other between tables, shrieking, at a peak of happiness but right on the precipice of melting down. I kept waiting for it, but they didn't. We went home, leftover balloons crammed into every available inch of my Prius. We let her watch *Frozen* alone, though not for long, because she could barely keep her eyes open. In the kitchen, my wife and I told each other that we'd done great, that she was a happy person with a good life.

During bath time, my wife and parents crowded around her. I walked down the hallway to our bedroom, unnoticed. It felt like I hadn't been alone in a long time. It's so easy to think of parenthood as a type of loneliness, and then in flashes, I realize all over again that I've never been less alone. I looked at pictures of my daughter from just a few hours earlier—a blur in her unicorn crown, huddled over a pinball machine glow with her friend, blowing out candles with only a little bit of her mother's help. Already, it felt like a fantasy. Already, I missed that moment we'd lived together. Already, the nagging fear of what might happen the next day, the disappointment of regular life, or at parent-teacher conferences the following week, and would it make this moment seem small? It was nice, too, though, to sit in the dark with my phone for a while.

I heard her voice calling down the hallway: she was looking for me.

Summer Diary; or: After Andy Warhol

Anything can be thrilling. I was at a house in Vermont with friends—thrilling! I used to think, What if someday, I became a person who went to a house in Vermont with friends? Coordinating calendars, catching up. And now I am that person! And my kid was there with my friends in this house in Vermont—thrilling! Tiring but also thrilling. My friend made a big batch of bacon, my kid ate the bacon, along with everyone else; out a window, we could see bales of hay. All my friends looked older than I remembered—not in a bad way; hot old—which means that I am also older than I remember myself to be. We went to a distillery, where my kid was . . . rambunctious. The sun was getting low in the sky; she was sprinting across the grass toward the parking lot because she'd peed on herself, and I was sprinting to catch her. When I caught her and carried her to the bathroom, I felt very visible and strong. There were my friends, and, wow, we'd been friends a long time, and they were eating flatbreads, drinking Negronis, and they were watching me, and maybe they were thinking about how miraculous friendship is the way I was, or maybe not. All these years, and I still don't feel comfortable asking something like that. I know it's kind of silly when absurdly young people do the whole last-night-was-a-movie thing on social media, but to be honest I am thinking a version of that thought all the time. That's the whole point of movies: a frame of reference. A long time ago, I did mushrooms in a park in Amsterdam with a lot of friends—someone puked, I saw a bulldog in a bike basket, etc., etc. It felt like a movie, of course! When we went back to the hostel, we invented a game where you play Guess Who, but the questions you ask are huge emotional and philosophical ones—does this person say they believe in God? Do they mean it? I remember, in that moment, thinking I was in a movie and also thinking, Wow, I've become the kind of person taking mushrooms in a park in Amsterdam with friends. Thrilling! When we came back from Vermont, I watched *The Andy Warhol Diaries*, which I thought was really beautiful, though that might have something to do with the fact that Warhol himself in his diaries called so many things beautiful. What a little sap! I guess that was always a critique of Warhol, but *The Diaries* made me think about sappy not as something surfacy but something deep and ingrained, a way of seeing. There's a scene where an AI Warhol narrator (not as bad as you'd think!) reads his diary entries about a Thanks-giving with friends in some country place that I don't think was Vermont but could have been. Warhol's partner was there and these friends, and they did all the things you do on Thanksgiving, ate all the things you eat. In the diaries, he writes about how happy he was; he notes how late it was in each of these moments, the exact time—when they finally left the table, when they played charades, when his partner got sleepy first, when Warhol himself trudged to bed at the end of the night. I don't know enough about Warhol to bring my own perspective in to mingle, maybe fight, with that of the documentary, but I was entirely taken by a cura-tor named Jessica Beck and the way she spoke about Warhol. It was a scholarship of tenderness—by this I don't mean *fawning*, I just mean *tender*. She was open to his best intentions; she as-sumed he really meant it, meant something, all the time. What a shift, to think about art or fame or genius or even companionship through that frame. In his own words, every time Warhol dropped a famous name, he seemed to me to be excited to be there, excited to know them, sad that the night had to end. He never seemed unimpressed. That's something I've been trying to embrace, though I haven't put language to it until right now. If I'm honest with myself, everything impresses me, I'm a sucker for everything. I don't think I come off that way, which makes me sad; I've got like fifteen years of coming off unimpressed that I'm working against. I want to say, That wasn't the real me! I was just very, very insecure! I still don't feel comfortable saying something like that. In Vermont, my friends talked about their lives and I thought, Wow! And I didn't think about my own life and disappointments in comparison to theirs, I just thought, Wow! That's a big deal for me! In a few days, I probably won't feel that way, but I did in the moment and I still do now. My friend and his girlfriend took pictures of my kid eating that special maple syrup ice cream they have in Vermont. I thought, I'm going to remember this. At the next table, hippie homesteader grand-parents sat next to more buttoned-up parents and then finally a kid in the middle, enjoying her ice cream, but on some level, I'm sure, deciding which type of person was a better thing to be. It was all thrilling! To be a life alongside those lives, as my kid wiped her ice cream face on my T-shirt and watched—I feel like that sounds stupid, but I do mean it. A thing about Warhol that's really poignant to me is how little he wanted to be alone. He wrote the diaries by calling his friend, a writer, and talking to her about what he did and what he felt, and trusting her to do the transcription. There's plenty of speculation in the documentary about how calculated, maybe even fabricated, his stories to her were, and also how visible her hand was in the final version published after his death—this is the least interesting part, by far. I'm just in love with the idea of a diary, theoretically the most private thing, turned into a way to feel less alone. It's brilliant, both as an emotional conceit and an artistic one. Me and my wife and my kid were in LA recently, and we saw a friend who'd been among those we did mushrooms with in the park in Amsterdam when it felt like a movie. I hadn't seen him in nine years. We had an Airbnb in Venice, and he came over, met our kid, told her he'd known her parents so long ago, and she grinned shyly, hugged my leg, and then we all hung out in this little yard that was full of hummingbirds. I watched her take in this new, old version of her parents, face pinched in concentration. We spoke a lot about how it didn't feel awkward to be together after all this time; we didn't have that many shared experiences to run through, we mostly had this shared sense that, somehow, even though perhaps we shouldn't, we cared for one another and thought about one another often. He confessed that when he was walking up to the door of the Airbnb, he'd been so anxious, which was exactly how I'd felt going to answer the door, and how my wife had felt in the bathroom washing her face. This made me want to cry, in a good way. He's an actor, which is what he'd been training to be all those years ago. He said it hadn't worked out for him yet, but honestly, it never stopped seeming like it might soon. I found this enormously inspirational; it made me grateful to know people who are artists. We felt so close after all these years, but I still wasn't comfortable enough to say something like that out loud. I recently read the latest Sally Rooney novel and said it sucked for the whole first half of the book, but I loved it so much by the end. This has been a recurring pattern lately in the books I've loved, or the art of any kind I've loved. Like I'm mid eye roll when suddenly I snap into focus, and it turns out that everything is profound. This is partially a *me* thing, of course, but I also think it's built into the form with an artist like Rooney—everything she makes is *very* close to being embarrassing, like Warhol. The thoughts and feelings expressed in her novels occupy this space right next to profundity, sometimes grazing it, but that proximity often only makes it seem sillier. Maybe that's the wrong word— *naked* is what I mean. I find her novels, particularly the latest, to be deeply uncool, though they are about cool and stylish people, and those who critique them often critique them with this weaponized idea of *cool*, which implies surface over substance, narcissism over curiosity. The main stylistic feature of the new one, *Beautiful World, Where Are You?*, is this long email correspondence between two friends, and when I read it, each time an email came, I was like, Oh, how thrilling! To get an email like that from somebody, the implication built into the overwrought tone of official correspondence that the writer is imagining you reading it, not just a friend but an audience whose approval means something. The language is clunky and effortful and tender; you can imagine these characters years later looking back through their Gmail and being like, Woof. There's a moment in *The Warhol Diaries* when these old documents are discovered in the attic of the mother of a lover of Warhol's, a longtime companion— vacation photographs, sun-drenched and haphazard, a dashed-off original Basquiat. And little poems sent back and forth between Warhol and this lover, which are not very good but make your breath catch. I've been too embarrassed to write much poetry. The first poem I ever wrote was for my wife when we were just babies, and it was terrible, and I meant every word of it. I wrote another one right after my kid was born, and it was terrible, and I meant every word of it. Earlier in my career, I tried to keep up correspondences; it was a thing I enjoyed and had the time for and—if I'm honest—felt like a confirmation of being a writer, as much as anything else. Imagine being the kind of person who *corresponds*. Thrilling! Like a version of hanging out, but only the non-awkward, just-drunk-enough moments. Now I'm a parent, so I don't do that anymore. That's a bullshit excuse but also true. I know the thing to say about being a parent is that you miss the moments alone, the quiet concentration, the intimacy of you and your own mind, but I don't miss that at all. I miss other people's voices, people I wouldn't say I love but who I love, the hum of inanity that, in memory, is allowed to turn into what it was all along: significant. I am old enough now to have a lot of people who meant something to me—past tense like that. Or they still do, but now the meaning is about absence. When I was with my friends and my kid in Vermont, another set of friends, from another time, was at a wedding that I wasn't invited to. There were pictures; everyone looked great. With one friend, I was like, Wow, *that's* what his hair looks like grown out? Good, just different than I would have thought. It made his whole face seem less . . . severe, and I missed him. When we were younger, we played croquet a lot; we talked about what we were reading. Over the years, when we've seen each other, we've had these conversations that almost feel saved up for one another, like maybe we were trying to impress each other, or at least I was, but also we were being honest. He held my kid when she was just a baby and I his, and we haven't seen each other since. I didn't feel envy looking at the wedding pictures or that I should have been invited, only that I wished I was there, which isn't fair, because I was with these other friends, thrilled to be *there*, but you really are always missing something, which is not exactly a revelation. Still, doesn't it hurt? Not in a bad way, more in a way that makes you amazed that there's enough fun in your world—and enough tenderness, too—that life can't hold it all, but still, doesn't it hurt? This was another thing that was so striking in *The Warhol Diaries*: because they were dictated, so many of the entries end in questions, and as audience, it can feel as though he's reaching out for confirmation, memory made instantly fallible. Afraid to stand on his own in that dark room of certainty. He's asking, Wasn't it beautiful then? Or Wasn't that amazing? A friend told me recently that there's a person in her life who she's known forever but is now probably her best friend, and it's because they use this app Marco Polo, which lets you have conversations through lengthy video updates about your life, back and forth, at whatever pace you desire. Just another way, I suppose, to mimic correspondence, which means mimicking the feeling of being very close to someone and missing them at the same time. I'm not shitting on it; it sounds fantastic. I think it's also a way to mimic documentary, a conversation made up of never-before-seen footage, the way we've been conditioned to watch something like that and let it feel like an elegy. A little archive of care stored up, like letters in an attic, or the closest you can come to it. You get to tell a friend a story, and also you get to hear yourself tell it—both of those actions and sensations can be equally thrilling. But there is risk to it, or that's what it seems like to me. Something naked and raw. I don't know if I could bring myself to ask someone to exchange these messages with me. That's asking if they might care about my life to the degree that I care about theirs. When I was in Vermont, I was driving to a lake with my friend and his girlfriend and my kid, who had passed out, her face still and soft, her breath just audible—the best way to be sure your friends think your kid is cute is if they're asleep. She was breathing, and we were speaking quietly; they were asking about my life, how it had been. It was overwhelming. I felt like I was saying too much suddenly, talking too fast, like when you let yourself get too hungry before a nice dinner and then the food comes. Then I asked about them, and they told me. I listened, and we climbed this road up a mountain until we saw the sun glancing across the valley below, and we all said it was beautiful, because it was. My daughter woke up as the light shimmered across her face. I read an essay recently by the novelist Alexandra Kleeman, which I both liked and disagreed with. She writes about the death of autofiction, a genre that was never well defined anyway, and whose most popular practitioners swore they weren't actually doing it. She talks about the COVID contraction of our worlds and how suddenly *every* (educated white-collar) person was reduced to a lonely, overthinking vessel in front of a computer screen. The bloom is off that rose now. Kleeman refers to this phenomenon, and how it happened for her, like this: *A sort of pixilation of the self.* This is exactly right—to see your little living room, your little flavored seltzer can, your little tilted screen prints, blending into the grid as everyone studies their own face on mute. It's impossible to feel remarkable in this world or that you are sitting on some insight that doesn't occur to the other shapes in their boxes, so the idea of the writer's mind as some special place is revealed to be bullshit. What Kleeman's interpretation hinges upon, though, is the belief that, before the smallness of our lives became so universally visualized, the power of these books came from the agreement that the writer was more aware of the world than everyone else, some isolated genius for

the reader to soak up. It never occurred to me that we were supposed to read the books this way. Kleeman mentions Rachel
Cusk's novels, which I read in fits and starts on that LA trip,
whenever we gave my daughter a little iPad time, and it seemed
to me like she just really enjoyed other people talking shit far
more than her own thoughts. Which I do, too; it's so fun! I hate
my hairdresser's ex, who I've never met, and his vaccine hesi-
tancy, and the way he was *work work work* with her, but now he's
mister stay-at-home dad with a little sports memorabilia business out of the garage for someone else. Fuck you, Brian! I really
mean it! What a thrill! To really mean that about this guy I've
never met, in defense of this person who I've seen every three to
four months for the better part of a decade, and once, I saw her
at a concert and it was so crazy, like seeing a celebrity. Sometimes, after a haircut, I'll tell my wife an update about these
people she doesn't know the same way she's gotten really into
hand-poked tattoos from this artist I've never met, but after a
tattoo, she'll tell me about how the artist is getting married soon
and the way she loves her dog and how it seems like she genuinely
thinks my wife is funny, and I'll say, Because you *are*. What I
mean is, Rachel Cusk wrote three novels in a row about being a
writer, and her narrator is never writing, because writing is boring and lonely, and it seems obvious that she doesn't like to be
alone. Me neither! Sometimes, when I'm out at the park with my
kid and there's all these other people there doing the same thing,
it's thrilling! Like, Look at all of us! In *The Warhol Diaries*, another curator, Donna De Salvo, says of Warhol's work, *You become an American by participating . . . he was so ahead of his
time to understand that.* There were times watching it that I for-
got he was an artist, to be honest, and certainly times where it

seemed that he did. But that assessment resonated—nothing commentary; participation only. The churning of experience, trapped inside one's self but eyes wide open. My father turned eighty. He said that's the decade when you get a call about someone dying and you can't be surprised. He'd always described himself—if not exactly proudly, at least unashamedly—as a man without friends, a man who could forget about other people for large swaths of time. But there was a party for his birthday; friends were there, they were toasting him and telling stories of versions of him, saying, Do you remember? Can you believe it? Listening, he looked small and bashful like a child who knew he'd done good. It broke my heart in a happy way. I was at a different birthday party this summer, and I tried ketamine for the first time out of one of those little necklaces with a hidden coke spoon that a stranger had around his neck. I was with friends, and it felt like we were older than everyone there, but it was kind of thrilling to try a drug for the first time as the old guy in the room—still got it, you know? House music was playing, which I love but never tell anyone I love, but I felt good enough to tell everyone then. We danced. A giant moth landed on my shirt, and people yelled like it meant something, like I was a kid in Amsterdam. I did more and danced more; I got to scroll through pictures of my kid on my phone and hear people I didn't know say she was beautiful. I was right on the edge of being embarrassed, but I felt grateful instead.

Acknowledgments

Some of these essays first appeared in other publications: "An Essay about Tiny, Spectacular Futures Written a Week or So after a Very Damning IPCC Climate Report," in *Literary Hub*; "An Approximate Hourly Record of Thoughts and Feelings during a Time of Intense Sleep Deprivation," in *Barrelhouse*; "An Essay about Watching Brad Pitt Eat That Is Really About My Own Shit," in *Hobart*; and "At the Playground," in the *Rumpus*. My enormous thanks to the editors who saw something in these essays and provided their guidance and support: Jonny Diamond, Tom McAllister, Aaron Burch, Robbie Maakestad, and Darcy Gagnon.

I'm also grateful to two editors who published parenting-related essays of mine that didn't end up in the collection but helped me hone my voice on the subject and emboldened me to keep going with it: Rebecca Onion at *Slate* and Medaya Ocher at the *Los Angeles Review of Books*.

To my agent, Victoria Marini, who's been a trusted reader, advocate, and friend since we were both babies: thank you for believing in this project, talking me through it, and sticking with me no matter what. I feel so lucky to have only ever worked with someone I like.

Thanks to Jim McCoy and the University of Iowa Press for seeing the potential in this book and treating it with such thoughtfulness and care. Thanks to Allison Means and Raj Tawney for your tireless publicity work.

Thanks to Molly McCully Brown, who read many of these essays and lent her time and brilliant mind to thinking about what they were trying to say and where they might find a home.

My immeasurable gratitude to the educators and staff at both Love 4 All Learning Center and the Dr. Pat Feinstein Child Development Center, without whom this book would certainly never have been written. Thank you for taking such good care of my kid during a literal pandemic. What a gift.

For a decade now, the University of Massachusetts Dartmouth has been my professional home. I couldn't imagine being a writer without being a teacher. I'm grateful to my students for sharing their lives and ideas with me, inspiring me to bring even a fraction of their courage to my own work, and always making me try to articulate, over and over, why this stuff matters. I am also grateful to be a member of a union and the protections that provides, including a contractually guaranteed sabbatical that allowed me to finish this book.

Thanks to my parents, Stu Waldman and Livvie Mann, and my brother, Peter Waldman, all of whom I love a lot.

And to Ottavia De Luca: I'm sorry I keep writing about our shared life. Honestly, I just don't have much of an imagination, and I like to think about our life because it makes me happy, but not in a way that I find boring. I adore you as a mom, a partner, a lover, an artist, and a friend.

And finally, to Matilda: my pal, my dude, my kid. Thanks for every second of it. Please keep being exactly yourself; yourself is the best.